The Unbeatable
4 x 4

K & J Slavin and G N Mackie

Foulis

Haynes

ISBN 0 85429 433 3

A FOULIS Motoring Book

First published, by Gentry Books Ltd, 1981
Second edition published 1984

Published by:
Haynes Publishing Group
Sparkford, Yeovil, Somerset BA22 7JJ

Haynes Publications Inc.
861 Lawrence Drive, Newbury Park, California 91320 USA

British Library Cataloguing in Publication Data
Slavin, Ken
   Land Rover. – 2nd ed.
   I.   Land-Rover truck – History
   I.   Title   II. Slavin, Julie
   III. Mackie, G.
   629.2'222   TL230.5.L3
   ISBN 0-85429-433-3

Editor: Mansur Darlington
Page layout: Teresa Woodside and Mike King
Printed in England by: J.H. Haynes & Co. Ltd.

Contents

Acknowledgements

We would like to express thanks to the following for their help in compiling this book: David Bowyer – Off-Road & 4-Wheel Driver, Alfredo Cassina – Santana, James Duckworth & Son, Richard Fisher, Glenfrome Engineering Ltd, Kathleen Griffiths, Tom Sheppard and Monica Wilks, and from Land-Rover: Tim Ackerley, Roger Ball, Stan Banting, Tom Barton, Roger Craythorne, David Crawley, Staff Dewson, Tony Gilroy, Michael Kennedy, Roger McCahey, Geoff Miller, Zoe Miller, Jack Reardon, Matthew Sharp, Linda Shear, A.B. Smith and H.J. Topping.

For their co-operation in supplying photographs for publication, we are indebted to the late Denis Lyons, to Harry Mills from Land-Rover's Photographic Department, The Ministry of Defence, Evers & Wall, Glenfrome Engineering Ltd, Laird's, Hotspur, Short Brothers, Jonathan Slavin, FLM (Panelcraft), Donald Miller (USA) and TAU – California (USA).

Special thanks to Squadron Leader Tom Sheppard for his help in supplying photographs and the report on the Joint Services' Expedition.

Introduction

For hundreds of miles around the terrain is scorched and unrelenting desert — volcanic mountains, immense slabs of cracked rock interspersed with scattered patches of sand, a lunar landscape in monotones of brown and grey. The only sound as we wait beside the deserted airstrip is the unfailing wind, until eventually the throb of an engine can dimly be sensed, and we know the aircraft is arriving. Then gleaming and shimmering through the haze of heat, it is bouncing gently towards us along the runway which is a glaring band of brightness in the harsh drabness all about.

It is 1969, in West Africa, and we are taking delivery of two prototypes of a 'revolutionary' new 4 x 4 design from the Land-Rover factory – for a month's field testing in the toughest conditions we can find ...

No other freight or passengers are unloaded, just two vehicles veiled in paper, ungainly packages with only their wheels visible. Once they are unmasked, we are looking, of course, at the earliest Range Rovers. The murmurs of cautious confidence in the factory before its release hardly anticipated the enormous impact this vehicle was to make both nationally and internationally, nor that it was to mark the dawning of an era in the 4 x 4 market: here was a cunning combination of style and strength, comfort and ruggedness that had evolved as an inspired development from the Land-Rover stable, while incorporating a V8 engine for greater power, and permanent 4-wheel drive, thus producing one of the world's most versatile vehicles – a Go-Anywhere car that was quickly to join the élite in motoring circles, and which, without the workaday Land-Rover, could never have been.

So let's go back to the real beginning ...

Authors note to the 2nd Edtion
Recently we drove across to Solihull, in our 1950 Series I 80-inch Land-Rover, to pick up a brand new automatic Range Rover from the factory to evaluate its performance. No one could fail to be struck by the extraordinary contrast in vehicles! Land-Rover Ltd. has come a very long way in 35 years. Up-dating this book has been an interesting exercise as, since its first publication in 1981 and the materialization of the £200 million investment programme, Land-Rover has evolved more than during the entire previous decade, and cataloguing the evolution has been a pleasure for all three of us.

Chapter 1
The Land-Rover Story

The Land-Rover has been so big for so long that it is hard to visualize life without it. There it is, daily, on the screen: a fire-engine copes with a blazing emergency, a convoy heads doggedly for some trouble-spot loaded with soldiers, an ambulance roars off bearing the wounded to hospital, the police arrive with blue lights flashing; and there it is again, pulling trapped cars out of the snow, moving a farmer's sheep to safety; now it's full of camping gear as an expedition gets under way, and – would you believe? – there's one disguised as a zebra, in an African Game Reserve.

The uses of the Land-Rover are so diverse as to be impossible to enumerate, which in itself is a good enough excuse to write a book about it, but now, after leading the world in the 4 x 4 market ever since the Second World War, its supremacy is being challenged as a host of competitors jostle for position: so let's look not only at what Land-Rover has meant in the past, but at what place it can hold in the future ...

The prime factor in the conception of the Land-Rover was, indirectly, the Second World War, although the idea emerged well after peace had been declared, and – at that stage – no military connection had even been imagined. To sketch in the background from which the Land-Rover was born, we shall have to go back a bit further, however, to Victorian England, when Coventry was best known as a centre for watch-making and ribbon-weaving.

Coventry's first-ever 'car' – a machine called the Rover Electric Carriage – was built in 1888 by JK Starley who founded the Rover company. Unfortunately this extraordinary vehicle, a battery-operated, electrically driven hybrid tricycle, was destined to die at the prototype stage, and the company did not start serious car production until after the turn of the century, in 1904. By then, the age of mechanization was dawning, and beginning to gain respectability, when even the King himself purchased a car (King Edward VII's example was to be followed, nearly 50 years later, by King George VI, who ordered his own

9

Land-Rover when it was still regarded as a very new phenomenon on the market).

Rover's first cars were a development from building motor cycles, which were a development from building bicycles, which were a development from building sewing machines, way back in the early 1860s. The designation 'Rover' emerged in 1884 with the advent of 'The Safety' – a tricycle produced that year which was considered to be ideally suited to 'roving' around the countryside. This machine was rapidly followed a year later by a 'Safety' bicycle – the forerunner of the present-day pedal bicycle, and successor to the acclaimed Compressus Ordinary, or Penny Farthing. The company officially became known as the Rover Cycle Company Limited in 1896, but this title was to be changed less than 10 years later to the Rover Company Limited, when production of motor cycles ceased.

The Rover Company experienced fluctuating fortunes through the first three decades of the century – firmly establishing itself as one of Britain's important car manufacturers in the years prior to the First World War, levelling out by the start of the 1920s, and in grave trouble by the time the Depression hit the world.

This then was the background of the business to which Mr Spencer Wilks was to harness his considerable talents when he made the decision to leave Hillman, where he had been Managing Director since 1919, and join the Rover Company in 1929. Mr A B Smith, who was Managing Director of the Rover Company from 1969 till 1973, recalls those distant days with clarity:

'I now know exactly how hard times were for Rover in those days. There were, of course, no labour problems as we know them today. Everyone's ambition was first to get a job and second to hold on to it. The people in authority were the foremen and the time-keepers who looked after the clock cards. It was difficult to find the money to pay the suppliers and the question arose of pleading with them for further extended credit. I have a recollection of Ted Commander – our Chief Buyer – offering to guarantee some supplier's account with his own pension fund! Spencer Wilks, Managing Director of Rover from 1933 to 1957, has often spoken of the drama that surrounded almost every weekly pay day in those early days. The appointment of Spencer Wilks was the first major step that saved Rover and even today his philosophy of building only quality cars has been adhered to strictly – to our very obvious benefit ... Spencer Wilks' brother Maurice joined Rover in 1931 and together with Robert Boyle assumed responsibility for engineering and design, and on the production side Spencer Wilks brought Geoffrey Savage from Hillman to become Works Director. This was really the team that put Rover back on their feet ...'

From 1933, when he was promoted to Managing Director, Spencer Wilks' consistent policy was to eliminate mediocrity from the firm and specialize in the production of prestigious vehicles. Very soon after his appointment, the name of Rover began to denote the respectability that its cars have retained to this day. One of his first actions when he took over the reins at the Rover Company was to form a new department for material control, the object of which was to time material flow precisely, in order to minimize work in progress and match production. This could well be regarded as a fore-runner of the computerized control systems of today, and thereby gives an idea of the breadth of Spencer Wilks' competence as the man in charge.

The outbreak of the Second World War, however, put an abrupt end to the steadily increasing sale of Rover cars, and for the time being Mr Wilks had to shelve his elaborate plans for expansion. As a result of his impact on the firm, the Rover Company had been invited to join the Government's 'Shadow Factories' scheme, to build aeroplane engines at two different sites – at Acocks Green as early as 1937, and at Solihull in 1939. All through the war years the company was stretched to capacity, fulfilling its commitment to the production of aircraft engines and a whole range of other military equipment which included, in the latter stages of the war, the Rolls-Royce V12 Meteor tank engine. Of this period, A B Smith recalls:

> 'At the end of the war we had a reservoir of highly skilled people, and pre-emptive rights on the buildings and plant from the Shadow Factories. Since our Coventry works (Helen Street) had been bombed in 1940, Spencer Wilks decided to come to Solihull, although I well remember him saying in despair to his brother, "We shall never be able to use a million square feet in all our lives! We shall have to let it out ..."'

So Helen Street was sold and the two new plants taken on at a 'peppercorn' rent, Acocks Green to continue with the production of the Meteor tank engine – the demand for which continued even after the end of the war – and Solihull as Rover's headquarters, where Spencer Wilks began to prepare for the renewed manufacture of his cars.

These preparations were on the ambitious scale of an annual output of 20,000 vehicles – 15,000 to the old Rover design, and 5,000 of a new design (the 700cc 6 hp 'M'-type) that his younger brother Maurice, by now Chief Designer for the Rover Company, was already working on. But all these plans were to be thwarted by the Government, which was hamstrung by the war-crippled economy. The great cry in these times was, not unlike today, Export! – but then it was to recuperate some of the monumental losses suffered during the preceding years. This in itself was made extremely difficult by the gross lack of raw materials, and of sheet steel in particular, without which cars such as Rover had hitherto produced simply could not be made. Government allocations of necessary materials including steel were made to those industries whose plans included a high level of export, but the new design that Maurice Wilks was developing, the 'M'-type, was considered unsuitable for the export market because of its relatively high cost; since nearly all its parts were brand new, the tooling costs were prohibitive. After building a number of prototypes, the reality of the necessary capital outlay finally sunk in, and the 'M'-type had to be cast aside. Until this period the Rover Company had never in its whole history designed or built a left-hand-drive vehicle, which serves to illustrate how un-export-minded they had always been (their own Export Department was not created until 1945).

Their application to build 15,000 of the old pre-war models per year was then squashed by the Government response that it could only allocate steel for the production of 1,100 vehicles. This was so far short of their target that Spencer and Maurice Wilks now came to realize that a compromise born of desperation must be achieved if the company was to have any hope at all of survival. Although their problems were pretty immense, they were not regarded as anything other than short-term. Once the country was 'back on its feet', production of motor cars could be stepped up again and the labour force usefully employed. But what, in the meantime, could they possible do with their factories and their men, and with all the restrictions of the age to contend with? Without question, a 'stop-gap' was vital – and one that met the essential requirement of export potential, without demanding the usual quantities of sheet steel for the body manufacture, or too much additional expenditure for its assembly. It had to be something that would utilize only what was already there. One way and another, a very tall order!

Maurice Wilks had a fairly big farm in Anglesey on which he found, in his spare time, that an old, beaten-up ex-WD Willys Jeep – one of the many that had become so familiar in Britain during the war – was a very useful thing to own, for many different practical purposes. Legend now has it that when this old vehicle was nearing the end of its usefulness, Spencer Wilks asked his brother what he intended to replace it with. Maurice answered that he would have to get hold of the same again as no alternative existed – though for such patriotic motor manufacturers as the Wilks, it went powerfully against the grain to buy any vehicle that wasn't British. Another factor not in the Jeep's favour at that time was the unavailability of spare parts; they could only be obtained in bulk, at sales of United States surplus stock – for instance, to get a replacement set of four spark plugs, a hundred had to purchased!

And so it was from this bald fact, that the American Jeep had no equivalent, that the original notion to design and build a purely agricultural vehicle is said to have sprung. All of a sudden, the Wilks brothers became conscious of a glaring gap in the market: a machine for the farmer that was not a tractor but something much more versatile, rugged without being too cumbersome, thus keeping pace with the increasing trend in the years after the war towards mechanized farming. As A B Smith told us,

'It is difficult today, to imagine the size of the gamble that was taken then. It all started when the Wilks brothers bought a war-time Jeep. It was constantly in trouble and they were forever having to bring it into the factory for some repair job or other, and I well remember Maurice saying to Spencer that if he couldn't make a better, more reliable vehicle he shouldn't be in the business!'

The governess to Maurice Wilks' three sons at that time was Kathleen Griffiths and she remembers, with affection, 'the insatiable boyish enthusiasm' with which Maurice tackled this (and every other) new venture. She recalls being bounced over sand dunes, bogged down on wet beaches and hurtled through the shallows in one of the first Land-Rover prototypes to be built.

The Rover Company was about to design a vehicle for the land – a 'Land-Rover', as Maurice Wilks had already christened the project. According to the minutes of the Board Meeting held in September 1947, Spencer Wilks recommended 'that the all-purpose vehicle on the lines of the Willys-Overland post-war Jeep was the most desirable,' and for some of the following reasons: 'The P3 engine, gearbox and back axle could be used almost in their entirety; little additional jigging and tooling would be necessary, and body dies would not be required ...' But by this time the first prototypes were already running, for Maurice Wilks had wasted no time in deciding the brief, in the spring of that same year. This was unusually broad:

'...to design a vehicle rather similar to a Jeep ...even more useful to the farmer ... a proper farm machine, not just another Jeep...Much more versatile, much more use as a power source ... able to drive things, to have power take-offs *everywhere,* and to have all sorts of bolt-on accessories, to be used instead of a tractor at times ... to be able to do everything ...!'

This was the outline he gave to Tom Barton, the man who over the years has earned himself the title of 'Mr Land-Rover' but who at that time was one of five section leaders to whom the job of designing and building the Land-Rover was handed. Maurice Wilks could afford to be confident in passing the project over to his team, which included Robert Boyle as Chief Engineer, Gordon Bashford as Research Engineer, Arthur Goddard as Assistant Chief Engineer, and John Cullen as Project Engineer for the Land-Rover, and to turn his own energies back towards the car market. All that Tom Barton and Co had to do now was to get their heads down and get on with it.

One of the most remarkable elements in the development of the Land-Rover was the speed with which plans and drawings became realities. Great urgency was imposed upon the project from the moment the Wilks brothers decided to make this the stop-gap vehicle they so badly needed: there was a work force to employ and the Rover Company simply had to have the export potential that this machine might provide. Even so, it is still quite amazing (especially by contrast with the standards of today) that while the concept was not thought up until early in 1947, prototypes were running by the end of the summer, and the first Land-Rover was shown to the public in April 1948! This is all the more impressive considering the traditional conservatism and cautiousness of Rover as a company – hardly known for making snap decisions and then implementing them!

Using the Willys Jeep as the jumping-off point, the design team had to scrutinize every detail of the American product and drive it about in all possible conditions to learn its limitations. Two Jeeps were acquired early on, solely for dissection purposes, but although certain of its stronger points were without doubt copied in the Land-Rover, the Rover team maintained vehemently that there was nothing on the Land-Rover that corresponded exactly to the Jeep. For one thing, the Land-Rover project was severely restricted by the conditions of its manufacture, which imposed a very/strict discipline upon the designers: wherever remotely feasible, existing Rover car components had to be used; the budget for alternative machine tools was meagre, and for press tools for the bodywork, non-existent. If the body panels, which were to be made almost exclusively of aluminium alloy, could not be formed by the simple bending method they were no use, and any form to be incorporated in the skin could only be achieved by using such machinery as they already had. With the earliest prototypes, bits of Jeep were certainly in evidence but these were used only to save time – for instance a Jeep chassis was 'borrowed' for the original vehicle, though most of its fittings were Rover's. When Rover started to build the Land-Rover its own chassis, there were more innovations as a result of the low-expenditure policy: the chassis frame side members were of box-section, built up from four plates of flat steel sheet, instead of U-section pressings. Olaf Poppe (whose Norwegian father Peter Poppe, engine designer, had joined the Rover Company in 1924, bringing with him his designs for the 14/45 engine that Rover used through the 1920s) devised this 'four-plate' concept which was, after much deliberation, taken up by Gordon Bashford – with surprising and lasting success, as is proved by the fact that it has endured to the present day on all the short wheelbase models.

One way in which even the earliest prototype Land-Rovers differed dramatically from the Jeep was in the engine: the Land-Rover engine was considerably smaller, allowing more carrying space. After a fair bit of trial and error, which determined the 1,389cc Rover 10 engine as lacking the necessary power and torque, the new 1.6-litre engine was fitted.

Always bearing in mind Maurice Wilks' original instructions 'to have power take-offs *everywhere!*', the first Land-Rover chassis to be built already incorporated the central power take-off, and, by the time that a number of pre-production vehicles were completed, the versatility that this afforded was being fully explored. Prototype 80-inch Land-Rovers with 4-wheel drive and power take-offs could be harnessed to a whole range of machinery, which made innumerable jobs a lot simpler and quicker to carry out, and their cross-

Side view of the first Land-Rover: the first appearance of the now familiar profile

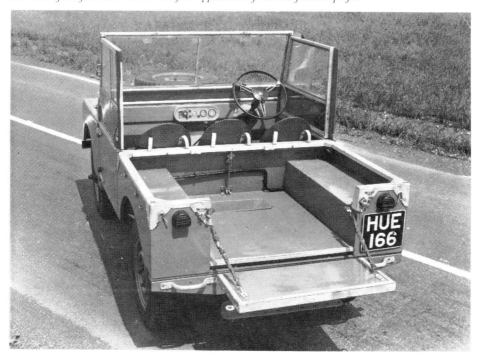

Everything about the first Land-Rover was purely functional.

15

A typical 1948 80-inch model in L.H.D. guise. Right from the start the export market was vital to the sales of the Land-Rover. Up to the present, over 70% of all Land-Rovers produced have been sold overseas.

country ability – from fording streams, crossing ploughed fields, to climbing steep hill-faces – was improving by the week. But the timing was becoming crucial. Spencer and Maurice Wilks were quite determined that the Land-Rover should be 'unveiled' at the Amsterdam Motor Show which opened on 30 April 1948, regardless of whether or not it was finished. The Show, which was of international interest, was far too good a promotional opportunity to miss for the launching of their new machine, and so this was the target to which the Land-Rover project team was committed. At this stage they envisaged building up to 50 Land-Rovers per week, but theoretically the state of the nation could hardly have been worse for new vehicle prospects: even if the interest was there and orders flowed in, without adequate materials to supply them, Rover would as quickly lose custom as they obtained it.

During the initial stages of construction, progress was disconcertingly slow. Because of the very complicated casting and machining operations to transmission casings, the first prototype took about six weeks to complete, and the second emerged several weeks after that. During this phase, however, the chassis jig had been designed and proved workable, so that the Land-Rover

Peter Wilks with his young son, Andrew, in 1964. Andrew is standing beside a miniature Land-Rover that was built as a gift for the King of Jordan's children.

team were then able to proceed with the production of their pilot-run vehicles, of which the intention was to build 50 – though finally only 47 or 48 were finished, probably because the components for the last few were 'sabotaged' to keep the existing vehicles running. These pilot-run or pre-production Land-Rovers varied in many particulars, as was required by the experimental and developmental purpose of their production – to the extent that the very first completed prototype had a central steering wheel, steering column and centrally positioned driving seat, with no doors! The common denominator, though, was always the galvanized steel chassis frame.

Of the pilot-run vehicles, only 25 had been finished before the official launching, which was in fact somewhat premature in that the company was hardly geared to forge ahead with production, but on the other hand they were deliberately awaiting the general public reaction before finalizing certain design details, since it was the first-ever 4-wheel-drive vehicle of this sort to have been produced in Great Britain.

It was decided that for the Amsterdam Motor Show, two of the 80-inch Land-Rovers would be exhibited, one right-hand drive for display, and a left-

Farmers were quick to recognize the Land-Rover's potential.

hand drive demonstration model. Now, at last, the Wilks brothers were to see whether or not they had backed the right hunch in creating this unusual machine ...

At its initial launching in Amsterdam, the Land-Rover was received with universal enthusiasm and very serious interest. The Land-Rover archives at Solihull bulge with press comment of the day, but *The Autocar* and *The Motor* magazines reported in depth, dwelling on the innovative aspects of the vehicle. 'An All-Purpose Rover', said *The Autocar* (30 April 1948), and proceded to describe it in the following terms:

'There is now something to describe which can either be regarded as a private car able to perform many most valuable duties other than sheer transport, or as a general purpose countryside worker which is also capable of providing comfortable and efficient transport. This dual role of the new Land-Rover, regardless of which range of duty is of the greater value to the owner, cannot be too highly stressed, because it opens up possibilities of the greatest value to those who live in the country, whether under cultivation or in the wild state. So much has been said and written in the past about the so-called People's Car, much of it nonsense, that the advent of a really practical British vehicle which goes far beyond that over-publicised proposal should be hailed with genuine acclamation ... It has been designed and built by the Rover Company, and that in itself is a guarantee of quality which will be instantly accepted by any British

18

motorist. Its appearance is starkly practical; there is nothing of the luxury vehicle about its looks. Nevertheless it is not ugly and has a distinctly attractive appearance all its own ... The Land-Rover can go through floods up to its wheel centres or deeper without trouble. The operative word about the whole car is "substantial". All these features alone make one think. If the world has to be strictly economical for years to come, is not this the sort of car that most of us need, one that is entirely practical and essentially usable? Washing is reduced to a minimum, and maintenance is easy; there is no carrying about of weight more or less uselessly devoted to fashionable appearance and not really essential luxury. And it is a car usable in open form or completely enclosed. These points alone proclaim themselves. But they only tell half the story. The Land-Rover is a mobile power station as well, and will tow or do a variety of useful work on the land over rough ground. It can drive a large circular saw and cut up timber for firewood. It can be used with trailers to transport heavy loads over ploughed fields or other hard going. As a mobile power unit it takes the power to the job. Through the power take-off it can be harnessed to drive a threshing machine, an elevator, or a chaff-cutter. It can draw a plough, and most other farm implements. It can perform all these tasks because it is specifically provided with a four-wheel drive, and a power take-off ... Provision is also made for a power-driven winch of the capstan type mounted at the front of the vehicle, which can be used for a variety of jobs from moving machinery in a factory to grubbing out old tree roots on the farm. It is a vehicle of almost unlimited uses ...'

The Motor presented a similar glowing account, over a full four-page report, calling it 'a go-anywhere vehicle with a plain utility-type body, a portable source of power, and an alternative to the light tractor' but finished by saying:

'In launching this new vehicle the Rover Company has displayed an enterprise which should be well rewarded, and there is no doubt that a big market, both at home and abroad, exists for a machine such as the Land-Rover. There is no doubt also that in its design the Rover Co has applied a wide knowledge and experience not only of vehicle manufacture, but of agricultural and industrial requirements.'

So, from the outset, it was established that here was something much more versatile than a mere agricultural machine. And the public pounced on it! Apart from its appeal on the grounds described in the above-quoted press comments, another favourable factor was its price – only £450 for the basic vehicle (though 'extras' such as passenger seat cushions, doors, heater, sidescreens, spare tyre – and even starting handle! – were additional):

Soon after its release, the Rover Company submitted two Land-Rovers to the National Institute of Agricultural Engineering and Scottish Machinery Testing

Station for thorough test-work to be carried out over a period of about nine months. Their impartial report on the two vehicles was published in 1949, and the following extracts, while rather long-winded by today's standards, give an idea of the extent of their probe, and their findings:

Report on test of PROTOTYPE LAND-ROVER
Manufactured by: The Rover Company Ltd., Meteor Works, Solihull, Birmingham.
Test requested by: The manufacturers.
Brief Specification: The Land-Rover is a light 4-wheel drive vehicle designed to transport goods and/or personnel by road or across country and for general use in farming operations. Two models were supplied for test purposes: one right-hand drive vehicle (Chassis No R.32, Engine No 33) and one left-hand drive vehicle (Chassis No L.31, Engine No 32).

Engine

Fuel	Pool petrol
Arrangement and number of cylinders	4 cylinders in line. 2.736 in bore x 4.134 in stroke. Aluminium alloy pistons.
Compression ratio	6.8 : 1
Valves	Overhead inlet, side exhaust
Engine speeds	Governed 3,000 $\pm$ 100 rpm. Maximum 4,500 rpm.
Carburetter	Solex 32 PBI down-draught including economiser and accelerator pump. Supplied by electric SU pump from tank via AC sediment bowl filter.
Air cleaner	AC Sphinx oil bath heavy duty type fitted with pre-cleaner.
Ignition	Lucas coil. Centrifugal and vacuum automatic advance and retard.
Lubrication	Forced feed from gear type oil pump delivering 160 gals/hour at 2,000 engine rpm. Filters on pump inlet and by-pass.
Cooling system	Centrifugal pump, pressurised radiator and fan with cowling. Thermostat control. (Fine mesh radiator screen available as extra.)
Electrical equipment	12v Lucas 51 amp/hour lead acid battery. Headlamps, side-lights, rear-lights, horn, instrument panel, windscreen wiper, socket for trailer light. Starter motor and dynamo.
Governor	Iso-Speedic. Driven by V-belt from crank-shaft.
Capacities	Fuel – 10 gallons
	Cooling water – 17 pints
	Oil – 10 pints

Chassis and Body

The chassis is made up of two longitudinal and five lateral members of 14 gauge steel box-section, welded throughout and galvanised. The fuel tank is underslung on the chassis and is provided with a double bottom carried up to form the mounting and guard. Suspension is by semi-elliptic leaf springs controlled by Monroe hydraulic dampers.

The scuttle and dash are of steel and the floor, seats, and rear section are of high tensile light alloy. The wings and bonnet are also of light alloy. The windscreen can be folded down on to the bonnet if required and a detachable fabric hood with Perspex side windows can be fitted for weather protection. Provision is made for carrying a spare wheel in the rear section of the body or extra fittings can be obtained for clamping it on the bonnet.

Overall dimensions of vehicle

(on 6.00 x 16 tyres at inflation pressure 24 lb/sq in).

Length	128½ in.
Width	62½ in.
Height	Without hood and windscreen folded down: 53½ in.
	Without hood and windscreen upright: 65¼ in.
	With hood: 72 in.
Ground clearance (on hard surface)	To bottom of differential housing: 7½ in.
	To bottom of spring clamp bolts: 7¾ in.

Overall dimensions of rear section

Length	42 in.
Width	60 in.
Depth	Centre portion: 14½ in x 34 in wide.
	Side portions (forming seats if required): each 5½ in x 13 in wide.
Capacity (to top of sides)	15½ cu ft (including spare wheel space)
Recommended pay-load	10 cwt.
Dimensions of tailboard	14½ in deep x 34 in wide

Transmission

Clutch	Single plate, dry. 9 in diameter. Foot operated.
Gearbox	A normal gearbox giving four forward speeds and reverse (synchro-mesh on 3rd and 4th gears) transmits power to a transfer box having

two ratios – high and low. From the transfer box output two Hardy-Spicer open propeller shafts drive the front and rear axles: a free wheel on the front axle drive is incorporated in the transfer box.

Oil capacity	Main gearbox: 4 pints
	Transfer box: 6 pints
Wheels	16 in rim fitted with Avon 6-ply 6.00 x 16 Traction or 7.00 x 16 Super-Traction tyres.
Brakes	Girling Hydrostatic on all wheels: foot operated. Girling mechanical handbrake on transfer box output shaft for parking.
Wheelbase	80 in.
Track (fixed)	50 in (on 6.00 x 16 tyres)
Drawbar	The drawbar consists of a lateral plate 29½ in long x 3 in wide welded to the rear chassis cross-member. Ten ⅞in diameter holes are drilled at 3 in centres. A cranked drawbar extension plate 16 in long is also provided for bolting to the drawbar when the pto unit is fitted. One ¾ in and one ⅞ in bolt holes are drilled at 4 in centres. The extension cannot be fitted centrally.
Height of drawbar above ground	(a) on hard surface with 7.00 x 16 tyres at inflation pressure 22 lb/sq in
	Body empty – 14 in.
	1,200 lb in body – 10½ in.
	(b) on hard surface with 6.00 x 16 tyres at inflation pressure 24 lb/sq in
	Body empty – 13¼ in.
	(c) height of extension plate, conditions as (b)
	Four positions giving 10½, 11½, 13½ and 14½ in.

Total weight (on 7.00 x 16 tyres without fuel, operator, or pto assembly but including oil, cooling water, hood, doors, and spare wheel on bonnet):

	Body empty – 2,780 lb.
	1,200 lb evenly distributed in body 3,980 lb.
Weight on rear wheels (conditions as above)	Body empty – 1,205 lb.
	1,200 lb evenly distributed in body 2,465 lb.
Weight on front wheels (conditions as above)	Body empty – 1,575 lb.
	1,200 lb evenly distributed in body 1,515 lb.
Power take-off and belt pulley assembly	The power take-off is driven through a Hardy-Spicer propeller shaft from the main gearbox

22

output and two interchangeable pinions giving two ratios. The pto gearbox casing is bolted to the rear chassis cross-member and an 8 in x 8 in belt pulley driven from the pto shaft through two bevel gears can be bolted to the pto gearbox casing.

The test-work carried out by the National Institute of Agricultural Engineering and Scottish Machinery Testing Station included comprehensive testing of the belt power and drawbar performance, road trials, and farm and field trials, applied to both the prototype Land-Rovers. The field trials involved ploughing, disc harrowing, drag harrowing, rolling and chain harrowing grassland, hauling a reaper and binder, rolling on a hillside, hauling a pto-driven muck-spreader, and potato harvesting and cultivation. At the conclusion of all these tests, the left-hand drive Land-Rover was dismantled at the manufacturers, and the component parts were inspected for wear and damage. Here is what the report had to say:

Engine

Cylinder block and crankcase:	Good condition
Cylinder bores:	Maximum wear 0.0015 inches above production limits
Pistons:	Very little carbon on crowns or in control rings. Dimensions within production limits
Piston rings:	No damage. No increase in side clearance. Maximum increase in compression ring gap 0.001 inch above production limits.
Gudgeon pins:	Good condition.
Crankshaft:	Some score marks on all journals particularly centre one which had one deep mark. No ovality on journals or crankpins. Maximum wear on crankpins 0.0005 inch.
Bearings:	Main: some score marks on all three, particularly centre (thrust). Maximum wear 0.004 inch (on centre bearing). No ovality.
	Big ends: within production limits. No ovality. Piece of metal broken out of No 3.
	Small ends: good condition.
Camshaft:	Very little wear on cams.
Cylinder head and gasket:	Good condition.

Valves:	Exhaust valves in need of regrinding. Inlet valves in good condition. Some play between stems and guides on all valves but new guides not required.
Tappet and push-rods:	Good condition.
Valve springs:	Within production limits.
Flywheel:	Starter ring in good condition. Score marks on clutch side.
Chain drives and sprockets:	No wear. Chain tensioning device in original position.
Carburettor:	Good condition. Fine dust present in float chamber.
Water Pump:	Good condition.
Oil Pump:	Good condition.
Oil filters:	Primary: clean and intact. Secondary: dirty and intact.

Transmission

Clutch:	Score marks on flywheel. Score marks on pressure plate and slight blueing. Clutch plate not very badly worn. Dirt and dust in clutch housing.
Gearboxes:	Gears in good condition except 1st in main gearbox on which leading edge of teeth broken. Some corrosion on springs and roller bearing housings.
Propeller shafts:	Good condition.
Front axle free-wheel:	Good condition.
Power Take-Off drive shaft:	Play in end coupling to pto giving rise to noise.
Front axle:	Shafts and Tracta joints in good condition. Some corrosion and score marks on swivel pin roller bearing housings. Differential not stripped (almost new).
Power Take-Off:	Good condition.

Steering

Steering box:	Good condition. Mounting on dash panel –bolts loose.
Steering relay box:	Good condition.
Linkages and pins:	Good condition.
Front wheel castor:	2°20′ (originally 3°).
Front wheel camber and toe in:	Within production limits.

Chassis and Suspension

Chassis frame:	Good condition except plates pulled out on rear cross-member. No corrosion.
Engine and gearbox mountings:	No appreciable deterioration. No distortion.
Exhaust pipe and mountings:	No appreciable deterioration.
Springs:	Rear offside set 3.69 in at 720 lb Rear nearside set 3.75 in at 710 lb (when new were 4.13 in at 750 lb) Both front 2.5 in at 520 lb (were 2.65 at 530 lb). No obvious wear on shackles, pins or Silentbloc pushes.
Shock absorbers:	Good condition.
Body:	Generally in good condition (this applies to both models) with no rusting or corrosion. Hood badly out of shape at rear and fasteners broken. Rear window gauze broken. Door catches no longer positive. Sidescreen steady arms broken and peg sockets strained.

Electrical System

Wiring:	Good condition.
Components:	All serviceable, no damage. One rear lamp missing (broken off). Mixture strength warning light fickle.

Wheels and Brakes

Brakes:	Hydraulic system in good condition. New brake linings were fitted during the tests.
Tyres:	Three badly worn but not completely unserviceable. One rear tyre worn down to canvas and replaced at 8,500 miles.

At the end of this report, the conclusions of the testers are listed as follows:

'The results of the test show that the Land-Rover is an excellent transport vehicle which can be used instead of a tractor for some agricultural operations including belt work. It is capable of carrying a load of up to 10 cwt across difficult conditions and of hauling trailer loads of the order of 4 tons. The fuel consumption on road work ranged from 30 mpg when driven unladen at an average speed of about 30 mph, to 21 mpg when fully laden and engaged on a long journey interspersed with some short runs. It is very suitable for the transport of livestock in trailers since the choice of gear ratios in the four-speed gearbox has been such that a constant rate of acceleration and deceleration can be maintained in traffic and when negotiating difficult corners. When not heavily laden and without a trailer, it can be driven at a cruising speed of 45-50 mph with a maximum slightly in excess of 60 mph. On one test run an average speed of 42.9 mph was maintained over a 162 mile journey. At the higher speeds necessary to maintain such an average, however, the vehicle was too noisy for comfortable travelling.

'One particular advantage of the Land-Rover for farm transport is its ability to go practically anywhere since its cross-country and hill-climbing performances are very good. It is very stable and has an obvious usefulness both for carrying small items of equipment across terrain which would otherwise require the use of a tractor and trailer and for internal and external farm transport. Its capacity for draught work is shown by the results of the drawbar tests in which maximum sustained pulls obtained when unladen and equipped with 7.00 × 16 tyres ranged from 2,200 lb on tarmac to 1,700 lb on rough cultivated loam.

An Evers & Wall conversion of a forward-control Land-Rover 250 Fertiliquid Sprayer, with boom in spraying position.

'The results of the belt test show that the Land-Rover develops sufficient power for many farm operations such as driving threshing drums or medium-sized hammermills although improvement to engine governing is desirable. The maximum power obtained was 27.3 belt hp at a belt linear speed of 3,840 ft/min and maximum equivalent crankshaft torque was developed at a belt speed of 2,525 ft/min. It is possible that a Land-Rover being used for agricultural purposes may spend an appreciable part of its time on stationary work and attention is therefore drawn to the need for some simple means, such as a locking device on the foot-brake pedal for securing the vehicle and to the necessity of advising operators on how to eliminate the rear axle springing for anything but light belt work.

'The vehicle, as tested, could be employed on many jobs where good manoeuvrability and row-crop wheel spacing are not required but its usefulness for farming operations would be improved by lower gear ratios. The results of the drawbar tests show that the factor limiting maximum sustained pull on all three types of land was engine stall and it is recommended that the practicability should be considered of modifying the transfer box low ratio so that the forward speeds of the vehicle on a hard surface are about 2.5 mph in L_1, 4 mph in L_2, and 5.5 mph in L_3, (ie about twice the ratio of the vehicle as tested). A modification of this nature would not only increase the usefulness of the Land-Rover for farm work but would also increase the maximum pull. The transmission differs from that of a tractor in that the pto drive passes through the gearbox so that, irrespective of the gear being used, the ratio of pto speed to vehicle wheel speed remains the same. Thus the normal tractor pto speed of 540 rpm is only obtained at one forward speed – about 4 mph – with new 6.00 x 16 tyres, dropping to 3.7 mph with the same tyres well worn. (The manufacturers have pointed out that, if required, their agents could interchange the gears in the pto assembly on any individual vehicle and the machine would then give 540 rpm of the pto shaft at about 2.7 mph.) This method of driving the pto would be a disadvantage on a general purpose tractor but is not expected to lead to difficulties with the range of pto driven machines likely to be used with the Land-Rover; it has the noteworthy advantage that, as the belt pulley attaches to the pto shaft, a wide range of belt speeds is readily obtainable for stationary work.

'The field trials showed that many farm operations other than heavy cultivations and row-crop work could be satisfactorily carried out with the Land-Rover. Disc and drag harrowing, rolling and reaping were successfully attempted and ploughing – except for the headlands – with a two-furrow mouldboard plough was found to be possible. The fuel consumption of the vehicle on drawbar work on conditions giving good adhesion was found to be good. The specific fuel consumption curves

27

obtained during the drawbar tests on grassland were flat over a wide range of pulls and the optimum consumption was more than 10 drawbar hp-hours per gallon. The fuel consumption when disc-harrowing and drag-harrowing in L₁ gear was 14.7 and 12.1 gallons per 8-hour day respectively, the average drawbar pulls being 950 lb and 730 lb respectively and the speeds approximately 3¾ and 3½ mph.

'The extensive and arduous nature of the tests to which the two models were subjected showed them to be very robust vehicles capable of heavy work with low maintenance requirements. The total mileage of the two vehicles during the test was 23,000 of which a considerable proportion was low gear work and the inspection of the left-hand drive model at the end of the performance tests and field trials showed it to be in very good condition. The use of light alloys and the heavy galvanizing of the steel components of the body and chassis had prevented any rusting or corrosion. The test showed the need for certain modifications and refinements, many of which are already being incorporated in production models. It is suggested that modifications to the drawbar, gear ratios, driving position and parking brake system are particularly worthwhile.'

Report No RT.1/49034: 27 August 1949

This very positive reaction to the Land-Rover was to be echoed by many other professional motor-vehicle assessors, but even apart from that, it seemed that the time was ripe for the general public to latch on to this new land-roving machine. Its reception both at home and overseas was immediately more enthusiastic than its makers had even dared to hope: after all, it was intended only as a hand-to-mouth emergency measure, and never as anything lasting or substantial in terms of Rover products. In Britain, the fact that during the post-war years the public was restricted to the purchase of not more than one new car every two years, and that Land-Rovers were classified as exempt from this ruling, gave the vehicle an unquestionable advantage which was at once reflected in the sales figures. In its first full year of production, it was to exceed the sales target of 5,000 vehicles by as much as 3,000, a figure way beyond everyone's expectations. In the second full year of production sales doubled, and by 1951 Land-Rovers were out-selling Rover cars at the rate of two to one. Once the dazed and delighted Rover people had grasped the implications of this success, plans were rapidly adapted in an endeavour to meet the orders that came pouring in.

Production got off to a very slow start. The launching at the Amsterdam Motor Show had been premature in that the company were far from geared to produce Land-Rovers in any quantity at that stage, but it served its purpose: while it attracted international attention, Rover got the feedback it needed, and production was able to begin, albeit haltingly. From that day to this, Land-Rover has never been able to match its production to demand.

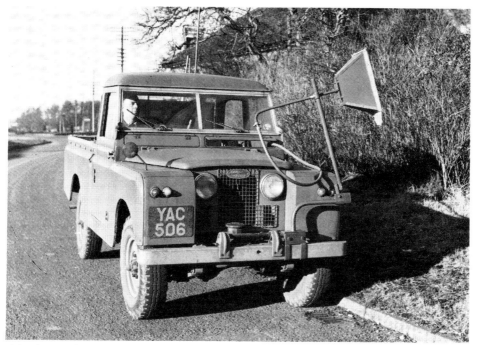

A Land-Rover fitted with a 'Fortemist' kerb unit in travelling position, converted by Evers & Wall.

Every Land-Rover built has found an eager customer waiting to buy it – and customer reaction has played a vital part in the vehicle's evolution. It became clear from the outset that it would be expected to function in widely differing spheres of operation, which was perhaps the least anticipated selling factor during the period of initial development. The clue to its unpredicted success lay in this breadth of its appeal – not just to farmers, but to police forces, armed services, building contractors, expeditions, rescue services, electricity boards, and private estates, to name just a few.

Later, another enormous bonus which further helped to indoctrinate the public into the everyday use of 4-wheel drive vehicles for road-going purposes, was the successful application to have Purchase Tax removed on those Land-Rovers that could be categorized in the commercial class as opposed to the private car class. Every motor vehicle had to be slotted into a category for the imposition of appropriate legislation, but the versatility of the Land-Rover made this an issue of extreme complexity, affecting not only its eligibility for Purchase Tax exemption, but the type of fuel on which it could be run (in the days of petrol rationing after the war, commercial vehicles could be run on the cheaper 'pink' petrol), and the maximum speed up to which it could be driven on the road (the speed limit for commercial vehicles was then 30 mph, which meant an unacceptably slow journey for the relatively spry Land-Rover). It was not until the mid-1950s that the position was eventually clarified, when it was prounced a 'dual-purpose' vehicle: if it was used for carrying freight, it was a commercial vehicle and free of purchase tax, while if it was used in place of an estate car, it was liable. After the introduction of the 12-seater Station Wagon in 1962, the authorities had to exempt this one because it was officially tagged a bus – which meant of course that this model became immensely popular, whatever its intended purpose, to the virtual exclusion of the 10-seater which didn't qualify.

One year earlier, nobody could have foreseen that by October 1948 a second type of Land-Rover would have been produced: a hard-top version of the 80-inch with a new light alloy body, new doors, horizontally split tailgate hinged top and bottom, and two inward-facing seats on each side of the rear, giving a seating capacity for seven passengers. In theory, this was an excellent first step in providing an alternative to the basic machine already in existence, but there was the problem of pricing. Because it had to include Purchase Tax of over £200, the final price was about £960 – compared to £450 for the open model. The latter was now extremely good value, especially as within a very short time Rover had included such 'extras' as the doors and sidescreens, passenger seat and seat cushions, spare tyre, spare wheel carrier, starting handle and driver's hood, without raising the overall cost of the vehicle. This first estate model effectively priced itself out of the market and by 1951 it was discontinued. Here was a lesson learnt, and no subsequent Land-Rover development has proved to be such an expensive and inglorious failure, thanks to much improved market research.

Having accepted that the Land-Rover was here to stay, and had indeed become a well-established part of the rural, industrial and military scene, the Wilks brothers realized that development was inescapable. They had simply got off on the wrong foot with their first attempt. Before the original Land-Rover was four years old, a different variation on the theme was available, and proving very popular this time. This sister model was a revised, cheaper version of the 7-seater Station Wagon in a much more basic form, with a hard-top and side windows – all built on the same 80-inch chassis and using the same 1,595 cc Rover P-3 engine. The only mechanical alteration to have taken place since the introduction of the Land-Rover was to the transmission in the front power line: with a more powerful engine in the offing, it was felt advisable to protect the transmission by making 4-wheel drive automatic in low transfer gear and splitting the torque. To do this, the free-wheel was dropped in favour of the system in use today, using a simple dog clutch. In 1952 the engine itself was changed to the larger, more powerful 1,997 cc unit because the physical demands being made of the vehicle were in excess of its capability. Once in possession of the innovatory machine, owners expected it to balk at nothing, and the company decided that, rather than trying to re-educate them, it would be justified in providing more power. This was only the start of the public dictating the direction in which Land-Rover was to evolve – but Tom Barton's engineering team were united behind the Wilks in

30

their decision only to implement such modifications as would improve the vehicle's versatility, durability and saleability. This most definitely did not include any refinements conducive to driver or passenger comfort.

Predictably enough, the 1950s were to prove the most dramatic decade for Land-Rover development, the era when it matured into the go-anywhere/do-anything transport for which it has become so famous. For several years the designers, engineers and planners scarcely had time to draw breath at Solihull – where by then the Land-Rover had become the principal product. The next customer quibble that had to be quietened was that there was insufficient length in the rear loading area. Initially, the solution to this problem was found to be in extending the wheelbase dimensions of the chassis, from the well-known 80 inches to 86 inches – technically a more exacting and costly development than it would seem – but this was accompanied by a far more daring and ambitious development: the long wheelbase Land-Rover. This model was born in 1954, simultaneously with the 86-inch short wheelbase. The extension of the short wheelbase model was effected by the addition of 6 inches between the bulkhead and back axle, with a further 3 inches of floor behind the axle, so that in practice the load space behind the seats was increased by 9 inches; the new long wheelbase model enlarged the load space by 21 inches more than that. The customers' complaint had been heeded, and most efficiently silenced, but at no small cost. Apart from the obvious requirement of new chassis members, the 86-inch version demanded a new propeller shaft, new springs (rear), new body panelling and a new exhaust system, not to mention a host of more minor modifications, which all added up to a high percentage of new components. The 107-inch long wheelbase, however, was a far larger undertaking. It shared common components with the 86-inch vehicle in the frame construction but the main side members had to be completely retooled, and in many other respects it was like producing an entirely new vehicle – though the end product was the familiar Land-Rover, only longer.

Both these extended versions were destined to be manufactured in this form for little more than two years, when further changes took place, this time partly to quell a totally different customer grumble. A demand had rapidly grown up for a diesel-powered Land-Rover. Many fleet-users were having to purchase petrol just for their Land-Rovers, and commonization of fuel was soon to be regarded as both practical and logical. The Rover Company had so far had neither use for nor experience of diesel engines, but with typical thoroughness it embarked on the arduous business of researching and developing its own design of light diesel engine, unique to the Land-Rover and very different from the existing petrol engine. During its development it became apparent that it was too big to drop into the existing engine housing, whatever they contrived to do with it: so the vehicle had to be enlarged yet again. Both 86-inch and 107-inch models had to have an extra 2 inches inserted in the chassis behind the front axle and in front of the toeboard, though for a year or so this mystified the public because the transfer of engine did not take place concurrently with the puzzlingly slight chassis extension. The new dimensions, of 88 inches and 109 inches, have existed ever since, for both petrol and diesel powered Land-Rovers.

With the implementation of all these developments, the range of options increased dramatically. Alternative power units and a choice of body styles ensured Land-Rover of ever expanding trade – but after 10 years it could not count on holding the centre of this particular 4 x 4 stage forever, and neither could it afford to rest on its laurels. The Series I model needed reappraisal. The challenge was given to the Rover's styling department: to do something with the vehicle's appearance, which had never before been under serious scrutiny at any time of its life. The subtlety lay in improving its style without damaging its rugged efficiency and without adding any superfluous trim for the sake of mere appearances; in other words, changes had to be discreet, and very carefully considered.

As the Rover diesel engine was introduced, a new Rover petrol unit was already in the pipeline, sharing many common features, engineering and production tooling with the diesel to replace the original P4-based engine. By now Land-Rover exploitation was rife, and everybody who owned one tended to expect more from it than it had been designed to provide: an increase in power was unavoidable. The power of the new 2,286 cc petrol engine compared with Rover's first diesel was as follows:

Maximum power:	*Maximum torque:*
Petrol: 52 bhp at 4,000 rpm	101 lb/ft at 1,500 rpm
Diesel: 52 bhp at 3,500 rpm	87 lb/ft at 2,000 rpm

This new unit provided the most significant technical difference in the revised Land-Rover, Series II. Evolved from the same basic layout as the Rover diesel engine, the 2,286 cc petrol unit had a bore and stroke of 90.47 x 88.9 mm (compared to 85.7 x 88.9 mm for the diesel), and it was bigger and stronger than its predecessor. The latter was by no means insubstantial, but it had been around for a long time – 10 years powering Land-Rovers and 10 years before that. Land-Rovers were ready to take on something more impressive, and the Series II was to provide the shell in which it would be accommodated.

In styling terms, the differences between the new Series II and the Series I which it was to supersede, were practical and in no way extreme: gentle reshaping of doors, wings (front and rear) and bonnet panel; sill panels fitted to conceal the exhaust system and chassis frame from view in profile (the designers felt that the vehicle was improperly dressed without this skirting below wings and doors); glass to replace the perspex of the sliding side windows; and several unseen improvements such as increase in wheel movement caused by relocation of rear springs, improved lock (reducing the turning circle by over 3 feet in the case of the short wheelbase model, and 5 feet on the 109-inch), and better ventilation through manually adjusted air-intakes along the base of the windscreen. From £450 for the 1948 80-inch Series I model, the 88-inch petrol Series II was introduced at £640, while the long wheelbase equivalent was £730. It is no coincidence that the Austin Gipsy appeared on the open market at about the same time as the Series II, but neither would it be fair to say that the threat posed by the Gipsy's appearance on the scene caused the Series II to be produced. Sales of the Series I were going well and a change of model was bound to cut back supply temporarily, but Land-Rover were in need of a competitor, and this product provided a necessary and healthy fillip to maintain Land-Rover's standards and keep its customers happy. Two years later the Home Sales Manager claimed that the changeover to Series II had caused home sales to double, so this policy was clearly the right one.

By the time its tenth birthday came around, the old 80-inch canvas-topped petrol Land-Rover had been replaced by two 88-inch Land-Rovers (petrol or diesel powered), and four 109-inch Land-Rovers (basic or de-luxe, petrol or diesel). However, by then the price the company was having to pay for its famous product was in having every other 4 x 4 machine ever invented being referred to as a land-rover. This caused the Rover Company to come up with the telling advertisement, 'When better land rovers are made, the Rover company will make them'. For the BBC, the problem had been reversed: because of their commitment not to advertise, they would not use the term Land-Rover, but – illogically – spoke freely of the 'Jeep', until the Rover

This Series II Land-Rover was specially customized for HM Queen Elizabeth II.

Company pointed out that in so doing they were inadvertently promoting an American product over a British one. Thereafter Land-Rover was given its rightful name.

The Series II Land-Rover sold over 28,000 in its first full year, and over 34,000 the year after. Just over three years after its introduction, the Series II was to be replaced by the Series IIA, but the only appreciable difference in this applied to the diesel engined version. In 1958 the Series II had introduced the up-graded petrol engine to increase commonization of tooling with the diesel unit, but now in 1961 it was the turn of the diesel 2,052 cc engine to be up-graded to match the bore and stroke of the petrol 2,286 cc unit. By the end of that year Series IIA Land-Rovers were rapidly replacing the original Series II off the production line. The following year, 1962, saw the introduction of the first 12-seater Land-Rovers seating three people in the front, three in the back on a forward-facing bench seat, and three on each of the two inward-facing seats accessible from the rear door. This meant that the vehicle fell conveniently into the category of a bus, as far as the authorities were concerned, and hence could be sold free of Purchase Tax. This ploy soon virtually killed any demand for the 10-seater on the home market as, naturally enough, the public opted for the cheaper vehicle which was otherwise identical – but it is doubtful (to say the least!) that these 12-seaters have always been used to transport twelve people at a time. Anyone who has tried being one of twelve passengers in a Land-Rover will confirm that it is far from ideal, especially for the six in the rear where the lack of headroom is only eclipsed by the lack of legroom. However, as a device to cut the purchase price for home market Land-Rover Station Wagons, it has continued to work very well for over 20 years.

The 12-seater was not the only new model to emerge from the Solihull plant in 1962. It was accompanied by an entirely different-looking Land-Rover – one that seemed at first glance to be more related to a truck than to the regular Land-Rover. This was the forward-control unit that grew out of the demand for a far more robust load-carrier, one that was capable of bearing up to 30 cwt in reasonable conditions and 25 cwt cross-country, with a much enlarged load-space. Basing such a requirement on the Land-Rover 109-inch chassis and engine meant total revision of layout, body style and transmission – the obvious first amendment being to the basic structure. In order to achieve the flat platform for additional load-space, a new frame was built to marry on to the existing 109-inch chassis. This proved to be much more economical than developing a completely new chassis for the purpose but resulted in a relatively heavy unit, given that the normal Land-Rover 2,286 cc petrol engine was to be used. This possibly explains the comparatively short production period of the vehicle in this form, from its announcement in 1962 at the Commercial Vehicle Show until 1966, when it was redesigned to offer the option of the diesel 2,286 cc engine and also a 6-cylinder engine. Because of the drastic changes in layout from the conventional Land-Rover plan, forward-control was incorporated at the outset, as well as heavy duty axles and much bigger tyres, but the majority of components were, surprisingly, the same as those used on the regular Land-Rover. The appearance was altered as much by the repositioning of the cab as by the increase in ground clearance and load-space area. The forward-control Land-Rover's cab was placed much further forward to allow load-space behind, and provided the only seating arrangements. Adapted from the existing cab, it could be either open or of the truck variety. Gear change linkage and the layout of the steering had to be redesigned among all the other more minor details, but the end result was still unmistakably a Land-Rover. When, four years later, it was altered to accommodate the 2,286 cc diesel engine option, it also became available with a 6-cylinder, 2,625 cc petrol engine that had been developed from the earlier Rover car P4/P5, noted for its reliability. The wheelbase was extended by 1 inch, and the wheel tracks by 4 inches for improved handling and stability. This model was to endure in its revised form until just before the introduction of the specialized forward-control military Land-Rover built on the 101-inch wheelbase, with the V8 3,528 cc engine, and constant 4-wheel drive – a far more sophisticated machine. Although a prototype was to be seen at the Commercial Vehicle Show in 1972, production didn't start until 1974/5. The new light-weight military 88-inch Land-Rover was introduced concurrently, and full descriptions of both these units are included in the Military chapter.

This same 6-cylinder 2,625 cc engine also became available in the 109-inch wheelbase of the conventional Land-Rover in 1967, to give it greater refinement. Being longer, it was a tight squeeze to fit it in but by allowing the space for bellhousing and clutch to be pared down to the barest minimum it was achieved without extending any existing dimensions. At the same time, both 88-inch and 109-inch models were treated to an internal facelift in the driving compartment, encompassing windscreen wiper, handbrake, controls, instruments, switches and dials, as well as vastly improved front seat cushioning which became available as an optional extra on all Series IIA models. None of these adjustments affected the external appearance of the Land-Rover which had remained basically unchanged since its initial restyling. In 1968, however, the headlamps on export models were to change their position, which noticeably altered the front view: having been mounted close together, deep-set between the wings and protected by the radiator grille, they were moved out to the wing position that they have held ever since. This was induced by specific legislation in certain overseas territories relating to motor vehicle lighting. A year later home market models were to follow suit and have wing-mounted headlamps as well.

The advent of the Range Rover in 1970 and its subsequent development is dealt with in detail in its own chapter, so we shall skip on to 1971 when the Series IIA Land-Rovers were replaced by the Series III, with the exception of the forward-control 109-inch vehicles. These continued to be produced in the Series IIA form until they were finally superseded by the 101-inch 1-tonne Land-Rovers.

A Series III Land-Rover cab interior with redesigned dashboard.

The Series III came about for reasons which were very similar to those behind the introduction of the Series II. While there was nothing in particular wrong with the current model, it was not noticeably moving with the times, had not undergone drastic changes or improvements since its beginnings, and was facing increasing competition with every passing year. This time, had the capital been available, perhaps a totally revamped version could have resulted from all the probing and questioning that took place behind the scenes at Solihull, but – as always – despite its success as an exportable commodity as well as on the home front, the cash to expand and develop was limited. Additionally, Land-Rovers buyers were not clamouring for radical change, because the old-style workhorse was still proving very popular. Thus, what eventually came about was not a remarkably restyled machine, but the Land-Rover as we know it today, which is still being assembled in ever greater quantities each year. It differs from its predecessor in many details, but the chassis, wheelbase dimensions, body styles, suspensions and general layout remained unchanged. One crucial difference was in the transmission: the original basic gearbox was finally discarded in favour of a new all-synchromesh design which was unique to the Series III Land-Rover within the Rover stable. With synchromesh on all forward gears, it had revised internal ratios (first and reverse ratios were much reduced), and a reduced low-range step-down ratio, which combined to uphold stoically the Land-Rover's climbing capability, while facilitating a smoother and quieter gear change, helped by the inclusion at this stage of a diaphragm spring clutch. Other mechanical alterations to the basic specification of the vehicle included the replacement of dynamos by alternators, improved brakes, and heavy-duty rear axles (and strengthened stub axles) fitted as standard on all long wheelbase models, while vacuum-servos were also standardized on all 6-cylinder models. Visually, there was little alteration externally, the principal difference being in the new radiator grille, but internally it was another story: the dashboard was completely redesigned, incorporating an open stowage locker, and the new steering-column switchgear and steering wheel (as well as steering lock) were prominent features. There was also a much better fresh-air heater. Land-Rover was beginning to recognize that its customers did not necessarily have to be penalized by undergoing a constant endurance test, but were quite entitled to their creature comforts, especially considering the hardships to be suffered in some areas of Land-Rover operations. The Series III even had provision for a radio to be fitted, which would have been laughable in 1948.

Before moving on to the 1970s, there is one other model to mention, dating from 1968. This is the heavy duty 1-ton Land-Rover, built on the Series IIA 109 inch chassis (and physically resembling this model on completion) but with much reduced overall gearing to allow for the loading and towing of increased weights. The '1-ton' description refers to the official maximum total payload, but like all official limits it has to err on the side of conservatism because it is bound to be exceeded – as Land-Rover manufacturers were to discover from the word go. The 1-ton took the wise precaution of bracing itself against such abuse: equipped with the heavy duty transmission components of the forward-control Land-Rover, it achieved overall ratios of 15.40:1, 23.10:1, 34.10:1, 55.3:1, and 46.4:1 in reverse when in low range, which effectively widened the potential of Land-Rover accomplishments. Although it never became a great seller, this unit held a much-valued place in the more specialized and rarified sector of the market, until it was replaced by the Series III equivalent model when these became standard in 1971.

In 1976 an auspicious occasion was celebrated at Solihull, with the production of Land-Rover Number One-Million. This was a short wheelbase 7-seater which was destined to join the very first Land-Rover, RO.1, in the Leyland Historic Vehicles Collection. The quarter-million mark had been reached in 1959, the half-million mark in 1966, and the three-quarter million mark in 1971.

From the point of view of product development, the next highly significant milestone was the introduction of the 109 inch V8 engined Land-Rover in 1979. The total 4 x 4 market had been growing rapidly and consistently and, accordingly, the product requirements had also been evolving. Interest

Note the redesigned front of the V8 Land-Rover.

stimulated by increased ecological awareness, and by increased leisure-use of 4-wheel-drive vehicles, coupled with the improved road networks in many overseas territories, imposed higher standards of performance and comfort both on and off the road. The Range Rover proved beyond all doubt that luxury and ruggedness could be successfully united, and that a market existed for this combination. What the V8 Land-Rover presented was the dependability, the load-space and the indestructability of the Land-Rover, combined with the proven power unit and drive-line of the Range Rover. Although the power output of the V8 was reduced to suit customer application of the new Land-Rover, it is still one-third up on the 4-cylinder model. The 3,528cc 8-cylinder light alloy petrol unit entailed under-the-bonnet enlargement of the standard 109 inch model (the V8 engine was not made available on the 88 inch chassis) which explains the frontal re-styling that distinguishes it so glaringly from all other Land-Rovers. The bonnet, fitted with a broad metal radiator grille, extends to fit flush with the wings, and the radiator is no longer recessed between the wings as has been the case on all former models.

The smoother, more powerful V8 engine enhances on-road performance and produces peak torque and power at exceptionally low engine speeds,

The V8 doesn't intend to be taken for anything else!

A V8 engine

Early V8 Land-Rovers fording a stream.

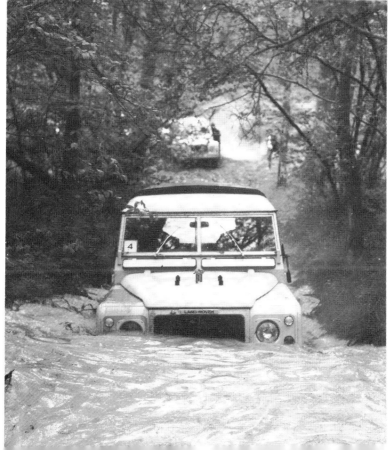

improving towing capability as well as the cross-country performance (this is dealt with in detail in the Expedition chapter). Like the Range Rover, the V8 Land-Rover offers permanent 4-wheel drive, and when the going gets really tough the centre differential can be locked for even greater traction. The engine gives a top speed of over 80 mph, and the ability to climb gradients as steep as 45° or 1 in 1. The introduction of the V8 Land-Rover was marked by new dazzling colour options – Java green, Masai red, Inca yellow, and Pageant blue – as well as the more sober selection of colours current on existing Series III models.

At this stage it should be pointed out that one great advantage of the 'meccano'-style design of the Land-Rover is that it can be exported in kit form and assembled overseas. A total of nearly 50,000 Land-Rovers are sold in this way every year, and about 2,300 Range Rovers. The following countries have their own Land-Rover assembly plants: Angola, Australia, Iran, Kenya, Malagasy, Malaysia, Indonesia, Morocco, New Zealand, Nigeria, Phillipines, Spain, Portugal, South Africa, Tanzania, Thailand, Trinidad, Zaire, Zambia, Zimbabwe, and most recently of all, Sudan. This is an aspect of Land-Rover exports which is constantly developing and growing – though it means that model changes are not always greeted with enthusiasm by the overseas factories: changes at home entail equivalent changes abroad, and the wisdom of it all is not always appreciated by those assembling Land-Rovers at long range!

Santana

In 1956 The Rover Company reached an agreement with a company in Spain called Metalurgica de Santa Ana, S.A., manufacturers of 4-wheel drive vehicles. Though BL is still today the largest single share-holder in the company that was formed then, 'Santana' Land-Rovers have evolved rather differently from their British-made equivalent models, mainly because of the markets into which they sell. The Spanish factories produce their Land-Rovers under licence, selling throughout the Spanish territories and exporting to 25 countries, predominantly in South America, Central America and North Africa. They also manufacture Land-Rovers in knock-down form for export to Morocco, Iran and Costa Rica, where they are assembled on arrival.

The original company was founded with a total capital of 3 million pesetas, but there are now four major Santana bases in Spain: two important manufacturing sites, a technical service centre, and the head offices in Madrid. Their output of Land-Rovers has steadily risen over the years, topping 18,000 by 1980, and the firm also makes gear boxes, over 93,000 of which were sold in that year.

Most Santana Land-Rovers are based on the Series III A unit, but are adapted to suit local market requirements and conditions. Nearly all their vehicles are diesel-engined as their order books always show a heavy bias in favour of diesel, so they haven't become involved with the manufacture of V8s, and they don't manufacture Range Rovers at all. Although there is an infinite

The Spanish-built Santana S-2000.

number of variations on the theme, there are five basic variations of the 88-inch, four of the 109-inch (with either 4-or 6-cylinder engine option) and two of their own model S-2000 which is an extremely tough and versatile forward control truck, not unlike the 101-inch 1-tonne Land-Rover that used to be produced for the military market at Solihull. For fans of the 101-inch, it is comforting that there is still a comparably resilient and powerful vehicle being manufactured by Santana, although production of the 101-inch itself has ceased, and their product is sold for use as anything from a tipper to a cattle- or vehicle-transporter, and – unlike the 101-inch – is also available with an extended cab incorporating a second row of seats.

There are instances where Santana has developed in areas that the British parent company has not, for example in taper leaf suspension, and their own turbo charged $2\frac{1}{4}$ litre diesel engine. If you come across a Land-Rover when you are abroad that has real leather upholstery and much more comfortable seats, or a polished wooden handle on the gear lever, you can be pretty sure that it originates from the Santana stable.

* * * * *

The £200 million investment programme, embarked on relatively soon after Land-Rover Limited was established as a self-governing company, was geared to encompass a series of new developments. Stage 1 gave us the V8; then came the 4-door Range Rover, which was followed by the up-market 'County' Land-

An early 110-inch prototype undergoing testing at Eastnor Castle.

Rover, and the High-Capacity Pick-Up, or HCPU as it quickly became known. This was followed, early in 1983, by the 110-inch model, a dramatically different vehicle planned to eventually replace all 109-inch Series III Land-Rovers, then, in 1984, the final stage of the investment programe was marked by the launch of the completely new model, the 90-inch, but let us first deal with the 1982 innovations.

The 'County' was introduced to bridge the 'comfort gap' between existing Land-Rovers and the Range Rover, focussing mainly on seating, upholstery, trim and noise reduction. The end result is certainly a Land-Rover with a difference, decidedly up-grading it, while only increasing the price by four-to five-hundred pounds above standard models.

The 'County' is easily distinguished from its sister-models by full-length side stripes running horizontally along the body, and also by such refinements as tinted glass windows, reversing light, rear mud flaps, side flashers and spare wheel cover, all of which are standard items. The seats in front are a new de-luxe design for far greater comfort, and all seats are upholstered in a grey-black tweed which is a very pleasant change from the cold black vinyl of the usual Land-Rover seating (though we were a bit worried about keeping the fabric clean and looking good: most attractive when brand new but perhaps less of an assett when grubby and stained). Instead of a centre front seat, a

Land-Rover enthusiasts meet to view the new 110-inch in 1983.

The 110 Station Wagon.

45

lockable box can be fitted, as in Range Rovers, and the position of both front seats can be adjusted forwards and backwards as well as having a reclining back: very good news for those of us who have suffered from 'Land-Rover Back' over the years, owing to the seat's hitherto uncompromising rigidity. It might look a bit gimmicky on such a work-horse of a vehicle, but, particularly on long slow towing journeys, the additional comfort makes for a much more relaxed driver (and passenger) at the end of the day. Engine noise reduction also contributes to the sense of well-being when driving this vehicle, and when 'County' trim is coupled to the 110-inch Station Wagon body and power-assisted steering (as was the case with the first one we drove), it is almost possible to forget you are in a Land-Rover at all! On all Station Wagons in the 'County' range, a Boge Hydromat self-levelling unit is a standard fitting, improving the ride still further. For power, lightness and classy detail this model seemed at once to be a sure winner.

As might be expected, the main feature of the High-Capacity Pick-Up is its increased and improved load space. The load bed is completely new, and there is an additional 7 inches behind the rear chassis member. No longer do you see full-length boxes on each side of the load space, the only boxed-in area being over the rear wheels themselves. Effectively the cubic capacity has been increased by 45%, and the tailgate, supported now by coated steel wire instead of the familiar chains, is 18 inches wider than on standard pick-ups. Number plate and light are mounted on the tailgate, and there are now tubular steel protective 'mini-bumpers' below both light panels. Another clever feature is in the load space having a double skin, so that scratching and denting of the interior does not mar the exterior appearance.

Now, what about the 110-inch, the long-awaited 'new' Land Rover? Before its unveiling, rumours abounded about this model, and personally we were quite worried that Land-Rover might have gone too far, firmly believing that any vehicle worthy of the name Land-Rover must be immediately recognisable as such. Luckily the apprehension was ill-founded, as all the external differences are relatively discreet, like the taller one-piece windscreen, flares over the wheel arches (in flexible polyurethane) and wider plastic, radiator grille and headlamp panel, while the more remarkable differences are concealed from view, like the superb coil suspension, permanent 4-wheel drive, 5-speed gear box on 4-cylinder models, and new disc brakes on the front. The interior, too, has changed. The hand brake has been modified, the dashboard panel updated, the heater improved, the doors lined with new one-piece trim and fitted with new handles and locks (all doors lock externally), and ventilation to the interior is improved by new sliding windows, whose locking device was initially disastrous but quickly remedied. From the driver's seat the windscreen's additional height and uninterrupted expanse can be fully appreciated; it improves visibility much more than the extra 2 inches in height would suggest, and makes older models seem very restricted in comparison. Power-assisted steering is optional on the 110-inch, and engine options are the

One of the most fundamental improvements adopted in the 110 was the coil-spring suspension.

A view of the 110's mechanical components.

47

4-cylinder, $2\frac{1}{4}$ litre petrol, $2\frac{1}{2}$ litre diesel, and the V8. At the time of its launch, people expressed disappointment that the overall dimensions and form of the 110-inch were not more drastically different, but since the model is intended to elbow the Series III out altogether through time, there are obvious practical and economic reasons why many Series III features should be retained. Gilroy has been quoted as saying, "The element of continuity is very important, because we operate in a conservative market that appreciates evolution rather than revolution ...", which we feel encapsulates Land-Rover's philosophy with regard to product development. Even though the approach has clearly been 'evolutionary' rather than 'revolutionary', the resulting model is without question the most important and striking single development from Land-Rover since it became established. Within a year of the 110's appearance on the market in March 1983 its impact was already being felt, not only at home but in Europe, the Middle East and Far East as well, culminating in an unexpected fillip to sales figures with a military order from the Far East for 900 110-inch units, well in advance of anticipated military sales, after what Tony Gilroy described as, "the most extensive testing and trials ever encountered".

For Land-Rover's management the other gratifying new area that opened with the 110-inch – especially with the "County" Station Wagon – was that of the large estate car, with which Land-Rover had been unable to compete in the past in terms of comfort; the 110-inch broke down those barriers to include a whole new market sector, and in the UK in 1983 Land-Rover had its best selling year since 1980 (one third of the units sold were 110-inch models which is not at all bad for a vehicle's first year!).

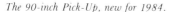

The 90-inch Pick-Up, new for 1984.

In May 1984 Land-Rover was ready to announce the first set of improvements to the vehicle, having evidently quizzed their customers extensively on
suggested further refinements. The up-shot was, for the first time ever, wind-
up windows on the front doors to replace the sliding type (which greatly
improves visibility, and makes putting your head out to reverse, or watch the
ground when negotiating 'rough-stuff' off-the-road, a great deal less
hazardous); new door trim to smarten up the interior appearance; new sliding
windows on the rear section of the Station Wagon which are easier to adjust,
and a new wash-wipe system on the rear door window which is also now
electrically heated. Keeping the rear window clean is a long overdue
refinement in view of the exceptionally wet and muddy conditions through
which many Land-Rovers travel in the course of a day's work. Added to all
this, in the 'County' version you find fitted carpets! When the Range Rover
turned up carpeted many years ago there were plenty of raised eyebrows, but
whoever would have guessed that this would be the way of the Land-Rover as
well? In practice, of course, it reduces noise levels still further, is a great deal
more comfortable, and looks very good. Gone are the days when Land-Rovers
were designed essentially for farming, though, of course, you can still get them
appropriately equipped just for that. Looking at the new 110-inch though,
every indication is that Land-Rover knows exactly where it's going, through
the eighties and beyond.

If the 110-inch seemed like a breakthrough in 1983, it was certainly rivalled
in 1984 by the startling arrival of its little sister, the 90-inch. Here was a vehicle
without comparison, a jaunty yet streamlined body sitting lightly on its
powerful coil springs, yet as tough and durable as any 4 x 4 anywhere,
designed to reach a ripe old age ("where others build in obsolescence, we build
in longevity" – Tony Gilroy) without losing any of its work-horse qualities.
The ingenuity entailed in conceiving such a vehicle, which combines old
attributes with new standards of comfort, efficiency and technology without
any evident compromise, in a much more compact package, is a measure of
the experience and expertise of the team behind it, who we reckon have earned
a standing ovation for this one, though when we said as much at the launch of
the new unit, the response of the management was, to a man, "never mind the
accolades, as long as we fill the order books!" It is, after all, a ferociously
competitive field, and to maintain its forward position Land-Rover has not
only to create innovative products, but sell them very hard. Nobody could
deny that the current models will stand them in excellent stead to combat
whatever opposition turns up.

The new 90-inch, or 'Ninety', may be much smaller than the 110-inch, but
it is actually nearly $4\frac{1}{2}$-inches longer than the Series III 88-inch and of its class
has unsurpassed payload potential with bigger cubic capacity and load length,
but one interesting feature of the model is that the rear overhang is $2\frac{1}{2}$ inches
less, which means the vehicle has an impressive departure angle of up to 52°,
as well as better towing ability. The model is manufactured with either a petrol

The interior shared by the 90 and 110, showing how far the Land-Rover has come over the years.

or a diesel 4-cylinder engine, the latter being the latest 2.5 litre diesel. The petrol engine develops 74bhp (55kw) and 120 lbf ft (163 Nm) of torque from its 2286cc. The 2495cc diesel engine, introduced only months before the 90-inch itself, gives 67 bhp (50kw) and 114 lbf ft (155Nm) of torque at only 1800 rpm, and is proving to be a very popular development, especially with those who use power take-off equipment, because of the economy and dependability it provides. Throughout the 90-inch range, which includes soft-top, hard-top, pick-up and 6- or 7-seater station wagon in both standard and 'County' versions, as well as chassis-cab for would-be converters, 5-speed transmission with 2-speed transfer box is fitted as standard, plus permanent 4-wheel drive. Power-assisted steering is available as an option for the first time ever on a short wheelbase, (and when combined with the top-of-the-range 'County' Station Wagon makes for phenomenally smooth riding and handling). Externally, the 90-inch has many features in common with the 110-inch: the flexible 'eyebrows' of the wheel arches, the flush black radiator grille, and of course the one-piece windscreen, which is increased in size by 25% over its Series III equivalent. Also in common with the revised 110-inch, there are wind-up windows and new trim on the doors (front passengers might miss the door's arm-rest, however), an improved heating system, decreased noise levels and an up-dated design of instrument panel in the dashboard. Also in common with 110-inch models, 90-inch Station Wagons have heated rear window-glass and a modern wash-wipe system – the water being very effectively squirted from the side of the glass instead of from the base. While on the subject of rear windows it is perhaps worth mentioning a fact that Land-Rover is rather pleased about, and that is the introduction of aluminium rear window frames as standard on pick-up cabs and Station Wagons, reducing the rust problem. Aluminium as a material has been a good friend to Land-Rover (and a good selling point over the years) so they are always glad to see the percentage of aluminium increased as their vehicles evolve. The 'County'

A Janspeed turbo installation on a 2¼ litre diesel Land Rover engine.

version, as on the 110-inch wheelbase, has its own special refinements: hard-wearing carpet front and rear, tinted glass, a quartz clock, spare wheel cover and radial tyres.

Physically a lot less obvious than all the above modifications, but one of the most significant features of the 90-inch range is the suspension, which is also shared with the 110-inch. The new front and rear long-travel coil springs, with 2-way hydraulic dampers, dramatically improve rider comfort both on-road and off, and make cornering and general handling far surer since the friction inherent in multi-leaf springs is eliminated. Another important innovation is powerful servo-assisted disc-brakes for the front wheels which resist fade, and take less time to dry out after passing through deep water than the Series III brakes. The drums at the rear have improved sealing (like the 110-inch) all of which provides remarkably good and steady stopping power, even when heavily laden, or towing. The discs and drums are supplemented by a 110 inch (254mm) transmission handbrake. The front wheels also have more room to manoeuvre on the new models because the track has been increased to $58\frac{1}{2}$ inches (2360mm), which makes negotiation of awkward spaces or dense traffic much simpler.

The payload of the 90-inch is another of its impressive characteristics (and one which proves that all the 'refining' has not been at the expense of work-horse capability, but rather in support of it). Where such competitors as Daihatsu carry 411 kg, the CJ5 Jeep 531 kg, the Colt Shogun 735 kg and even the Galaendewagen by Mercedes-Benz only 805 kg, the 90-inch exceeds even its own predecessor – the 88-inch Series III – by achieving a payload of 917 kg, and can tow an unbraked trailer of up to 750 kg, or a fully braked unit of up to 4 tonnes. The key to this unprecedented strength lies in the immensely

Two 90-inch variants; the luxurious 'County' and the soft-top workhorse Pick-Up.

robust separate, box-section ladder-type steel chassis which is in effect just a shortened version of the 110's (useful commonality for servicing and spares), and is designed to protect the 12-gallon, side-mounted fuel tank as well as to provide front and rear jacking points.

Colour options for the 90-inch are those available for the rest of the range which was revised on all Land-Rovers in the Spring of 1984 to offer the following: Ivory, Masai Red, Stratos Blue, Marine Blue, Trident Green, Roan Brown and Slate Grey.

TECHNICAL DATA

2,286cc 4-CYLINDER DIESEL ENGINE

Engine, Diesel models

Bore	90.47 mm (3.562 in)
Stroke	88.9 mm (3.500 in)
Number of cylinders	4
Compression ratio	23:1
Cylinder capacity	2,286 cc (139.5 cu in)
BHP	67 (50 Kw) at 4,000 revs/min
Torque	14.5 kg m (105 lb ft) at 1,800 revs/min
Firing Order	1, 3, 4, 2
Tappet clearance, inlet	0.25 mm (0.010 in) } Engine at running
Tappet clearance, exhaust	0.25 mm (0.010 in) } temperature
Valve timing (No. 1 exhaust valve peak)	109° BTDC
Oil pressure	2,5 to 4,5 kg/cm² (35 to 65 lb/sq in) at 50 kph (30 mph) in top gear with engine warm
Lubrication	Full pressure
Oil filter, internal	Gauze pump intake filter in sump
Oil filter, external	Full-flow filter

BHP and maximum torque figures are derived from bench tests and do not allow for installation losses in the vehicle.

Fuel system, Diesel models

Fuel pump	Mechanical with hand primer (high pressure type)
Air cleaner	Oil bath type with integral centrifugal pre-cleaner
Fuel filters	Paper type element and sedimenter on export models

Injection system, Diesel models

Injector pump	Distributor type, self-governing
Injectors: Type	CAV Pintaux, nozzle size BDNO/SPC 6209
Start of injection	13° BTDC

2,625 cc 6-CYLINDER PETROL ENGINE

Engine, 6-cylinder Petrol models

Bore	77.8 mm (3.063 in)
Stroke	92.075 mm (3.625 in)
Number of cylinders	6
Cylinder capacity	2,625 cc (160.3 cu in)
Compression ratio	7.8:1
	7.0:1 (optional)
BHP } *BHP and maximum torque figures are derived from bench tests and do not allow for installation losses in the vehicle*	95 (71 Kw) at 4,500 revs/min
Maximum torque }	18.5 kg m (134 lb ft) at 1,750 revs/min

Firing order	1, 5, 3, 6, 2, 4
Sparking plugs	
7.8:1 and 7.0:1 compression ratio	Champion N5
Sparking plug point gap	0.75 to 0.80 mm (0.029 to 0.032 in)
Distributor contact breaker gap	0.35 to 0.40 mm (0.014 to 0.016 in)
Ignition timing static and dynamic	
7.8:1 compression ratio	2° ATDC 90 octane fuel United
	6° ADTC 85 octane fuel Kingdom
7.0:1 compression ratio (optional)	2° BTDC 83 octane fuel } use 2 star
7.0:1 compression ratio (optional)	TDC 80 octane fuel } grade fuel
Tappet clearance, inlet	0.15 mm (0.006 in) Engine hot
Tappet clearance, exhaust	0.25 mm (0.010 in) Engine hot or cold
Valve timing (No. 1 exhaust valve peak)	
7.8:1 compression ratio	105° BTDC
7.0:1 compression ratio (optional)	105° BTDC
Oil pressure	2.8 to 3.5 kg/cm² (40 to 50 lb/sq in) at 50 kph (30 mph) in top gear with engine warm
Lubrication	Full pressure
Oil filter, internal	Gauze pum intake filter in sump
Oil filter, external	Full-flow filter

Fuel system, 6-cylinder Petrol models

Petrol pump   Electric, located at chassis side-member
Carburetter   Zenith Type 175 CD 2S single horizontal
     dust-proof
Air cleaner   Oil bath type with integral centrifugal
     pre-cleaner

SERIES III SHORT-WHEELBASE LAND-ROVER

Engine 2.25-litre (Petrol)

Type	4-cylinder petrol	
Bore	90.47 mm (3.56)	
Stroke	88.9 mm (3.5 in)	
Capacity	2286 cc	
Compression Ratio	7:1	8:1
Maximum Power	47.8 kW (64 bhp)	51.5 kW (69 bhp)
	at 4000 r/min	
Maximum Torque	154 N m (113.5 lb ft)	159 N m (117.2 lb ft)
	at 2000 r/min	
Firing Order	1, 3, 4, 2	

Engine 2.25-litre (Diesel)

Type   4-cylinder diesel
Bore   90.47 mm (3.56 in)
Stroke   88.9 mm (3.5 in)
Capacity   2286 cc
Compression Ratio   23.1
Maximum Power   41.9 kW (56.2 bhp) at 4000 r/min
Maximum Torque   137.3 N m (101.3 lb ft) at 1800 r/min

Lubrication

Nominal Pressure   Engine warm at 2000 r/min
     2.46–4.57 kg/cm^2 (35–65 lb/in^2)
Oil filters internal   Gauze pump-intake filter
         external   Full flow oil filter

Fuel System (Petrol)

Carburettor   Single Zenith 361V
Petrol Pump   Mechanical with priming lever and sediment
     bowl

Fuel System (Diesel)
Injectors   CAV Pintaux
Fuel Pump   Mechanical with priming lever
Injector Pump   Self-governing D.P.A. distributor type

Cooling System
Type   Pressurised with pump, fan, thermostat and
                             expansion tank
Working Pressure   0.63 kg/cm² (9 lb/in²)
Thermostat   82°C

Transmission
Clutch   Diaphragm spring, single dry plate
Diameter   241 mm (9.5 in)
Main Gearbox   4-speed and reverse
                             Synchromesh on forward gears
Transfer Gearbox   2-speed reduction on main gearbox output.
                             Two-/four-wheel-drive control on transfer box
                             output
Differential Ratios   Both Axles   4.7:1
Front Axle   Hypoid spiral-bevel, with fully-floating shafts
                             and enclosed universal joints
Rear Axle   Hypoid spiral-bevel, with full-floating shafts
Propeller Shafts   Open type 50.8 mm (2.0 in)

Steering
Type   Recirculating ball, worm and nut
Lock-to-lock   3.5 turns
Steering Damper   Optional – fitted to drag link (standard for
                             certain export markets)
Turning Circle   11.60 m (38 ft)

Wheels
Type   Steel-ventilated disc
Fixing   5 stud
Size   5.00F x 16 in
Tyre Size   6.00 x 16 in

Brakes
Type   Hydraulic drum
Drum Diameter   254 mm (10 in)
Brake Shoe Width   38 mm (1.50 in) front and rear
Handbrake   Mechanical – on transfer box output

Drum Diameter	228.6 mm (9.00 in)
Brake Shoe Width	44.5 mm (1.75 in)

Electrical – Petrol

Type	12-volt negative earth
Battery	58 amps/hour
Ignition	Coil
Alternator	16 ACR – 34 amp output
Starter Motor	Inertia type

Electrical – Diesel

Type	12-volt negative earth
Battery	95 amps/hour
Ignition	Compression ignition
Alternator	16 ACR – 34 amp output
Starter Motor	Pre-engaged type

Capacities

Cooling System (petrol)	8.1 litres (14.25 pt)
(diesel)	7.8 litres (13.75 pt)
Engine Oil (including filter)	6.85 litres (11.5 pt)
Main Gearbox	1.5 litres (2.5 pt)
Transfer Gearbox	2.5 litres (4.5 pt)
Rear Differential }	1.75 litres (3 pt)
Front Differential }	
Fuel Tank	45 litres (10 gal)

SERIES III LONG-WHEELBASE LAND-ROVER

Engine 2.25-litre (Petrol)

Type	4-cylinder	
Bore	90.47 mm (3.56 in)	
Stroke	88.9 mm (3.5 in)	
Capacity	2286 cc	
Compression Ratio	7:1	8:1
Maximum Power	47.8 kW (64 bhp)	51.5 kW (69 bhp)
	at 4000 r/min	
Maximum Torque	154 N m (113.5 lb ft)	159 N m (117.2 lb ft)
	at 2000 r/min	
Firing Order	1, 3, 4, 2	

Engine 2.6-litre (Petrol)

Type	6-cylinder	
Bore	77.8 mm (3.06 in)	
Stroke	92.07 mm (3.62 in)	
Capacity	2625 cc	
Compression Ratio	7:1	7.8:1
Maximum Power	53.7kW (72 bhp)	57.4 kW (76.9 bhp)
	at 4200 r/min	at 4500 r/min
Maximum Torque	160.9 N m (118.6 lb ft)	164.8 N m (121.5 lb ft)
	at 2000 r/min	
Firing Order	1, 5, 3, 6, 2, 4	

Engine 2.25-litre (Diesel)

Type   4-cylinder
Bore   90.47 mm (3.56 in)
Stroke   88.9 mm (3.5 in)
Capacity   2286 cc
Compression Ratio   23:1
Maximum Power   41.9 kW (56.2 bhp) at
                         4000 r/min
Maximum Torque   137.3 N m (101.3 lb ft) at 1800 r/min
Firing Order   1, 3, 4, 2

Lubrication

Nominal Pressure
2.25-litre engine   Engine warm at 2000 r/min
2.6-litre engine $2.46–4.57 \text{ kg/cm}^2$ (35–65 lb/in^2)
Oil filters internal $2.81–3.51 \text{ kg/cm}^2$ (40–50 lb/in^2)
             external   Gauze pump-intake filter
                           Full flow oil filter

Fuel System 2.25-litre (Petrol)

Carburettor   Single Zenith 361V
Petrol Pump   Mechanical with priming lever and sediment bowl

Fuel System 2.25-litre (Diesel)

Injectors   CAV Pintaux
Fuel Pump   Mechanical with priming lever
Injector Pump   Self-governing DPA distributor type

Fuel System 2.6-litre (Petrol)

Carburettor   Single Zenith 175-CD2S
Petrol Pump   Electric dual inlet

Cooling System

Type	Pressurised with pump, fan, thermostat and expansion tank
Working Pressure	0.63 kg/cm² (9 lb/in²)
Thermostat	2.25-litre engine 82°C
	2.6-litre engine 78°C

Transmission

Clutch	Diaphragm spring, single dry plate
Diameter	241 mm (9.5 in)
Main Gearbox	4-speed and reverse – synchromesh on forward gears
Transfer Gearbox	2-speed reduction on main gearbox output
	Two-/four-wheel-drive control on transfer box output
Differential Ratios	Both Axles 4.7:1
Front Axle	Hypoid spiral-bevel, with fully-floating shafts and enclosed universal joints
Rear Axle	Hypoid spiral-bevel, with fully-floating shafts
Propeller Shafts	Open type 50.8 mm (2.0 in)

Steering

Type	Recirculating ball, worm and nut
Lock-to-lock	3.5 turns
Steering Damper	Optional – fitted to drag link (standard for certain export markets)
Turning Circle	14.3 m (47ft)

Wheels

Type	Steel-ventilated disc
Fixing	5 stud
Size	5.50F x 16 in
Tyre Size	7.50 x 16 in

Brakes

Type	Hydraulic drum
Drum Diameter	279.4 mm (11 in)
Brake Shoe Width	
4-cylinder models	57.15 mm (2.25 in)
6-cylinder models	Front 76.2 mm (3 in)
	Rear 57.15 mm (2.25 in)
Handbrake	Mechanical – on transfer box output
Drum Diameter	228.6 mm (9.00 in)
Brake Shoe Width	44.5 mm (1.75 in)

Electrical – Petrol

Type	12-volt negative earth
Battery	58 amps/hour
Ignition	Coil
Alternator	16 ACR – 34 amp output
Starter Motor	Inertia type

Electrical – Diesel

Type	12-volt negative earth
Battery	95 amps/hour
Ignition	Coil
Alternator	16 ACR – 34 amp output
Starter Motor	Pre-engaged type

Capacities

Cooling System	
(2.25-litre petrol)	8.1 litres (14.25 pt)
(2.25-litre diesel)	7.8 litres (13.75 pt)
(2.6-litre petrol)	11.2 litres (20 pt)
Engine oil 2.25-litre engine	6.85 litres (11.5 pt)
(including filter) 2.6-litre engine	7.3 litres (13 pt)
Main Gearbox	1.5 litres (2.5 pt)
Transfer Gearbox	2.5 litres (4.5 pt)
Rear Differential	2.5 litres (4.5 pt)
Front Differential	1.75 litres (3 pt)
Fuel Tank	68 litres (15 gal)

STAGE 1 V8 109 INCH

Engine

Type	V8, overhead valves, water cooled
No of cylinders	8
Bore	3.5 in (88.9mm)
Stroke	2.8 in (71.1mm)
Cylinder capacity	215^3 ($3528cm^3$)
Piston area (total)	77 in^2 ($497cm^2$)
Compression ratio	8.13:1
Maximum power BHP	90.7
Maximum power PS	92 } @ 3500 rpm
Maximum power KW	67.7
Maximum torque	166.4 lbs/ft. (23 MKg) @ 2000 rpm
Maximum rev/min	5,000

Firing order	1,8,4,3,6,5,7,2
Crankshaft	Spheroidal graphite – iron; number bearings – 5.
Main and connecting rod bearing	Lead bronze, lead indium overlay.
Pistons	Aluminium alloy.
No of compression rings	2, top ring chromium plated.
No of scraper rings	1
Cylinder head	Aluminium alloy
Cylinder block	Aluminium alloy, with dry liners.
Camshaft	Position central, five bearings steel shells with white metal.
Valves	Overhead operation by hydraulic lifters and rockers.
Seat angle	45° inlet and exhaust.
Valve timing inlet opens	30° BTDC
closes	75° ABDC
Exhaust opens	68° BBDC
closes	37° ATDC
Valve Lift	0.39 in (9.9mm) inlet and exhaust.
Ignition Control	Ballasted Coil.
Ignition Timing	Detox TDC
	Non Detox 6° BTDC
Sparking Plugs type	N12Y
gap	0.025 in (0.65mm)
Distributor contact breaker gap	Static 0.014 in – 0.016 in (0.35mm – 0.40mm). or 26 – 28° Dwell meter setting at 550 – 650 rev/min.
Cooling system type	Pressurized with pump, fan, thermostat and expansion tanks and cross flow radiator.
Max working Pressure	15 lb/in² (1.05 Kg/cm²).
Thermostat	Wax type.
Setting	Open at 82°C.
Water pump	Centrifugal, driven by 'V'.
Fan	Detox, Seven blade plastic overall diameter 16 in (406mm) driven through a 5,000 centi-stoke viscous coupling. Non-Detox five blade steel overall diameter 16 in (406mm).
Capacity of System	17 pints.
Lubrication system type	Pressure.
Nominal Pressure (@ 2400 rev/min)	30-40 lb/in² (2.1 – 2.8 Kg/cm²).
Warning Light	Red light on instrument panel operates when pressure drops below 10 lb/in². (0.70 kg/cm²).

Oil Filters	Gauze pump-intake strainer, full flow external.
Capacity	10 pints (5.68 litres).
	Including 1 pint (0.568 litres) in filter.

Fuel System

Carburettors	Twin Zenith-Stromberg.
Type	Detox CDSE
	Non-Detox CDS3
Needle	BLEW
Jet Size	0.100 in.
Damper Oil	SAE20
Cold Start Control	Variable jet size with manual control and amber warning light on dash.
Air Silencer and Cleaner	Standard Detox AC Delco paper element. ADR27A and non-detox. AC Delco cyclone type, metal encapsulated paper element.
Petrol Pump Type	Bendix Electric.
Max. Working Pressure	$3.5 - 5.0$ lb/in^2 ($0.25 - 0.35$ Kg/cm^2).
Filters	Tank filter, tank suction pipe, AC Delco paper element.
Petrol Tank Capacity	15 gallons (68.25 litres).
Engine Mountings	Four – Point rubber mountings.
Exhaust System	Single cross-over type with front exhaust pipes, main silencer and tail silencer.

Transmission

Clutch	Single dry plate, diaphragm spring type 10.5 in (267mm) diameter. Operation, hydraulic by pendant pedal (hydrostatic).
Main Gearbox	Four speed and reverse, synchromesh on all forward gears. Control by floor-mounted gear change lever.
Transfer Box	Two-speed reduction on main gearbox ouput. Control is by a heel board located between them. Front and rear drive is permanently engaged with a lockable third differential. Differential locked by vacuum control from a heel board mounted switch.
Capacity	Main gear box oil 4.5 pints (2.6 litres). Transfer box oil 5.5 pints (3.1 litres).
Propeller Shafts	Open type, 2 in diameter, front prop. shaft has a double hookes joint at the gearbox end and gaiter is fitted to the sliding coupling.

Rear Axle type	Hypoid: fully floating shafts	
capacity	4.5 pints (2.6 litres)	
ratio differential	3.5385:1	
Front axle type	Spiral bevel, enclosed constant velocity joints.	
capacity	3 pints (1.7 litres)	
ratio differential	3.5385:1	
Steering lock angle available	26°	
Gearbox Ratios: Main	Top	Direct
Gearbox	Third	1.5049:1
	Second	2.4480:1
	First	4.0691:1
	Reverse	3.6643:1
Transfer Box	High	1.3362:1
	Low	3.3206:1

Steering

Steering type	Burman Recirculating Ball, worm and nut.
Steering wheel diameter	17 in
Number of turns lock to lock	3.5
Steering damper	Fitted to drag link.

Wheels and Tyres

Type of wheel	Ventilated disc.
Wheel size	5.50 in F x 16 in.
No. of fixing studs	5 per wheel – M16 x 1.5
Tyre size	7.50 x 16 in.
Standard Tread	Avon Ranger HS nylon Mark II.
	Goodyear Hi-Miler S & G.
Pressures unladen	Front: 25 lb/in^2 (1.76 Kg/cm^2)
	Rear: 25 lb/in^2 (1.76 Kg/cm^2)
laden	Front: 32 lb/in^2 (2.24 Kg/cm^2)
	Rear: 42 lb/in^2 (2.94 Kg/cm^2)

Brakes

Type	Girling
Footbrake	Hydraulic, Servo assisted.
Brake Drum Diameter	11 in (279.4mm).
Brake Shoe width	Front 3 in (76.2mm).
	Rear 2.25 in (57.1mm).
Frictional Lining area	222 in^2 (1432cm^2).
Hand Brake	Mechanical, Lockheed 7.25 in (184mm) diameter, 3 in (76mm) width, duo-servo drum brake on rear of transfer box.

Electrical System

Type	Negative earth.
Voltage	12 volt.
Battery capacity	58 amp hour C9 Lucas.
Ignition System	Ballasted Coil.
Alternator	18 ACR Lucas Model.
Alternator Ouptut	45 amp.
Starter Motor Type	3M100 Lucas pre-engaged.

Capacities

Engine Oil (sump)	10 pints (5.68 litres).
Main Gearbox	4.5 pints (2.6 litres).
Transfer Box	5.5 pints (3.1 litres).
Rear Differential	4.5 pints((2.6 litres).
Front Differential	3 pints (1.7 litres).
Swivel pin housing	1 pint (0.5 litres).
Fuel Tank	15 gallons (68.25 litres).
Cooling System	20 pints (11.37 litres).

Overall Dimensions

Wheelbase	109 in (2770mm).
Track	52.5 in (1334mm).
Ground Clearance	8.25 in (209mm).
Turning Circle	47ft (14.3mm).
Overall Length	177 in (4445mm).
Overall Width	66 in (1690mm).
Overall Height (max)	79 in (2006mm).

Internal Dimensions

Height of body sides	19.5 in (495mm).
Interior width between cappings	57 in (1447mm).
Floor width between wheel boxes	36.25 in (921mm).
Width of wheel boxes	13.75 in (349mm).
Interior length between cappings	72.75 in (1847mm).
Height of wheel boxes	9 in (229mm).
Height of Floor to Roof	48 in (1219mm).

Weights
No. 1 881 Basic rhd Spec. truck cab.

	Front Axle	Rear Axle	Total
Showroom weight	828 kg	712 kg	1555 kg
EEC kerb weight	854 kg	810 kg	1679 kg
Laden GVW	1000 kg	1710 kg	2710 kg

No. 2 886 Basic rhd

	Front Axle	Rear Axle	Total
Showroom weight	820 kg	920 kg	1740 kg
EEC kerb weight	846 kg	1018 kg	1864 kg
Laden GVW	1000 kg	1710 kg	2710 kg

Note List (1) includes the following extras as basic equipment:

E1178/79A	Towing equipment
E6557	Rear mudflaps
E6731	Lifting and towing rings
E1050/1356	Truck cab and fittings
E1072	Rubber pedal pads
E1185	Sun visors
E6773	Interior and exterior mirrors
E6846	Bonnet lock
E6864/5	Deluxe seats
E1550	Astrolan application
E6758/60	Speedo with trip
E6775	Hazard warning system
E6797	Reversing lights

List (2) includes the following extras as basic equipment:
As list (1)

plus E1015	front mud flaps
less E1050/1356	truck cab and fittings

Showroom weight figures do not include driver or fuel.
EEC kerb weight includes driver + full fuel tank.

110 INCH

Engine, V8

Type	All-aluminium water-cooled V8 with overhead valves and central camshaft.
Bore	88.9 mm
Stroke	71.1 mm
Capacity	3528 cc
Compression ratio	8.13:1
Maximum power	114 bhp (85 kW) at 4000 rpm
Maximum torque	185 lbf.ft (251 Nm) at 2500 rpm
Firing order	1-8-4-3-6-5-7-2
Carburettors	Twin Zenith Stromberg 175 CDSE
Main bearings	Five
Fuel	Petrol (low octane)
Lubrication	Pressure-fed wet sump.

Engine, 2.1/4-litre Petrol

Type	Cast-iron, water-cooled, inline four-cylinder with overhead valves.
Bore	90.47 mm
Stroke	88.9 mm
Capacity	2286 cc
Compression ratio	8.0:1
Maximum power	74 bhp (55 kW) at 4000 rpm
Maximum torque	120 lbf ft (163 Nm) at 2000 rpm
Firing order	1-3-4-2
Carburettor	Single twin-choke Weber 32/34DMTL
Main bearings	Five
Fuel	Petrol (low octane)
Lubrication	Pressure-fed wet sump

Engine, 2.1/4-litre Diesel

Type	Cast-iron, water cooled, inline four-cylinder with overhead valves.
Bore	90.47 mm
Stroke	88.9 mm
Capacity	2286 cc
Compression ratio	23:1
Maximum power	60 bhp (45 kW) at 4000 rpm
Maximum torque	103 lbf ft (140 Nm) at 1800 rpm
Firing order	1-3-4-2
Fuel injectors	CAV Pintaux
Main bearings	Five
Fuel	Diesel
Lubrication	Pressure-fed wet sump

Transmission, V8 model

Clutch	Borg and Beck diaphragm spring.
Clutch plate diameter	10.5 in (266.7 mm)
Main gearbox	Single helical constant mesh with four forward and one reverse ratios.

Ratios	: Fourth	1:1
	Third	1.50:1
	Second	2.44:1
	First	4.06:1
	Reverse	3.66:1

Transfer box	Two-speed reduction on main gearbox output, permanent four-wheel drive with lockable differential.	
	Ratios: High	1.34:1
	Low	3.32:1

Overall ratios	**High range**	**Low range**
Fourth	4.72:1	11.74:1
Third	7.11:1	17.68:1
Second	11.57:1	28.76:1
First	19.23:1	47.81:1
Reverse	17.32:1	43.05:1

Front axle	Land Rover spiral bevel
Front axle ratio	3.54:1
Rear axle	Salisbury 8HA hypoid
Rear axle ratio	3.54:1

Transmission, Four-cylinder models

Clutch	Borg and Beck diaphragm spring.
Clutch plate diameter	9.5 in (242.1 mm)
Main gearbox	Single helical constant mesh with five forward and one reverse ratios.

Ratios	: Fifth	0.83:1
	Fourth	1:1
	Third	1.50:1
	Second	2.30:1
	First	3.58:1
	Reverse	3.70:1

Transfer box	Two-speed reduction on main gearbox output, permanent four-wheel drive with lockable differential.	
	Ratios : High	1.66:1
	Low	3.31:1

Overall ratios	**High range**	**Low range**
Fifth	4.90:1	9.76:1
Fourth	5.89:1	11.74:1
Third	8.89:1	17.70:1
Second	13.57:1	27.02:1
First	21.14:1	42.11:1
Reverse	21.82:1	43.47:1

Front axle	Land Rover spiral bevel
Front axle ratio	3.54:1
Rear axle	Salisbury 8HA hypoid
Rear axle ratio	3.54:1

Electrical System

Type	12 Volt negative earth
Battery	Petrol, 55 amp/hour (9 plate)
	Diesel, 96 amp/hour (15 plate)
Ignition	Petrol, coil
	Diesel, compression ignition
Alternator	**Petrol Diesel**
2.1/4-litre	34 amp 34 amp
V8	45 amp –
Fuses	12 Cartridge type.

Suspension

Type	Beam axles front and rear with coil springs controlled by hydraulic telescopic dampers.
Front	Transverse location of axle by Panhard rod, fore and aft location by twin radius arms.
Rear	Fore and aft location by twin tubular trailing links, lateral location of axle by central 'A' bracket. Boge self-levelling unit optional on all models and standard on County Station Wagon.
Wheel travel	Front, 7 in (180 mm)
	Rear, 8.25 in (210 mm)
Approach/Departure Angles	Approach angle 50°
	Departure angle 35°
Ground clearance	8.5 in (216 mm)

Brakes

Type	Dual, servo-assisted system with tandem master cylinder and pressure differential warning actuator.
Front	11.81 in (300 mm) disc
Rear	11.00 in (280 mm) drum
Handbrake	10.00 in (254 mm) transmission drum type

Steering

Type	Manual, recirculating ball. Power assisted steering optional.
Lock-to-lock turns	Manual, 4.37 Power assisted, 3.0
Turning circle	42 ft (12.8m)

Wheels and Tyres

Type of wheel	Steel ventilated disc
Wheel size	5.50 x 16 in
Tyre size	7.50 x 16 in

Tyre type fitted according to customer requirements.

Capacities

Fuel	17.5 gallons (79.5 litres)
Engine oil	9 pints (5.1 litres) for V8.
	11 pints (6.00 litres) for four-cylinders.

Dimensions

	In	mm
Wheelbase	110.0	2794
Track	58.5	1486
Soft top		
Length	175.0	4445
Width	70.5	1790
Height	80.1	2035
Cargo bed length	74.8	1900
Pick-Up		
Length	175.0	4445
Width	70.5	1790
Height	80.1	2035
Cargo bed length	74.8	1900
High Capacity Pick-Up		
Length	184.0	4669
Width	70.5	1790
Height	80.1	2035
Cargo bed length	79.2	2010
Hard Top		
Length	175.0	4445
Width	70.5	1790
Height	80.1	2035
Cargo bed length	74.8	1900
Station Wagon		
Length	180.5	4580
Width	70.5	1790
Height	80.1	2035

Towing Limits

	On Road	**Off Road**
Unbraked trailers	500 Kg (1102 lb)	500 Kg (1102 lb)

Trailers with over-run brakes	3500 Kg (7716 lb)	1000 Kg (2205 lb)
4-wheel trailers with coupled brakes	4000 Kg (8818 lb)	1000 Kg (2205 lb)

Vehicle Weights
Gross vehicle weight:

Standard Suspension	3050 Kg (6724 lb)
Levelled Suspension	2950 Kg (6504 lb)

90 INCH

Engine, 2.3 litre Petrol

Type	Cast-iron, water cooled, inline 4-cylinder with overhead valves.
Bore	90.47 mm
Stroke	88.9 mm
Capacity	2286 cc
Compression ratio	8:1
Maximum power	74 bhp (55kW) at 4000 rpm
Maximum torque	120 lbf ft (163 Nm) at 2000 rpm
Firing order	1-3-4-2
Carburettor	Single twin-choke Weber 32/34DMTL
Main bearings	Five
Fuel	Petrol (2-star)
Lubrication	Pressure-fed wet sump

Engine, 2.5-litre Diesel

Type	Cast-iron, water cooled, inline 4-cylinder with overhead valves
Bore	90.47 mm
Stroke	97.0 mm
Capacity	2495 cc
Compression ratio	21:1
Maximum power	67 bhp (50 kW) at 4000 rpm
Maximum torque	114 lbf ft (155 Nm) at 1800 rpm
Firing order	1-3-4-2
Fuel injectors	DPS
Main bearings	Five
Fuel	Diesel
Lubrication	Pressure-fed wet sump

Transmission

Clutch	Single dry plate hydraulic
Clutch plate diameter	9.5 inches (241 mm)
Main gearbox	Single helical constant mesh with five

	forward and one reverse ratio	
Ratios:	Fifth 0.83:1	
	Fourth 1:1	
	Third 1.51:1	
	Second 2.30:1	
	First 3.59:1	
	Reverse 3.70:1	

Transfer box	Two speed reduction on main gearbox output, permanent four-wheel drive with lockable differential.
Ratios:	High 1.41:1
	Low 3.32:1

Overall ratios	**High Range**	**Low Range**
Fifth	4.15:1	9.77:1
Fourth	4.99:1	11.75:1
Third	7.52:1	17.71:1
Second	11.49:1	27.03:1
First	17.40:1	42.11:1
Reverse	18.48:1	43.47:1

Front axle	Land-Rover spiral bevel
Front axle ratio	3.54:1
Rear axle	Land-Rover spiral bevel
Rear axle ratio	3.54:1

Electrical System

Type	12 Volt negative earth
Battery	Petrol, 55 amp hour (9 plate)
	Diesel, 95 amp hour (13 plate)
Ignition	Petrol, Coil
	Diesel, Compression ignition
Alternator	Petrol, 34 amp Diesel, 34 amp
Fuses	Cartridge type (20)

Suspension

Type	Beam axles front and rear with coil springs controlled by hydraulic telescopic dampers.
Front	Transverse location of axle by Panhard rod, fore and aft location by twin radius arms.
Rear	Fore and aft location by twin tubular trailing links, lateral location by central 'A' bracket.
Wheel travel	Front, 7.2 in (182 mm)

71

	Rear,	7 in (178 mm)
Approach and Departure angles	Approach angle,	51 degrees
	Departure angle,	52 degrees
Ramp break over angle	150 degrees	
Ground clearance	9 in (229 mm) minimum	

Brakes

Type — Dual, servo-assisted system with tandem master cylinder and pressure differential warning.

Front — 11.75 in (298.5 mm) disc

Rear — 10 in (254 mm) drum

Handbrake — 10.00 in (254 mm) transmission drum type

Steering

Type — Manual, worm and roller. Power assisted steering optional.

Lock-to-lock turns — Manual, 4.4
Power assisted 3.0

Turning circle — 38 feet

Wheels and tyres

Type of wheel — Steel ventilated disc

Wheel size — 5.50 x 16 in

Tyre size — 6.00 x 16 in

Tyre size (County Station Wagon) — 205 x 16 in

Capacity

Fuel — 12 gallons (54.5 litres)

Dimensions

	in	mm
Wheelbase	92.9	2360
Track	58.5	1486
Soft Top		
Length	146.5	3722
Width	70.5	1790
Height	77.4	1965
Cargo bed length	45.0	1144
Pick Up		
Length	146.5	3722
Width	70.5	1790
Height	77.3	1963

Cargo bed length	45.0	1144
Hard Top		
Length	146.5	3722
Width	70.5	1790
Height	77.6	1972
Cargo bed length	45.0	1144
Station Wagon		
Length	151.9	3858
Width	70.5	1790
Height	77.3	1963

Towing Limits

	Petrol	Diesel
Unbraked trailers	750 kg	750 kg
Trailers with over-run brakes	3500 kg	3500 kg
4-wheel trailers with coupled brakes	4000 kg	3500 kg

Vehicle Weights

Standard Suspension *(gross vehicle weight 2400 kg)*

	EEC Kerb (kg)	EEC Payload (kg)
Soft Top:		
2.3P	1606	794
2.5D	1643	757
Pick Up:		
2.3P	1635	765
2.5D	1672	728
Hard Top:		
2.3P	1648	752
2.5D	1685	715
Station Wagon:		
2.3P	1690	710
2.5D	1727	673

High Load Suspension *(gross vehicle weight 250 kg)*

	EEC Kerb (kg)	EEC Payload (kg)
Soft Top:		
2.3P	1633	917
2.5D	1670	880
Pick Up:		
2.3P	1662	888
2.5D	1699	851
Hard Top:		
2.3P	1675	875
2.5D	1712	838

Station Wagon:

2.3P	1717	833
2.5D	1754	796

SANTANA S-2000 MODEL

Engine, Petrol

Type	6-cylinder	
Bore	90.47 mm	
Stroke	88.90 mm	
Capacity	3,429 cc	
Compression ratio	8:1	
Maximum power	@ 4000 rpm	77 Kw
Maximum torque	@ 1500 rpm	240 Nm

Engine, Diesel

Type	6-cylinder	
Bore	90.47 mm	
Stroke	88.90 mm	
Capacity	3,429 cc	
Compression ratio	23:1	
Maximum power	@ 4000 rpm	70 Kw
Maximum torque	@ 1800 rpm	207 Nm

Dimensions

Overall length	4949 mm
Overall width	1960 mm
Overall height	2235 mm
Overhang at front	1186 mm
Wheelbase	2565 mm
Overhang at rear	1283 mm
Front track	1461 mm
Rear track	1486 mm
Ground clearance	265 mm
Turning circle	7 m

Weights

Net weight in chassis	2360 kg
Maximum authorized weight	4360 kg
Maximum towing weight	3315 kg

Brakes

Hydraulic on all four wheels and mechanical on the transmission.
Independent dual circuit system with servo.

Electrical

Negative earth. 12v charging circuit. Alternator with electronic regulator incorporated.

SANTANA 109 INCH MODEL

Engine, Petrol

Type	6-cylinder	
Bore	90.47 mm	
Stroke	88.90 mm	
Capacity	3,429 cc	
Compression ratio	8:1	
Maximum power	@ 4000 rpm	77 Kw
Maximum torque	@ 1500 rpm	240 Nm

Engine, Diesel

Type	6-cylinder	
Bore	90.47 mm	
Stroke	88.90 mm	
Capacity	3,429 cc	
Compression ratio	23:1	
Maximum power	@ 4000 rpm	70 Kw
Maximum torque	@ 1800 rpm	207 Nm

Dimensions

Total length	4440 mm
Total width	1676 mm
Total weight	2050 mm
Length of rear body	1850 mm
Width of rear body	1450 mm
Height of rear body	1200 mm
Wheelbase	2768 mm
Track	1310 mm
Ground clearance	210 mm
Turning circle	6.85 mm

Weights

Unladen	1820 kg
Maximum authorized weight	3150 kg
Maximum towing weight	2645 kg

Brakes
Hydraulic on all four wheels and mechanical on the transmission. Independent circuit system with servo.

Electrical
Negative earth. 12v charging circuit. Alternator with electronic regulator incorporated.

Chapter 2
The Special Projects Department

The idea for a Land-Rover Special Projects Department was discussed initially between Peter Wilks, the nephew of Spencer and Maurice Wilks, and myself when we were winding up our Marauder car business in 1952. We both thought such a proposition might work, but on further reflection came to the conclusion that at the time there weren't enough Land-Rovers about to justify it. Five years later the advent of the diesel engine and the increased numbers of Land-Rovers in circulation made me think again.

The diesel engine was an introduction sparked off by the Sales Director, Alan Botwood, who had been brought in by Spencer Wilks to strengthen the Board on the Sales side. In turn, Botwood brought in Geoffrey Lloyd-Dixon as General Sales Manager, and following him quite a lot of new people were taken on in the Sales Division, which was considerably strengthened up. Increased sales activity resulted in much more work for the Engineering Division, as the new sales people wanted to exploit the Land-Rover to the full to justify their existence. It wasn't long before Maurice Wilks began to realize that all the special requests from Sales to the Engineerng Department were beginning to interfere with overall development: at the time, cars and Land-Rovers were not separated, so that activities for Land-Rovers also tended to have an influence on car development and generally slow things up.

This seemed to be a good moment to approach him with a suggestion that this special work should be hived off, and separated from Engineering. Traditionally, the selection of equipment that Rover recommended for use with the Land-Rover was handled by the Service Department. This was ill-equipped to undertake the work, and hadn't enough staff anyhow to devote to it, and so would be quite happy to let it go. Added to this was the fact that, since the early days of the Land-Rover, we had been trying to market certain special vehicles – a special compressor vehicle, a special welding vehicle, and a special fire appliance. The first two had got nowhere because of the lack of a diesel engine, and the fire appliance was unsuccessful because most fire officers wanted their own particular specification, while our objective was to build one basic vehicle for the lowest possible price. All in all, I think Maurice Wilks felt that he could clear up all these outstanding nuisances by lumping the whole activity into one Special Projects Department.

When I approached him about this, he was kind enough to say he would be perfectly happy to leave it all in my hands, providing that the Sales Department were in agreement – the reason for this being that he intended to form a Technical Sales Department and place all this activity within it. I had to spend about a year lobbying around the Sales Department to get them interested, which I eventually did, but at the eleventh hour Lloyd-Dixon said he didn't want this activity as the responsibility of his Sales Division. This looked like 'curtains' for the whole project, but I decided there was nothing to be lost in appealing to Maurice Wilks again. Rather to my surprise he still supported me and said he would do his best to persuade Lloyd-Dixon and the Sales Division to take the job over. They finally agreed to comply, and in January 1957 Special Projects (or the Technical Sales Department, as it then was) was set up.

It might be helpful here to clarify and define the Special Projects Department, and its activities, because Land-Rovers are built to so many specifications that the whole enterprise might almost be described as a special project. Of the Land-Rovers built in the factory, there is a clear division between those built to Rover specifications, and those built to approved specifications on the military and para-military side, for British and foreign governments or para-military fleet-users. But in addition to this, there are many specialist firms who make equipment or undertake vehicle conversions which when applied to the Land-Rover further increase its versatility.

This activity needs feeding with information and advice; liaison between Rover, the outside manufacturer and the sales network is essential; and incoming inquiries must be dealt with without disrupting the overall engineering development programme. It was soon seen to be desirable to exercise some form of control over this work and after studying the manner in which tractor manufacturers faced similar problems, I decided to institute an approval scheme which would evaluate, test and record details of all equipment and conversions which passed our acceptance trials satisfactorily.

Besides protecting the Land-Rover warranty in such circumstances and relieving basic vehicle development personnel of these problems, our approval, which came to be known as Special Projects Proprietary Approval, meant that:

1) A conversion or piece of equipment would be sold under the maker's name and warranted, sold and serviced under the maker's arrangement.

2) We in Special Projects would ensure by appropriate tests that the approved item would not be detrimental to the vehicle, in the context of the operation(s) the conversion or equipment enabled it to perform, and so invalidate its warranty.

3) Performance and fitness for purpose of the equipment or conversion would be evaluated to satisfy ourselves that what was to be offered had acceptable marketing quality.

4) An agreement had to be reached between Rover and the approved manufacturer covering these and other aspects. Also it was important to safeguard Rover as far as possible against possible litigation from an approved manufacturer or his customer.

It took a little time for the foregoing to evolve into a satisfactory formula but when they did it was seen that:

1) Such a system was generally well understood and appreciated in the retail trade, and by removing uncertainties over possible warranty claims added to their freedom of action when pursuing business.

2) Adjudication of warranty claims for service department personnel was simplified.

Besides testing items for approval, we also had to respond to many queries from prospective customers concerned with 'work horse' applications for the Land-Rover which they had under consideration.
Here is a typical example of such an inquiry:

Typical Enquiry
Customer: Tanzania Water Authority
Requirement: Equipment carried and powered by a Land-Rover to
pump 600 gallons of water per hour from a well 240ft deep.

Action
A. Search and Find
1) Acknowledge enquiry.
2) Circulate pump manufacturers to find suitable equipment.
3) Tabulate data – power, weight, dimensions, cost, etc.
4) Decide on equipment to be recommended: eg series of 12 pumps electrically driven in series.
B. Prepare Land-Rover Basic Specification
1) Basic vehicle: 88-inch or 109-inch
2) Engine type: Petrol or diesel
3) Body type: Pick-up, hardtop, or special body
4) Suspension: Standard, heavy duty, extra heavy duty
5) Brakes: Standard or servo
6) Cooling system: Standard, heavy duty, oil cooler

C. Negotiate SID (Special Installations Department) Non-Standard Items
1) Extra fuel tank
2) Split charging circuit for floodlights
3) Blank off spare wheel well
D. Prepare Ancillary Proprietary Equipment Specification
1) Hydraulic winch with shear legs to raise and lower pumps down well.
2) Centre pto to drive generator.
3) Hydraulic lower centre pto to drive winch.
4) 10 kva generator to power pumps.
5) Air conditioning.
E. Compile Draft Specification and Drawings
1) For customer.
2) For Rover Co Ltd.
3) For proprietary equip manufacturers.

To appreciate the vast and varied range of specifications, one should bear in mind that Land-Rovers are sold into more overseas territories than almost any other single product. Over the years, they have in fact been sold into 150 overseas territories – and since the total classification of such territories is, I believe, 152, that's a pretty good span of exports! (I can even recall having correspondence about how to fit an independent fuel burning heater to a Land-Rover Station Wagon – with Her Majesty's Plenipotentiary for Outer Mongolia! Or maybe it was Inner Mongolia ... Presumably the vehicle was his mobile consulate as well as his means of transport – but we never heard whether our instructions were successful.)

When we started up we discovered that a certain number of firms were already 'approved' in a fashion. Some of them are still with us today, and include British Films, who do mobile cinemas, Pilchers, who do a large range of ambulances and are now known as Pilcher-Greene (whose 109″ 'Popemobile' conversion is illustrated), Evers & Wall, who do crop-sprayers, and Dixon-Bate, who do towing gear. The initial staff consisted of myself, Herbert Topping (who is still there today), Harry Lenton, Neville Mewse, Stephen Savage (son of the late Sir Geoffrey Savage who had been Personnel Director and Production Manager), and a secretary. We were issued with some new vehicles on which we could start work for special adaptations and equipment, either having the work done ourselves or lending the vehicles out to suitable manufacturers. The diesel vehicle had just been announced and the first ones we were issued with were quite outstanding for noise level – it was fabulous! I recall an occasion when Herbert Topping and I went to visit British Films in a diesel Land-Rover: on arrival, we drew up in their yard between two bricks walls and the noise was deafening. As I switched off the engine, I paraphrased the saying which was rife at the time on the BBC 'In Town Tonight' programme: 'No need to halt the mighty roar of Rover's diesel, we can hear who's in town tonight!'

1950 Land-Rover 80-inch basic model. (Neill Bruce)

1949 Land-Rover 80-inch Chassis. (Neill Bruce)

An early 80-inch station wagon. (David Bowyer)

The new models at the launch of the Ninety, and improved One-Ten at Eastnor Castle in Spring 1984.

One of the first Ninety models.

Glenfrome's 'Ashton' power-operated convertible.

Glenfrome's 'Facet' built on the Range Rover chassis, a bold step into futuristic design. (Andrew Morland)

The Pilcher-Greene 'Popemobile' built on a 109-in chassis.

One of the things I wanted to ensure was that we had advertising literature to let everybody know what we were doing, and what was available on our approved list. It seemed to me that the way to do this was to get a clause put in a legal agreement with the manufacturer, once he was approved, stipulating that he would at his own expense print a leaflet to our format, advertising his merchandise and giving pertinent specification data. We would then have the leaflet distributed to all our dealers, fleet-users, etc. This made the agreement rather a cumbersome affair, especially when the Sales people wanted to tack on a whole number of clauses covering the selling conditions, but nevertheless it was a way of getting the scheme started and known about in the widest possible way, and was probably rather more effective than ordinary straight-forward expensive advertising. Apart from this intervention by the Sales Division, we were mercifully left comparatively free to develop our new activity along the lines we thought best.

One of the items that we took over from the Engineering Division when we were formed was the question of a drum winch for the Land-Rover. It had not been possible at that time to find anything on the British market, and apart from mechanically driven drum winches available in the States, which were rather expensive, we had no alternative but to develop our own. When Herbert

Topping joined us he brought with him details of a hydraulically operated winch that he had been working on. It was decided that we should go ahead with this, finish the scheme off and make arrangements for it to be marketed as a Land-Rover drum winch to give support to the capstan winch we were already marketing. Dowty's were keen to sell their gear-type pumps and motors which were extremely reasonably priced, partly due to the lower efficiency inherent in gear type units. However, in this particular context this was not important as, willy-nilly, the horse-power available from the Land-Rover engine was enough to overcome this reduction in efficiency.

The use of winches on Land-Rovers has taken up much of our time over the years. It is a fascinating occupation which at first sight appears quite simple; the more involved one becomes, however, the more interesting it turns out to be. There are two simple types of winch which mount on to the front bumper of the Land-Rover – the most popular position. The capstan winch is a simple bollard that can be turned mechanically by a pto drive from the engine; if a suitable rope is wrapped round it two or three times, enough friction will be caused for the rotating bollard to pull the rope along with it. The alternative is a drum winch. This again is mechanically driven from the engine of the vehicle, but winds the cable up on to a drum which is all part of the winch assembly. Both have their advantages and disadvantages and a choice between the two really has to be made according to the purpose for which the winch is required. Such purposes often involve what is known as self-recovery. It is slightly ironic that a 4 x 4 vehicle is usually purchased for its ability, when necessary, to leave the tarmac road and go off across country, but however good its traction and ground-clearance may be, there will doubtless come a moment when it loses

The standard capstan bollard is nine-sided. This improves grip on the rope but when the operator releases tension to induce slip the change-over may cause some initial rope snatch.

The smooth surface on this bollard permits more precise control of rope tension by the operator.

Left: Components of the Fairey drum winch hydraulically driven from the centre pto.
Right: Components of the Land-Rover drum winch hydraulically driven from the centre pto.

its ability to proceed, due to digging in, bogging down or bellying on the ground. In fact the more efficient and cross-country-worthy an all-wheel drive vehicle is, the further it will go before it comes to a halt, which in turn makes it harder to pull out again. If it is unaccompanied, the driver then has the task of winching himself back on to firmer ground where he can regain traction.

Having said this, it is rather extraordinary that nearly all self-recovery winches are mounted on the front of the vehicle and can only pull it forward, and that the demands for a backwards pull facility are comparatively rare. We thought our hydraulically operated drum winch, with its flexible hydraulic transmission facilitating various mounting positions, would fulfil a much wanted need, but in the event, that need turned out to be a very minor one and the great majority of winches are mounted at the front of the vehicle.

Besides vehicle recovery, much use is made of winches by electricity boards, for instance, to help in the erection of small poles for overhead electricity power lines, and to pull up transformers on to H-poles. I well recall being told by a procurement officer of one of the electricity supply boards that he had heard of our work developing a hydraulic drum winch, but that he couldn't

Hydraulic operation of a separate capstan unit designed to operate below ground level on building estates, for installing electricity supply cables.

Very effective ground anchors. When the winch pulls the vehicle forward, the chains prevent it over-running the anchors and cause their leading edges to dig in. The winch is the Land-Rover hydraulically driven drum winch.

understand why we had bothered. He claimed that such a winch would be too expensive for his people and that they would stick to mechanical operation. This rather shook me but we were so near to completing our work that we carried on. Eventually this same supply board became thoroughly converted and used the hydraulic winch in large numbers. In fact they found they could often use just one 109-inch Land-Rover for winching on an off-road site as well as for transport for the working party, instead of having to take a tractor-mounted winch in addition to the transport vehicle.

The Post Office also uses winches fairly frequently, for pulling in multi-core telephone lines in underground ducts. In forestry work they are used for hauling the cut timber from the forest to the roadside, where it can be stacked awaiting collection by the timber lorries. Some of these industrial uses call for somewhat more sophisticated winches than the simple drum or capstan, the main problem being the amount of cable required on a particular operation, and a method of storing and handling it. This can be achieved in various ways, one of the most ingenious being that employed by the Swiss Plummet winch. This is virtually a capstan winch but once it is in motion, the rope coming off the capstan is fed straight through to a revolving storage drum on which it is laid. The cable storage drum is coupled to a slipping friction pad which tries to rotate the drum at a slightly faster speed than that imparted by the capstan to

The standard appliance marketed by Rover before the business was handed over to the specialist manufacturers.

the incoming cable. This in turn creates tension to the cable between capstan and drum thereby creating sufficient friction at the capstan to cause the cable to be gripped and hauled in. Secondly, it causes the storage drum to revolve and pay on to itself the incoming cable. With this system the storage drum can accommodate 750 to 900 feet of cable depending on diameter, which is a great advantage, but it does present another problem. When a cable several hundred feet long is being payed out, it becomes extremely heavy. To assist the operator, the capstan is made reversible. A freewheel in the friction pad drive prevents the storage drum rotating but the friction pad itself maintains cable tension between drum and capstan. When he pulls on the cable, he will generate friction at the capstan sufficient for it to pull cable off the storage drum and pay it out. When the operator has gone as far as he wants to and stops pulling, the cable will then slip on the capstan and stop paying out. The Plummet system avoids the use of expensive mechanical storage drum cable-laying attachments and has been used on Land-Rovers for many purposes.

Electrically powered and compressed air-driven winches are also available, though the latter are normally used only as a convenient adjunct when compressed air is required in a major role, such as operating paving breakers or underwater tools. The electrically powered drum winch has much to recommend it. It shares with hydraulic operation the flexible choice of mounting positions, installation is often faster, and it has the advantage over hydraulics in that no oil reservoir is required. It does, however, need a robust battery and the number of pulls is limited according to the battery capacity.

As we had decided that we were not well-equipped to sell fire appliances based on Land-Rovers, it was a question of selecting a certain number of specialist manufacturers to undertake this work. I had my first slight clash of policy here with the Sales Division, who beat me to it, and made an agreement with Carmichael and Sons, of Worcester, as the exclusive converters of fire appliances for three years. I thought this policy a bad one – no reflection on Carmichael's – simply because fire officers tend to have their favourite manufacturers to whom they go for repeat business, and it is difficult to persuade them to go somewhere else. My intention had been to approve about three or four different manufacturers. However, we were tied to Carmichael's for three years, which at least simplified our work-load as we had to deal with only the one firm to get specifications, overall conversion matters, and any engineering problems sorted out.

Unusual by UK standards was the supply and drive of a front-mounted water pump on the Land-Rover. These installations were fairly popular in Scandinavia and America but little known in the UK, and posed the problem of whether we could drive and take full torque from the front of the crankshaft of the Land-Rover to drive the pump. With true Rover caution, the engine people would not commit themselves without some rather extensive testing, but in the end we were able to accommodate the demand – not a big one – for such an installation, provided a special torsional vibration damper coupling was inserted between the pump and the engine.

I cannot claim to be an expert on all aspects of fire appliance specifications. Indeed I have always been at pains to make it clear that we regard the specialist manufacturers as the experts in their field, with Special Projects providing engineering support service with the Land-Rover. However, in the course of our work we obviously learnt quite a lot about the various specialized activities of these manufacturers, so much so that I sometimes wondered if we weren't in danger of becoming a unit getting to know less and less about more and more!

We also gained insight into many of the problems which apply to the fire prevention field, such as the intricacies of Home Office grants (in simple terms a government subsidy to public authorities who purchase equipment approved by the Home Office), problems created by the development of pedestrian shopping precincts and the difficulty of access for fire appliances to 'incidents', restrictions of movement caused by the ever-increasing traffic density in built-up areas, the arguments for and against the various fire extinguishing chemicals and the introduction of 'light water' – a product of the 3M company which creates about the most effective flame smothering foam available today.

*The specialist manufacturers produced
many more varieties than Rover would
have found economical to handle.*

A factory fire appliance.

All these problems seemed to point towards an increase in the use of smaller, more mobile fire appliances, but an important obstacle was that the Land-Rover did not at the time have Home Office approval, their thinking being that it was too small to be effective. Nevertheless several brigades found its usefulness justified purchase without a grant, quite often as a communications centre for the officer in charge.

As a fire appliance for factory complexes the Land-Rover was and is very popular and, by the same token, for military depots and air-fields. In the latter case there are two fairly distinct roles, one of protection for plant and equipment, and the other as a first rescue vehicle for crashed aircraft in and beyond the air-field perimeter. When Carmichael's made the 6 x 4 Range Rover available (see page 170) for fire fighting duties, it was immediately seen to be an ideal vehicle for first rescue. It had all the speed, cross-country ability, load capacity and engine power for pumping purposes that such a vehicle required in order to control an incident until the second rescue vehicles – the heavy brigade – arrived on the scene. Indeed it was hoped that the quick action the first rescue vehicles could take might, in many cases, literally take the heat out of the situation, completing rescue and immediate salvage and maybe even making it unnecessary to call out the heavy brigade.

The Carmichael prototype 6 x 4 Range Rover appliance.

At the time this 6 x 4 Range Rover was introduced, airport authorities were becoming increasingly aware, as more and more larger aircraft were being put into service, of the awful consequences awaiting them should there be a major disaster. One scheme that was considered was the possibility that each of the major airports should have anything up to six of these Range Rovers permanently available. If an incoming aircraft signalled that it was in trouble, they could then station themselves at the beginning of the runway, with engines running, ready to pursue it and get into position almost immediately the craft came to rest.

I was presented with what was for me an unusual situation on policy when I was approached by the Ministry of Defence, who wished to purchase a quantity of 6 x 4 Range Rovers for RAF air-field use. I found that it was not sufficient to point them in the direction of Carmichael's to whom we had given our approval for this conversion after our joint, lengthy, cost-sharing development programme. The Ministry insisted that their ground rules made it mandatory that they should purchase the 6 x 4 chassis direct from us, though we could use Carmichael's as our sub-contractor if we wished, and go out to tender for the body and equipment to the specialist fire appliance builders. The fact that Carmichael's were the only specialist builder with our approval at that time and that the vehicles would almost certainly be cheaper if purchased as a single package failed to sway them.

So, contrary to our normal practice with approved conversions, we had to become involved with shipping Range Rover chassis to Carmichael's, together with the additional axles, wheels, suspension units, etc, that they required for the conversion; receive the vehicles back after conversion for the usual Rover and Ministry quality acceptance tests; and then, when a body builder had been

90

In the end the Ministry got what they wanted.

selected, be concerned with yet another test and approval procedure, as the Ministry insisted that they would require full standard warranty cover from us on the converted chassis component of the complete vehicle. This wouldn't have been so bad if the body specification had been the same as the Carmichael conversion which we had previously tested, but unfortunately it differed sufficiently to come out somewhat heavier, and a period of testing had to be gone through and some compromise reached before all parties were satisfied.

In the end the Ministry got what they wanted at extra cost, Carmichael's had to accept a slowdown in the rate of recovery of their development costs, and Rover suffered a (probably unidentified) rise in their overheads. But Gloster Saro Ltd, the firm who were awarded the contract for the body and equipment, gained an expanded market for their products, and Rover will benefit in the long run by having another reputable firm as a 6 x 4 Range Rover chassis outlet.

It was becoming clear as the years sped by from 1948 that the original idea of using Land-Rovers as an alternative to tractors in agriculture wasn't really taking off. As a workhorse, the vehicle was being used far more by public utilities, and by industry. In the farming world, apart from a few dedicated people who insisted on doing everything with their Land-Rover, we found that the vehicle was being used for personal transport and for towing horseboxes and trailers, while tillage work, or any farming activity of that nature, was left to the tractors. We looked at various fertilizer spreaders and grass-cutting and

Left: 'Adrolic' 3-point linkage operated by a hand pump situated on the wheel box behind the number plate.
Right: SMOMOT.

Left: Our tests showed a two-furrow plough to be a reasonable limit on medium soil.
Right: A granulated fertilizer spreader which can be effectively operated. A hydraulic pto is required to raise the loading shovel attached to the rear of the trailer.

hay-making equipment, but found that the farming world was becoming much more mechanized in the battle to cut down on labour costs. To this end, tractors were becoming bigger, but the Land-Rover stayed the same size, and so from that point of view it was losing the race to become an agricultural tool. The price of tractors and Land-Rovers increased over the years, and at one time it looked as if we might find further outlets in the agricultural field when the law requiring tractors to have safety cabs came into effect. But although this put up their price considerably, the demand for Land-Rovers didn't seem to increase. Had we been able to produce bigger 4 x 4 vehicles, as I had at one time hoped, the picture might have been a bit different, but even then I think we would have had to pioneer a new system, based on the SMOMOT (see page 145) principle of a good 4 x 4 lorry chassis – very adaptable – and utilizing the swop-body concept in the main.

Another item which had been the subject of much discussion was whether a 3-point lifting linkage, of the type that was then becoming commonly available for tractors, should be made available for the Land-Rover. A firm up in Scotland called Adrolic Engineering developed a unit which we had for trial and evaluation. It wasn't terribly successful and – although we weren't convinced at the time – with hindsight one can see that a Land-Rover in its present specification isn't really a suitable vehicle on which to fit such a unit. However, having possession of this mechanism did enable us to fit implements to the back, such as ploughs, harrows, etc, and to evaluate the Land-Rover's pulling performance when carrying out jobs of this sort.

For a brief period it did look as if a system which encouraged improved grassland husbandry might be particularly adaptable to the Land-Rover. Grass grown for fodder has to be cut and partly wilted before it is lifted from the field, the wilting operation being speeded up by crushing parts of the grass stem. A system for economizing and speeding up these two operations was developed by a Mr Murray who farmed in Gloucestershire near a village named Paradise!

We decided to cooperate with Mr. Murray.

A mobile workshop with electrical services. Compressed air and oil hydraulic services are also often provided.

His system was to use a light 4 x 4 chassis, to the driver's side of which he attached a mower cutter bar. Immediately behind this, trailed by means of an offset tow bar attached to the rear cross member of the vehicle, was towed the crimping machine for the wilting process. As his mower, Mr Murray had adapted a cutter bar with two reciprocating knives instead of the single knife and guide fingers used in other mowers. He claimed two advantages for this double knife bar: it could cut at a much faster rate than the single knife mower, and it was available with a hydraulic motor drive which simplified the problem of the side mounting. A chassis with wheel suspension was desirable owing to the higher speed of operation.

We decided to co-operate with Mr Murray, who was also receiving some sponsorship from one of the oil companies, and devised a hydraulic drive and side mounting for the mower. Preliminary tests showed that any significant increase in ground speed for this operation was going to demand extra concentration by the driver on navigation, that there were problems in maintaining an acceptable consistent height above ground for the cutter bar, and that the power required to propel the vehicle, operate the cutter bar and tow the crimper, was going to tax the Land-Rover to the limit.

By the time we had got this far, new types of rotary grass mowers were beginning to emerge. These machines were less prone to blockage, simpler to maintain, and, besides cutting, able to windrow the grass for the first drying

94

The V blade: an effective shape for rural work. The blade shape imparts sufficient momentum at the right speed to cause snow to be deflected several feet on each side.

operation. Although they are generally more costly to buy and use more fuel than the reciprocating knife mower, they have rapidly gained in popularity. Their arrival and popular acceptance prompted new approaches to grassland harvesting, and Mr Murray's scheme had perforce to lapse.

As mentioned earlier, the Land-Rover's contribution to operations of a specifically agricultural nature is not as great, after all, as was originally visualized. But in these mechanized times, it is used for several operations performed by non-farmers which have an agricultural flavour, such as semi-mature tree transplanting (see page 159), mobile workshops for repairs in the field, and winching operations. Some counties retain farmers to use their Land-Rover with a snow plough attached, to clear country lanes and secondary roads – operations hardly conceived in 1948 but playing an important part in rural activities today.

In the early part of 1958 it was pointed out to us that the Commercial Vehicle Show would be taking place in September and we ought somehow to cash in with our new scheme of approved implements and conversions. Eventually we put up a suggestion to the Sales people that for the period of the Show we should take over part of the service area at Seagrave Road, London, which at that time was a solely Rover-owned establishment. In the event, we took over the workshop for the whole ten days and wrought a transformation. I think even the mechanics there, who were pretty scornful of the whole idea, were rather amazed when they saw the place transformed, with bunting, flags, decorations and an impressive display of the equipment that we had been able to assess and approve in our first two years. We had a gratifying number of visitors, including some fairly senior ones. Spencer Wilks was one who came and had a look round, and seemed suitably impressed. (He was always interested in this activity, and even after his retirement to Islay I continued to have correspondence with him regarding winches and special cross-country tyre equipment for the Land-Rover.) A chap called Manby, from Silsoe, also came to have a look at us; it was he who had put his signature on the Report on the first Land-Rover, submitted to Silsoe for test purposes in 1948, and which is quoted in Chapter I.

In 1961 it was decided that we should introduce an enlarged version of the diesel engine, up from 2 litres' to 2¼ litres' capacity. The Publicity Department were somewhat at a loss to know how best to put this across and get maximum

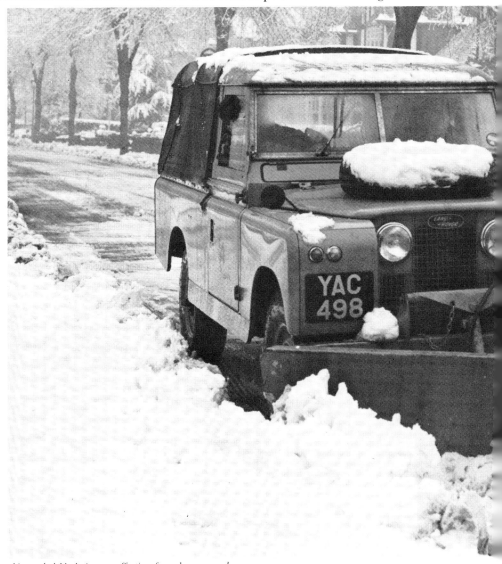

This angled blade is very effective for urban snow clearance.

press coverage, because the engines looked pretty much identical externally to the uninitiated. During discussions I pointed out to them that we had for some time been doing tests with another firm who wished to put some equipment on the market to convert Land-Rovers to operate on railway lines. What better, said I, than to have a demonstration of Land-Rovers pulling rolling stock up and down the railway line, as a means of planting the idea into the heads of the astounded onlookers of what a powerful gain we had made in our diesel engine! It is a fact that with rubber tyres in contact with steel rails the adhesion factor is relatively much greater than with steel wheels on steel rails, and conventional railway rolling stock has to depend on the massive weight of its engine to make up for this lower adhesion. We found in our experiments that we could start moving 50 or 60 tons dead weight in rolling stock without much trouble. (It wasn't quite so easy to stop it all again, but that's another story!)

Anyhow, my idea was accepted, and over the weeks it snow-balled mightily. Eventually, we ended up with a programme which started with hiring a special train to bring the delegates, Press, fleet-users, overseas distributors and dealers

Operations like these were carried out satisfactorily but the cost of buying and fitting the 3-point lifting linkage and hydraulics was too high.

Left: Powered mowers which are trailed for transport between sites suit the Land-Rover well.
Right: In addition to the hydraulic digger, a hydraulically operated concrete breaking hammer was also fitted, making the whole unit useful for construction and repair work.

who happened to be in the country down from London to Knowle & Dorridge Railway Station. The train was drawn by a steam locomotive to which was affixed a rather incongruous notice which said 'Land-Rover Diesel'. When they arrived we took them across to a siding and demonstrated 'Land-Rover on the Railway Line' operations to them. We also had elevating platforms and mobile workshops mounted as equipment for operating on the railway line, so that we could show them how the workhorse capabilities of the Land-Rover could be used for railway maintenance. Once this episode was completed, we took the delegates by bus to a nearby hotel, Chadwick Manor, out in the country, which was fortunate in having fields alongside which sloped gradually down to a lake at the bottom. At this lake we were able to demonstrate all manner of fire pumps and appliances, general purpose pumps, and a certain amount of wading and water-proofing, before we took the delegates back to the hotel for a drink and a meal. After lunch we took them out again to the same field, which was a very effective arena, where we had erected a covered grandstand –not necessary, actually, as the weather was perfect. From here we were able to parade past them all the other wheeled conversions and equipment that we had been able to muster. The finale was provided by the Royal Air Force, who sent a helicopter unit over, giving us one of the earlier demonstrations of how

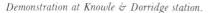

Demonstration at Knowle & Dorridge station.

Finale at Chadwick Manor.

they could lift Land-Rovers with their special lifting gear and transfer them from A to B. In this case they whirled the Land-Rover around the arena (narrowly missing some of the super-grid power cables, it seemed to me!) and then neatly deposited it back on the ground in front of the grandstand.

I happened to be talking to our Chief Security Officer sometime during the summer of 1965 when he mentioned the fact that the farmers who farmed all the adjacent land to the Solihull factory were pulling out. He suggested that I make a bid to the management to take over the care and maintenance of this land, amounting to about 100 acres, so that we could have close at hand facilities for field trials, demonstrations and so forth under our own control. I thought this was a good idea and made a bid, without much hope of success. Much to my surprise, I was told that I could go ahead – I think by A B Smith, who was General Manager at the time. He said he would like it kept in 'a park-like condition, with not too much agriculture' as he didn't want to sub-let it again in case we got planning permission to build extensions – agricultural tenancies were so complicated that it could take years to get a tenant farmer off the land. So with this brief I set to work. The place was in a bit of a mess and it was rather difficult trying to visualise quite how it would end up. We looked at various farming possibilities. One chap in the factory was very keen to join me – he was more of a farmer than a car-worker – and he set up a scheme for a mixed farming plan. I wasn't too sure about this, and happened to mention it to Maurice Wilks one day. He replied, 'Oh no, you don't want to get involved in that sort of thing. Your life won't be your own once you start getting animals on the ground. You'll find you'll be called out on a Sunday afternoon to take Daisy to the bull, and then Daisy will have trouble giving birth ... No, don't do that! Keep it all as simple as you possibly can.' This seemed like sound advice to me, so we just started to tidy the place up, verges, hedges and so on.

A high-speed perimeter road had already been built round the farm for testing production cars and Land-Rovers. The only problem with this was when slow-speed agriculture cut across the path (quite literally) of high-speed motor cars and Land-Rovers. Our Security Officer was a bit worried about this, and one particular incident had occurred to justify his concern. We had been out on one of the fields, looking at a granulated fertilizer spinner attached to the back of a Land-Rover, and discussing its merits with the farmer who had his horse and cart with him – his standard equipment! While we talked one of my chaps inadvertently coupled up the spinner to the rotating pto of the Land-Rover. It immediately started to discharge pellets of fertilizer over a wide area, and unfortunately caught the faithful old Dobbin of a carthorse right across his arthritic knees. Dobbin didn't like this, and although he had never been known to do other than walk, in a lazy sort of fashion, to our amazement he took off at a loping trot across the field! Before we could gather our wits he was out of reach, heading for a gate that led onto the fastest section of the perimeter track. The fates, however, were kind to us that day and no vehicles bore down on Dobbin as he lumbered across the road – but this incident clearly indicated that we had to become more security-conscious on Foredrove Farm in the future.

During the course of these preparations, I learned from my good friend Peter Pender-Cudlip, who was in charge of Military Sales for Land-Rover, that an organization I had never heard of, called Western European Union, was having its annual conference in the United Kingdom in 1966. It seemed probable that during a week's visit by representatives of their members they would give one day to visiting a commercial enterprise. As it seemed probable that the Ministry of Defence would tell them to visit the Rover Company, we decided we ought to make plans to put on a really good show. We had to have some suitable buildings erected for exhibition purposes and prepare some pretty comprehensive demonstrations. It was decided that we would join forces with Alvis who had merged with Rover a few months earlier, and have their armoured cars and other fighting vehicles along as well. So, the stage was set. The location was first class, the audience was of a very high level, with ambassadorial status for the leader of the Western European Union party, and the exhibits were of extreme interest to our visitors, totalling some 80 or 90, of which nearly 50 were mobile.

The weather was absolutely appalling, but fortunately trouble started the previous day at the dress rehearsal and not on the day itself. The static display area was becoming so bogged down that it seemed doubtful whether the exhibits would be able to move from that area to line up for the parade past the grandstand, according to the programme. But the Army came to our rescue, and the ordnance people sent a squad of soldiers along to put down some wire mesh matting to enable the vehicles to keep on the surface, and not dig in. This required a lot of man-power which fortunately the Army was able to provide. We dug trenches in front of the grandstand to enable the Alvis people to show the trench-crossing abilities of their 6-wheel all-wheel-drive vehicles, and we also arranged two items with the RAF: one was that they would fly in the Minister of State for the Army at an appropriate time, to land in front of the grandstand and welcome the visitors; the second was that they would carry out an up-dated helicopter lift of a Land-Rover as part of the demonstrations.

On the day in question everything was going like clockwork, and our mobile demonstration was well underway when we got a radio signal from the RAF, reporting that they were ahead of schedule, only 10 minutes flying-time away, and could they bring the Minister in early? 'No!', we said, 'Keep away! Our show's running to time, so we'd like you to land on time too.' This they managed to do, breaking through the cloudbase to land in the arena bang on schedule (which very much impressed our visiting dignitaries). In the afternoon we had arranged for the Alvis people to do their show, which consisted principally of a ditch crossing demonstration. Two ditches had been dug, one 4 foot wide, and the other 5 foot, in front of and at right angles to the spectators. The earlier 6-wheel-drive vehicles were capable of crossing the 4 foot ditch, and the latest vehicles the 5 foot ditch. As soon as the first vehicle started towards its target, it was apparent that something was wrong: it was going far too slowly. It gracefully tilted itself into the ditch, and – sure enough – there it stuck, nose down at a 30° angle in front of the entire audience. It could

A model was made of our exhibition area. The two buildings on the right foreground were permanent, the others to be temporary structures according to the size and scope of the display required.

102

The RAF delivered the Army Minister precisely on time. He is seen here on the left of the picture being met by Sir George Farmer (Rover Chairman), William Martin-Hurst (Managing Director) (holding umbrella), and the WEU delegation leader, who was later to have his umbrella turned inside out.

not recover, so, unabashed, the Alvis commentator called forward the later vehicle to cross the 5 foot ditch. This approached quite a bit faster, but not fast enough! Its front and middle axles crossed over safely but then it lost momentum, so that its rear axle subsided into the ditch – and we had another Alvis in front of the grandstand, this time with its nose pointing up into the air at a 30° angle! The problem was that while all the tests and practice had been carried out by Alvis drivers, it had been decided that Army personnel should do the driving on the day. They had hardly had enough opportunity to become conversant with how hard the vehicles should be driven, and had simply been too cautious. So there were these two mighty vehicles stuck in front of our distinguished audience, whose attention now had to be distracted at all costs!

In desperation, we called on the RAF to give us a low-flying demonstration of helicopters with Land-Rovers dangling from the bottom. They readily rose to the occasion – actually I suspect they must have risen from the beer tent, because by the time they had finished they had swooped down so low that the downward force of the air from the rotors, and consequent up-draught as it bounced off the ground, had lifted the fibre-glass roofs from the mobile latrines we had parked by the grandstand and sent them flying! Had they looked like flying saucers I'm sure the audience would not have been surprised by this time. Most regrettably, that wasn't all: the delegation leader's umbrella was also caught up in the air current and turned neatly inside out as he held on to it ... However, we managed to fix him up with a new umbrella, and by the time the excitement was over, Alvis had recovered themselves and offered the audience rides around the arena. The day finally ended very satisfactorily and to my mind the gefuffle over the Alvis vehicles just helped to make it more memorable without seriously detracting from their obvious ability to perform as per requirement.

In October 1972 we became involved in another military exercise, this time a very interesting and commendable operation named "Helping Hand" which took place at Ash Vale, Aldershot. In his Foreword to the report of this exercise, Lt Gen Sir Norman Talbot, Director General of Army Medical Services, described the objectives as follows:

> 'During Exercise 'Helping Hand' we studied the role of the medical services of the Armed Forces in disaster relief.
>
> 'The theme was provoked by our personal experience of impotence in the face of disaster, impotence arising from the reluctance of a stricken country to see the soldiers of a foreign power on their devastated soil, even to accept material aid which might be represented as demonstrating a political or international bias.
>
> 'As medical men it had seemed to us tragic that our affiliation to the Armed Forces, an affiliation itself dictated by humanitarian principles, should prevent our offering a helping hand to those in distress.
>
> 'We therefore decided to use the whole of our biennial study period in ventilating this problem; in showing what we had to offer; in drawing upon the lessons of the past; in exploring more effective measures for applying aid quickly where most needed; in identifying the problem areas and considering the means to overcome them.
>
> 'We were encouraged and stimulated by the participation of leaders of the medical services of other national Armed Forces, of leading representatives of our own national Voluntary Societies, and of the great international organizations, the United Nations and the League of Red Cross Societies.
>
> 'The two main lessons learned were firstly, the importance of co-ordination of relief effort on an international basis and secondly Humanity's need for a formula to enable medical services formed and trained to care for the sick and wounded in war without discrimination, to be used in peace for the benefit of mankind.'

The report included a list of the exhibits and for the Rover Company the entry was as follows:

Land-Rover and Range Rover Special Conversions
The Rover Company Ltd., Sales Department,
Solihull, Warwickshire.

The vehicles displayed included emergency, crash and rescue vehicles, and were capable of fulfilling many roles in a disaster, such as aiding and evacuating injured, clearing blocked roadways, clearing of flooded areas, and fire fighting, to name but a few. They were not all manufactured by the Rover Company and the individual exhibitors included:

Pilchers (Merton) Ltd, Victoria Road, Burgess Hill, Sussex.	Ambulance
Herbert Lomas Ltd, Handforth, Wilmslow, Manchester.	Ambulance
Spencer Abbott & Co Ltd, 51 Tyburn Road, Erdington, Birmingham B24 8NN.	Ambulance
Fuller Lucas & Co Ltd, Crowborough Cross, Eridge Road, Crowborough, Sussex.	Plumett Winch
H C B Angus Ltd, Totton, Southampton.	Fire Appliance
Air Drive Ltd, Davenport Vernon Trading Estate, London Road, High Wycombe, Bucks.	Excavator/ Digger
Evers & Wall Ltd, Lambourn Woodlands, Newbury, Berks.	Decontam- ination Sprayer
Cintec Ltd, 1-7 Ernest Ave, West Norwood, London SE27	Video recording and Communic- ation
Carmichael & Sons (Worcester) Ltd, Gregory's Mill Street, Worcester.	Fire appliance
Ledger Equipment Ltd, Airfield Estate, White Waltham, Maidenhead, Berks.	Mobile crane

Our mobile sales team who periodically carried out winter sales tours remember with some fervour the year of the Meat Pie Tour. We had for appraisal a refrigerated box body made specially for the Land-Rover, and the tour organizer thought it would be both novel and cost reducing to take this unit along, laden with deeply frozen sustenance for tour personnel. He accordingly made a bulk purchase deal with a local meat pie manufacturer and stocked the container full of pies. He may have been carried away by the large reduction in cost for bulk purchasing, for try though they did, the team were unable to consume all the pies. On occasions, tired and dispirited by bad weather and long hours at the wheel, they came near to lynching the organizer! The pies were going off a bit too, towards the end! We never heard that the makers of the container ever did much good with it either.

It was in 1958 that the Series II Land-Rover was introduced. We knew that Austin were thinking of introducing their 4 x 4 vehicle, the Austin Gypsy, in competition with us. Although the Series II design of the Land-Rover had been under consideration for some time, there was a reluctance to introduce it and disrupt production, which was then booming and getting in sight of the 1,000-a-week target. However, the advent of a little competiton from Austin proved a marvellous tonic, and the Series II was put into production to counteract any loss of sales that might be incurred because of our rivals' new model. There was some initial opposition from our fleet-users, who didn't like, among other things, the slight tumble-home given to the side of the vehicle to make its styling a little more acceptable. They rather over-looked the fact that the curve at the waist-line went outwards from the original body side so that there was no actual loss of capacity within the vehicle – it was just that much wider overall.

By now the Land-Rover's versatility – hitherto unprecedented in the world of 4 x 4s – had really gripped the public's imagination. The many enquiries that were coming in for different conversions and adaptations meant that we were obviously going to have to determine just what sort of a workhorse our vehicle really was, and where it would slot into the general scheme of things. We spent the late 1950s and early 1960s doing this, and also tried out a number of different activities during this period. With the demise of our own marketed

The meat pie job!

Land-Rover compressor vehicle, we were soon approached by Alfred Bullows, the paint people, who had developed a new type of compressor, rotary rather than reciprocating as previous ones had been. It was very much smoother, and vibration-free, and because of this capable of being mounted on the rear tail-board of a Land-Rover, driven from the rear power take-off. Some quick tests of this installation proved the point that with a special tailboard frame, on to which the compressor was mounted, one could be in operation very fast without making any drastic alterations to the vehicle, other than substituting tailboards and coupling up the belt-drive. This principle of tail-board mounting then led to thoughts of other items which could be similarly attached, such as water pumps, vacuum pumps, welders and generators of various sizes, and it began to look as if we might have a completely new system here which we could develop.

Water pumps were useful for municipal and public service use on maintenance and first aid. The advantages of mobile welders and generators speak for themselves, while the vacuum pump installation was developed to go with a gully-emptying trailer, so that small units could be used in outlying villages for cleaning up foul wells, gullies, and so on.

During the course of our experiments with these installations, we found a need to have what is known as a 'creeper gear'. In other words, we wanted plenty of torque from the Land-Rover engine but at a much lower ground speed than was available through the normal transmission. As a quick experiment we obtained a small 8 hp single-cylinder engine, mounted it on one of these special tailboards, fitted it to the back of the vehicle, and then used this engine to drive the Land-Rover through the power take-off system. We found we could have a very low speed, ½ mph or something like that, at 8 bhp, with full tractive effort. This was quite a useful experiment which we were to fall back on in the future.

There was also a demand for bigger compressors rather beyond the scope of our tail-board mounted units, and we carried out development work on these with Broom & Wade and Consolidated Pneumatics. An interesting side-line here was that with these bigger compressors permanently mounted in the vehicle, it should have been possible to use rebatable fuel, using the tax paid fuel only for propelling the vehicle along. However, it seemed that the authorities were not going to be sympathetic to this ploy as the basis of the equipment was the well-known Land-Rover. It came into effect only at about the third attempt – this time by Broom & Wade – when the tax authorities were approached from a different angle. What Broom & Wade did was to go to the tax people and say, in effect: 'You know our trailer compressors which we tow behind light vans and lorries: we don't have to pay any tax on fuel we use in those trailers; supposing we make the compressor self-propelled, would we have to pay tax on the fuel in this?' 'No', said the authorities, 'You would not'. So, without any mention of the Land-Rover name, Broom & Wade got a concession to use rebatable fuel on their Land-Rover compressor vehicle. The mistake made by the previous applicant had been to talk about adapting a Land-Rover for the job, and this of course introduced the subject from a completely different, and less favourable angle.

We made two special servicing vehicles for Donald Campbell's land-speed record-breaker. They supplied electrical starting requirements for the gas turbine engine, large amounts of air to cool the brakes at the end of each run, and hydraulic jacks to aid wheel changing.

Our representative in the United States, Gordon Munro, appealed to us for help with a problem he was having in what he called the Blue Grass Country in America. It was the fashion there for the horse-riding and breeding fraternities

1

2

3

4

Various pieces of equipment which could be mounted on the tailboard frame: (1) welder; (2) small reciprocating compressor; (3) rotary compressor; (4) vacuum pump. If the compressor at (3) is replaced by a small petrol engine driving the rear pto, the principle of our 'creeper' gear experiment becomes apparent. This principle was used later to achieve creeping speeds for a snow blower conversion.

110

to have British equipment. Rice trailers and all the tack were of British origin. The trouble was that with the long distances they normally have to cover in America, and the high speeds which are therefore necessary, they found that horse boxes – particularly a two-horse box – were prone to create a rather dangerous swaying effect, something which is not unfamiliar to those who tow caravans in Great Britain. Gordon asked us if we could develop some sort of damper to overcome this problem. After tests with various friction-damping devices, we eventually developed a horizontally positioned telescopic shock absorber, which connected between the A-frame of the trailer, and the rear cross-member of the Land-Rover. This was a great improvement – in fact it virtually damped out any swaying tendencies on a normal combination. We didn't feel inclined to market such a device ourselves, and we were eventually successful in selling the patent rights to Girling, who make quite a lot of trailer gear, and they decided to manufacture and market it. I think they paid us £3,000 for the patent rights.

Throughout these activities it was becoming fairly clear that although the Land-Rover was adaptable or convertible for a huge variety of uses, some of them would be ruled out on cost. For example, to fit up a Land-Rover to compete with tractors – which seemed to be a lingering dream with many – would involve:

1. Modifying the rear end to support a 3-point linkage.
2. Supplying a 3-point linkage.
3. Supplying a hydraulic source for operating 2 above.
4. Transmission modifications to obtain a lower set of gear ratios.
5. Spring lock-outs for the rear axle.

Even then, the vehicle would still be left with only a ground speed rear pto, not so universally useful as a live or engine speed pto, and a relatively large turning circle. (If the pto is engaged when the Land Rover is on the move, the speed of the pto output shaft can only rotate in relation to the vehicle's ground speed. An engine speed pto will rotate in relation to engine speed at all times. Both types can be engaged for stationary operation.) It can easily be realized that the cost of these modifications, carried out in small numbers and after-market, would be sky high.

When we were presented with a prototype Shorland armoured car conversion to test for approval I became rather uneasy. The military scene was not ours and was unlikely to become so in any volume, and the complexity of the conversion, due to the measures necessary to support the much increased axle loads, made me feel that we could become so deeply involved that our other activities would suffer disproportionately. However, a talk to Tom Barton, who fully appreciated my viewpoint, ended with him agreeing that the work should be handled by his military development section.

One of the problems that always intrigued me was how all the advantages of a 4-wheel drive, cross-country vehicle, moving very well across rough terrain, could be virtually nullified when a trailer was attached. The loss of traction always seemed out of all proportion with the fact that there was at least still 4-wheel drive in a 6-wheel unit. We consulted various papers on the subject of supplying power to the trailer wheels as well and came to the conclusion that it was considered to be not a very practical proposition. However, some of the documents were so long we just didn't understand them, and it seemed to me that the easiest thing to do was to build a trailer and find out for ourselves. So simple was it, in fact, that I entrusted the job to our young apprentice, Stephen Savage. He got himself a simple channel-section frame, to which he attached a Land-Rover rear axle assembly and a Land-Rover rear body, and we were just starting to build the trailer drive when the Commercial Vehicle Show for 1960 turned up.

During this Show, I was introduced to a Major Kitchen who at that time was Sales Manager for Scottorn Trailers Ltd. He had just returned from New Zealand where he had been negotiating a contract for trailers to go behind the New Zealand Army's Land-Rovers. The New Zealanders had told him that they wanted a really tough trailer that would be appropriate for the Land-Rover, and he wasn't quite sure what he ought to provide them with. The only thing I could suggest was that he should take over our project for a powered-axle trailer, see if the New Zealanders liked the concept, and if so carry on with the development, with all our hardware and our blessing.

This policy was eventually adopted, and Scottorn completed the trailer with the aid of a chap called Rex Sewell – an ex-Chobham man, retired, and a specialist in trailers, who was taken on by Scottorn as a consultant to help them do the final design work on the trailer drive. The unit that Scottorn developed had an effective working angularity of 60° between Land-Rover and trailer, and this was felt to be quite adequate for all reasonable cross-country usage; indeed, in tests by the Ministry at Chobham it passed all their requirements satisfactorily. However, when they came to offer it to units in the field, they were informed that the trailer had to be soldier-proof and therefore would have to have a much greater effective operating angularity to its drive, as it was liable to get turned over or jack-knifed, in the hands of the ordinary driver. The Scottorn system could not accommodate these requirements, so Chobham decided that they would have to design something. In due course they did: they produced a very elegant design which catered for 360° angularity, but demanded a specially adapted vehicle for attachment purposes, and a special trailer, neither of which were compatible with other units already in use. This meant, of course, that the trailer Chobham had developed could not be used by any of the other armies throughout the world which were already operating Land-Rovers.

At about this time the Ministry of Defence also wanted a new kind of tractor unit for towing a new gun which they were just bringing into service, and for

The trailer drive came from the centre pto and for the initial tests a Land-Rover box was used to synchronize trailer axle speeds with the Land-Rover.

The production design had a below floor transmission, a simplified transfer box and a coupling with the trailer permitting articulation of 60° in the drive line.

which no suitable towing unit existed. This eventually led to the development of the 101-inch, 1-tonne Land-Rover, which was at the same time adapted for powered-axle trailer operation. As a 6-wheel drive unit for cross-country work this was extremely effective and performed very well – in fact almost too well. In order to get the maximum cross-country performance, the ground clearance was raised, which in turn meant raising the height of the chassis frame and therefore the trailer hitch point. One day, at a demonstration, the inevitable happened. As the outfit proceeded down a steep slope with a sharp turn at the bottom, the extra traction momentarily exerted by the trailer at right angles to the Land-Rover had the effect of pushing it at the hitch point, which was rather

113

Testing with a V8 Land-Rover. The extra power available makes this all-wheel-drive combination extremely effective off the road.

high, and therefore turned it over! The realization of this danger point, coupled with the very high cost of the Land-Rover as a special vehicle only for the Army, and the even higher relative costs of the trailer as a special trailer only for use with this particular Land-Rover, got through to the book-keepers at the Ministry, and the upshot was that the powered-axle trailer concept was abandoned. While all this development had been going on, Scottorns had not been able to make much progress with their own design but now, with the abandonment of the expensive Ministry concept, they were able to come out from under, as it were, and start developing their own powered-axle concept again.

One of the earlier approaches for a special conversion came from a manufacturer of trailers, Ibbett Engineering from Bedford. Ibbett had come across a unit called a TempoWerke made in Germany, which was a light front-wheel-drive truck. The beauty of this was that you could chop the chassis off behind the cab and put on a very low floor. Ibbett provided the rear suspension from one of their trailers, which have the capability of being loaded at ground-level. The complete outfit therefore consisted of a front-wheel-drive cab unit and a very low rear platform, with hydraulically retractable rear suspension allowing the body to be lowered to ground level, the body floor then becoming a shallow grade loading ramp. Ibbett wanted to purchase

Land-Rovers from us, and then saw them in half, retaining just the power pack, cab and front-wheel drive. This was an interesting proposition but not quite suitable for our own units. At the time we were just changing over from constant velocity 'Tracta' joints on the front axle of the Land-Rover to the ordinary Hooke-type joints. We found that if you put full torque through a normal Hooke-type joint on the front axle, the kick-back on the steering wheel was quite unacceptable, and thus front-wheel drive could only be applied with constant velocity joints. The other problem was that the rear suspension supplied by Ibbett, although adequate for trailers, gave a very firm, limited travel ride which was hardly suitable for a complete vehicle. Added to this, payload space was diminished by the intrusion of the fully bonneted Land-Rover layout within the wheel base. The ideal is to get a forward control cab with the maximum weight over the front driving axle, then the pay-load space, and then the rear wheels as far back as you can possibly get them consistent with the turning circle, again to ensure that you have weight transfer on the front driving axle for maximum traction. None of these criteria did we quite meet, and this project was not, alas, a successful one.

I did, however, try to interest the Rover management in looking at a fresh concept of a front-wheel-drive commercial vehicle, utilizing our knowledge of transmissions and front-wheel drive as well as our units and facilities for manufacture. Front-wheel-drive vans are very popular on the Continent, particularly in France where Citroen and Peugeot have made many thousands – in fact, they are almost the standard French light van unit.It seemed to me that we could create a demand in the UK for a front-wheel-drive unit, and quietly put it on the market, rather as we had done with the Land-Rover in the

A front-wheel drive, low platform vehicle recovery unit. The vertical quarter-eliptic rear suspension spring is fixed to a pivot on the frame mounting and the rearwards inclined tie bars locate the other end. To retract the wheels the tie bars are hydraulically disengaged from the spring and the forward inclined hydraulic rams contract, causing the spring to rotate on the pivot to which is fixed the link supporting the wheel hub.

beginning. By feeding it in gradually, we could evade expensive market research, and expensive launch programmes. We were certainly getting a demand from other sources for a vehicle of this nature, particularly from public utilities and other similar services which were constantly loading and unloading heavy goods and equipment but didn't necessarily take them off the road. I talked to Maurice Wilks about this but although he could see the sense of it, I don't think he wanted to extend our engineering effort too far beyond what he considered to be our capabilities at that time. He also, light-heartedly, made the comment that if we started sawing our Land-Rovers in half and selling the front halves, what were we going to do with all the back-ends lying about the factory? To this I replied that we could use them up by making them into powered-axle trailers! This then became a minor crusade of mine in later years: one of my ambitions was to be so versatile in Special Projects that we could even saw Land-Rovers in half and sell the front half for one job and the back half for another. In a way, I suppose we have made it – in that we now sell front halves of Land-Rovers for a half-track military vehicle, and a certain number of Land-Rover units to be added to a powered-axle trailer. Later on we followed up the front-wheel-drive concept again, even going so far as to ask our distributors in France to purchase a Citroen H-type van on our behalf. This was shipped over to us at Solihull and we kept it for about six months for evaluation, before shipping it back to France for resale. But still no dice: the Sales Department were quite at a loss as to how to consider such a vehicle; they were still very much more motor-car orientated, handling the Land-Rover reluctantly, but light vans and commercial vehicles – never!

When the Range Rover was being prepared for production, I realized that several items we hadn't had before were now becoming available, such as constant velocity joints on the front axle, a better turning circle due to the greater angularity through which the front wheels could be turned, and a much improved suspension potential which would make such a vehicle, when finished, something that would meet the criteria of the ambulance world. The Miller Report of 1966, a Government-sponsored investigation into the whole UK ambulance field, came down heavily in favour of a low-platform, front-wheel-drive chassis on which ambulance bodies could be built – as is shown by the following specification, extracted from the Report:

Outline Specification for Type I and Type II Ambulance
1. An ambulance should be a simple and reliable vehicle, easy to drive and maintain. It should have adequate space for the treatment and nursing of patients during the journey and for storage of the equipment necessary for these functions. It should be safe and manoeuvrable in modern traffic conditions and so constructed as to encourage the highest standards of cleanliness.
2. The specific data given below were supported by much of the evidence we received and the answers to the questionnaire which we sent to

116

ambulance authorities. These answers also contain much information on points of detail (such as ancillary equipment for vehicles, body materials and construction, design of windows, doors, rear steps, etc.) which may be of value as the project we recommend develops. This material is in the possession of the Ministry of Health.

Ambulance (type I chassis)

3. A special chassis for Type I ambulances should include the following:-

(a) *Wheelbase*

This should be long enough to allow a patient to lie entirely between the axles and to minimize pitch. Current experience points to a length of approximately 10'3". Rear wheels should be set as far back to the rear of the chassis frame as possible to minimize inconvenience from wheel arches.

(b) *Turning Circle*

Not more than 40'.

(c) *Engine*

Smooth running and adequate power are highly important and the power output should be related to gross weight of the finished vehicle. It should be a petrol engine since, after many years of experience with both petrol and diesel power units, authorities are almost unanimous in their preference for petrol.

(d) *Drive*

Front wheel drive, by eliminating the transmission to the rear wheels, enables a vehicle to be designed with a lower centre of gravity, thus reducing the effects of pitch and roll, and with a lower floor making for easier loading. There would be a need for trials of front wheel traction.

(e) *Suspension*

Independent on all wheels and designed so as to provide a comfortable ride under all conditions of loading.

(f) *Brakes*

Fitted with pressure limiting device to provide even braking over the whole of the braking distance and to reduce the risk of skidding.

(g) *Fuel tank*

To hold sufficient petrol for 200 miles.

(h) *Road wheels*

14" wheels.

(i) *Driving position and cab*

Forward, or semi-forward, with ease of access of crew.

(j) *Transmission*

Fully automatic or semi-automatic gearbox to reduce driving fatigue and give a smoother ride.

117

Dual Purpose Ambulance (Type II Chassis)
4. The outline requirements given in paragraph 3 above would be suitable, subject to modifications because of the heavier loads to be carried. A self-levelling device should be incorporated.

Type I   An ambulance specially designed for a maximum of two stretcher patients, with seats for a maximum of two escorts, and with sufficient width and height to enable nursing and treatment to be given during the journey; there would thus be a maximum of six persons including crew.

Type II A dual purpose ambulance adaptable for:-
either 2 stretcher patients
or 1 stretcher patient and 4 sitting patients
or 8 sitting patients.
There would thus be a maximum of ten persons including crew.

In so far as vehicles then in use were concerned, the report summarized the position as follows:

Ambulances at present in use for stretcher patients have been widely criticised because:
(a) the centre of gravity is too high and this exaggerates the effects of pitch and roll with consequent sickness, distress and unnecessary suffering for recumbent patients;
(b) the wheel base is too short, resulting in excessive jolting in recumbent patients, who cannot avoid being partly over the rear axle;
(c) the types of suspension and springing used, even when modified, are designed for sitting passengers or inert loads and are not appropriate to the needs of recumbent patients;
(d) heating and ventilation are unsatisfactory.

I rather hoped that with our Range Rover units we would be able to move into this market. The GLC were interested in exploiting this possibility too and we discussed it with them at some length, also constructing various mock-ups of specifications which could be considered. However, in this case, finance put paid to the project. No matter how clever you are, nine times out of ten, if you are only building in small quantities, the price simply has to go way up compared to that offered by more conventional competitors.

When talking to the GLC we mentioned the fact that none of us knew what an ambulance performance – in respect of ride and suspension – was like. We suspected that most of them, being built on commercial vehicle chassis, must have given a very hard ride, beautiful as they looked. The GLC kindly arranged a little demonstration for us and drew together a variety of different makes of ambulance in which we all rode round, both on the stretchers and in the driving seats. Our suspicions were confirmed, and so we went back to our drawing boards. We eventually devised a lay-out which placed the Rover V8 engine ahead of the front axle, with the short prop shaft from the engine passing the side of the off-set differential to an automatic gear box – another thing the ambulance people wanted – with a transfer box behind. There was a bit of a problem here, because the transfer box had to be far enough back to allow for the angularity limits necessary for the propeller shaft driving forward to the live front axle. At this time Rover were developing their next new car, code named P8, which amongst other things was to have a ride-levelling rear suspension. Examination of this suspension led us to believe that we could adapt some of the components for the rear suspension of the ambulance; ride-levelling seemed to be essential, bearing in mind the very low platform and floor that we were going to have with this front-wheel-drive unit. However, no sooner did we begin to see a solution than it was decided to abandon any further development of the P8 Rover car. We now had no hope of obtaining a reasonably priced, off the shelf, rear suspension assembly for our chassis, and this, coupled with the inevitably high cost of small quantity units anyway, made the ambulance authorities with whom we were in contact reluctant to commit themselves to a project of this nature.

When the Land-Rover was first launched, the supply of a 2-wheeled, 1-ton or 15 cwt trailer of Land-Rover origin for Land-Rover and its dealers was something of an innovation. This trailer was actually made to our design by the Brockhouse Corporation, and Rover would buy it in quantity from time to time for Sales stock along with spares for the Parts Department. As time went on, the trailer became rather expensive, and demand was patchy – one would get an order from a fleet user for perhaps a hundred, and then probably nothing for a year or two. The Service Department was fidgeting a bit about having to service this trailer, and the upshot was that it gradually died out, and was deleted from our sales literature as we pulled out of this market. As soon as this became known, we were assailed on all sides by other trailer manufacturers requesting Special Projects' engineering approval for their own units. It soon became apparent that this was not on. A trailer for the Land-Rover has to be tested rather more thoroughly than perhaps a normal road-going type. This entails a lot of cross-country work, pave, wading, and so on, and, as a trailer is not a self-propelled item, I was finding that Land-Rover were having to supply the vehicle to tow the trailer along. At the end of the test the cost of the repairs to the damaged Land-Rover generally came to several hundred pounds more than the cost of the trailer manufacturer's contribution, so we were really doing development work for them. It seemed sensible to me to rule out all conventional trailers, and confine our approval to trailers specially built for the Land-Rover that couldn't be used with any other vehicles. By so doing we curtailed our activities at that time to two trailers, the powered-axle trailer made by Scottorns, already referred to, and an articulated trailer made by Dixon Bate Ltd of Chester, also a 'special' and made for the Land-Rover only.

The articulated trailer attached to a converted 88-inch Land-Rover.

Note the trailer's high swan neck attachment to the Land-Rover for cross-country articulation clearance, and the rear overhang to minimize excessive nose weight and diminish vehicle front axle traction.

Special pole carrying trailers for off the road use ...

The latter was made possible by the availability of what one might call a mini-sized turn-table coupling which was mounted on to the back of the Land-Rover, to which the trailer was attached. Weight distribution was always a tricky problem, as too much weight on the turn-table not only easily overloaded the Land-Rover but tended to reduce the traction on the front axle, making it not much better than a conventional vehicle. These trailers were used mostly by electricity boards, who wanted them for off-road, cross-country pole transport when erecting overland, overhead lines. Since the all-up weight wasn't great, load carrying capacity was not an important factor for them, but with a 4-wheel-drive tractor unit they could probably get a bit further a bit faster with a bit less effort than with any other system available.

A unique adaptation of this idea came from the Race-Horse Betting Levy Board. They wanted to use a standardized form of starting gate at horse-race meetings, but couldn't find enough race-courses with enough money to install them. Instead, they made up mobile starting gates which were towed by Land-Rovers from race-course to race-course through the medium of a fifth wheel coupling. I don't know whether this system is still in operation today, but it was quite a big thing in its time.

Shortly after the advent of gas-turbine-engined motor-cars, the organizers of the Le Mans 24-Hours Race in France offered a prize for the first gas-turbined car to complete the run. The Rover Company, in conjunction with Rubery-Owen, eventually devised a scheme to get a bit of publicity, whereby Rubery-Owen adapted one of their Grand Prix car chassis to take a Rover-built gas-turbine engine and entered it for the race. The first year it ran, it completed the course satisfactorily but for technical reasons was unable to use the designed heat-exchanger and the fuel consumption was therefore heavy. The following

... and a trailer with a rather special chassis!

year they decided to have another go, and arranged for the car to be tested over the course during the practice period organized by the Le Mans authoritiy in April, preceding the main race in June or July. The Rover gas-turbine BRM was transported to Le Mans by means of a Land-Rover and trailer. Unfortunately, on the way back afterwards, the driver experienced a phenomenal avoidance situation. This provoked such a severe swaying action on the part of the trailer that it went off the road and overturned. The major damage was to the gas-turbine car itself and there was no way it could have been made ready for the real race in a month or two. Before the next year's race, when the car had been rebuilt and put back into working order, our gas-turbine people asked me if, through my contacts with the trade, I could find a trailer which was suitable to transport it safely to Le Mans. My reaction was that, since we had already had trouble with a trailer, to try to do the same thing again was perhaps rather mistaken. Instead, I thought they ought to build a transporter to lift the vehicle, preferably a front-wheel-drive ground-level loading job, which I considered to be a great deal safer.

We were able to build this transporter using a spare set of components of similar specification to the splendid 4-wheel-drive, forward-control SMOMOT vehicle. It was built with a special frame to make a front-wheel-drive chassis unit, and used Ibbett trailer ground-level loading suspension units at the rear, which had the capability of retracting the rear wheels when required, thus lowering the rear cross-member down to ground level. It took the Grand Prix car easily and duly set off for France, where I am told (although I didn't attend the race) that it caused more interest in the paddock at Le Mans than almost anything else – almost as much as the exotic racing machinery! Upon its return, after the Rover/BRM's satisfactory completion of the 24 Hours, the

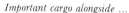

Important cargo alongside ...   *...ready for loading*

124

transporter was used for a long time for the Engineering Department's general transport duties before it was eventually broken up after wearing itself out in service. Although this vehicle amply demonstrated the potential of front-wheel drive, the message didn't get home that here was a possible extra market for front-wheel-drive vehicles. It now looks as if there has been a hole in this market in the UK for many years, which is at long last about to be exploited by Renault, who have just introduced a new range of front-wheel-drive vans into the British market.

We certainly cannot deny that it is a varied life in Land-Rover Special Projects – from boat-builders to mine-vehicles – and at one stage I have to confess that I even ended up in the maternity wing of University College Hospital in London! This came about in the early days of the Range Rover, when we were looking into the ambulance potential. Our Styling Department had come up with a sketch of a possible 12-seater Range Rover, intended as an up-market counterpart to the 12-seater Land-Rover, and we were looking at its potential as an ambulance, though it would have to go on an extended wheelbase chassis. One day I was visited by one of our British Leyland representatives from Switzerland. He happened to see this sketch and said he thought it would make a first-class ambulance, especially for the Swiss market. He thought we ought to build one and take it over to Switzerland the following year to an ambulance show that was scheduled to take place in Lausanne. We thought this would be a good introduction to the market as a whole, since with the help of our Swiss people we could try to tap the Swiss market for a start, and so we embarked on building it. It then transpired that the exhibition was a very special one, termed a Peri-Natal Medical Exhibition – in other words it was confined to matters concerning childbirth, before, during and after. It struck me that if we were putting a Range Rover ambulance on the stand it would be better if it were fitted out internally with appropriate equipment, so off I went to seek advice, having obtained an introduction to the Chief Gynaecologist at University College Hospital. I spent about an hour looking at incubators in the maternity unit, as the general idea was that the vehicle should be fitted with an incubator and used to rush premature babies to hospital for further treatment. I can't say I very much enjoyed my hour in the Maternity Unit – it wasn't really my scene – but the doctor did tell me about a firm building an incubator to his own design, which he hoped would be ready in time for us to take to Switzerland in the Range Rover. This all seemed highly appropriate, and when I contacted the firm they were only too willing to co-operate.

Eventually, after a strenuous effort, the ambulance was completed in time and we set off to Switzerland, with the prototype incubator inside. The manufacturers had equipped this with a celluloid dummy of a very life-like new-born baby, with tubes and things running from it to various junctions within the incubator. This hardly being our usual metier, we were all looking forward to getting through the Show as quickly as possible and then heading for home. It ended on a Saturday afternoon, and we left Lausanne at about

4 pm. When we came to the customs post outside Geneva we had a bit of a shock: as we were in charge of a commercial vehicle rather than a private car, we had had to use the carnet system to get through customs, but the commercial section had closed down for the week-end and would not reopen till Monday. We weren't going to stand for that but didn't know quite what to do, until eventually I said, 'Come on, chaps: let's motor round the edge of Switzerland till we come to a nice quiet little crossing point where they might let us through, not being so caught up with headquarters administration ...' We motored for about half an hour and, sure enough, we came to just such a crossing point. There were four of us altogether: one driving, one in the passenger seat, one in the attendant's seat in the back and the fourth on the stretcher, opposite the incubator. We got through the Swiss side alright, but when we got to the French side, two dear old French customs men, togged up

The first ambulance on the 10-inch extended wheelbase Range Rover which we took to Switzerland.

in nice blue uniforms, came to have a closer look. As soon as they saw an ambulance with a man lying on the stretcher, they wanted to know whether he was 'très malade' and if there was anything they could do to help him, which was very nice of them. However, the chap on the stretcher, being the party's wit, said – in the most execrable Solihull-French – thank you very much, but he was alright; it was the baby in the incubator that we were worried about ... These two customs chaps looked at the incubator, looked at the chap on the stretcher, looked at us four men in charge of a premature baby, and then, with a lovely Gallic shrug and an 'eh bien', they got out of the ambulance, closed the doors and waved us on! I never knew whether the penny dropped or not, but we got home in time for tea on Sunday after all. However, it was rather a near squeak, not knowing whether they were going to lock us up for taking the mickey out of them, or what!

A 28-foot operating height and considerable reach.

The hydraulically elevating work platforms, as made and marketed by Simon and others, were also becoming popular at this time. One of our fleet-users, the Southern Electricity Board, was very keen to have one of these mounted on a long wheelbase Land-Rover, for off-road use on overhead power-lines and transformers. The manufacturers of the platforms were strangely reluctant to work on this, not seeing any future in it, and it was not until our fleet-user had specifically ordered the manufacturers to have a go at it that any action was taken. Progress was made eventually, and proved highly successful: in fact the firm concerned was kind enough to admit at a later date that for many years it was the most successful line of platforms it manufactured.

We experienced a rather tense period with these people because, parallel with their marketing of their Land-Rover-based platform, we had also been doing tests with a chap who appeared from deepest Cornwall, with a device which he had fitted to his Land-Rover for lifting hay bales, picking them up and placing them on lorries for transport from the fields to the barns. We thought this was rather an expensive way of picking up bales – as far as I remember it only picked up one at a time, and was a little bit slow and cumbersome. However, when the chap concerned saw our experiments with the elevating platform, he reckoned he could make a platform out of his bale-loader which would not lift quite as high but would be much lighter, easier to

The converted straw bale loader.

128

A Ministry of Transport snow blower in operation.

slip on and off the Land-Rover, and sell for a lot less money. So he disappeared off to Cornwall again and about six months later, hey presto! – he turned up with his loading platform. Although this particular project was not successful, our investigations were sufficiently long-running for our original platform people to get to hear of it, and they became rather annoyed with us for actually talking to another manufacturer about a competitive unit. This was a somewhat parochial approach by today's standards but nevertheless very pertinent at the time. I never was able to convince them that we had no intention of doing any such thing, and that we could not help it if a man who produced a bale-loader for us to look at suddenly transformed it into a competitive working platform!

A very interesting project that arose during this period was one for operating snow-blowers. These are used in places such as Scandinavia, Switzerland and North America where they have large, predictable quantities of snow. They take the form of, you might almost say, an enormous cylinder lawn mower, which is pushed along in front of and driven from the operating vehicle. The snow is milled down by the cutting cylinder, and then blown forcibly through a chute and sideways over the hedge to get it well out of the way. We were approached by the Swiss firm of snow-blowing manufacturers, Rolba, who were interested in doing a small unit based on the Land-Rover, and we went to work. The concept was that these units would be kept at certain depots throughout the country, so that when a big snow-fall was reported in an area, the allotted depot's unit could quickly be trailed to the scene of operation, coupled up and put to work.

The system that Rolba suggested we develop was to have a separate engine mounted in the back of the Land-Rover with a propeller shaft driving forward through the cab and over the bonnet, to propel the cutting cylinders of the snow-blower that was being pushed in front of the vehicle. There were two snags to this: the engine in the back of the Land-Rover was not something that could be quickly removed and replaced, and making holes through the cab and the windscreen was not acceptable: in any case the Land-Rover would not really go slowly enough. Coupled to this was the inevitable delay in operation on arrival at the point of work, where there would be snow and slush about and miserable working conditions, amidst which the Land-Rover would have to be uncoupled, the unit turned round, and everything coupled up again, before the clearing could start. There was also the question of the low, or 'creeper' speed required for this operation.

Our final solution was to trail the blower behind the Land-Rover in the normal way to the point of operation. There the trailing wheels were removed – quite simply because the blower itself was height adjusted by hydraulic skids which could be used as jacks when removing the wheels. The trailer coupling was made rigid so that it was part and parcel of the Land-Rover. The driver then moved across into the passenger seat which was a swivel seat, enabling him to swivel round 180° and look out through the back window and over the rear floor and snow-blower. He coupled up a steering wheel mounted on the rear cab so he could steer the unit, while the blower itself was driven at a constant speed from the rear power take-off, which also drove a variable control hydraulic pump. By connecting it to a hydraulic motor coupled to a secondary lower power take-off it was possible to transmit drive through the vehicle's transfer box to the road wheels. Thus we achieved an infinitely variable 'creeper' gear to adjust the speed of the unit, forwards and backwards, through control of the flow from the pump.

Initial tests in the UK came at a time when there was just no snow about anywhere. The snow-blower people told us to try to find a water splash instead, as this would work almost as well as snow, and show us how effective our combination was. We found one at the Motor Industry Research & Proving Ground, and when we pushed the blower into it, it was so effective that it very nearly emptied the water splash completely. Our next move was to take the vehicle out to Switzerland and try it out in real snow. It worked well, but one could not help feeling that the Land-Rover was just a little bit too small and under-powered and that the whole unit was not quite up to scale. This was

Once the blower has been trailed to the point of operation, its wheels are removed ...

... the operator's seat is made ready and the steering wheel connected to the vehicle's steering column ...

... tie bars are put into position to lock the blower rigidly to the vehicle and the skids are set at the operating height and it is driven into work.

highlighted the next year, 1962-3, when we had terrific snowfalls in the UK. One of the northern county councils had some of these Land-Rover blowers in operation, but they were simply not hefty enough for the mountainous snow drifts that they had to move. In fact, the vehicle was almost in danger of milling its way underneath the snow drift and burying itself. All in all, it was just too much of a good thing, and of course it was a pretty pricey little outfit. Since then, the demand has never been as strong and we have never had a winter quite like that of 1962-3 again.

Land-Rover-on-the-Railway lines had been a dream for many people, and eventually we were approached by a firm of railway equipment manufacturers who had formerly made steam engines for the Indian railway system. They felt that a light unit for small sidings, generally private ones owned by manufacturing organizations, could be of interest as the normal small shunting engine was hideously expensive. In addition, it was thought that specially equipped road/rail vehicles that could easily get on and off the railway lines and take people to a point where maintenance was required, could be of interest to British Rail. In a way, the shunting unit proved the most difficult, because to get any traction at all with such a light tractive unit, it was necessary to make flanged railway wheels to replace the standard Land-Rover wheels. These had to have a special composition of rubber tyre shrunk on to give the necessary co-efficient of friction. The wheels also had to be dished out by 3 inches on either side in order to match the standard railway gauge, and it was feared that this would throw extra stress on the wheel hub bearings. Furthermore, when braking it was only too easy to lock the wheels with the standard automotive brakes, and any harsh application leading to wheel lock immediately caused a flat to appear on the rubber composition tyre, and set up unacceptable

Shunting and marshalling.   *Inspection.*

The road/rail vehicle lowering its front guide wheels prior to moving off.

vibrations. The standard rolling stock was also much too big for the Land-Rover which would have to be equipped with buffer gears to match up with the rolling stock buffers. Some form of braking system was required to operate the rolling stock which was equipped with a vacuum-braking system, as it was not considered to be wise to operate it with the old rolling stock which didn't have vacuum-brakes. Then again, when you go up a railway line you can't just turn round and come back; you have got to return in reverse. The vehicles were just not made for sustaining long periods in reverse: the speedometers got a bit upset for a start, and the speed wasn't very high, so something would have to be done about that. The real thought behind this whole project had been to see if something could be offered to fit on the smaller gauge railways throughout the world, at a much reduced cost, but the major 'carve-up' required in order to reduce the track of the Land-Rover made it quite uneconomical and eventually it had to be abandoned.

With what we called the Road/Rail Vehicle, things were much more interesting. These vehicles were made so that when they were on the rails they actually rested on their tyres, and the tyres in turn rested on the rails. The wheels had to be packed out to match the railway gauge, and small guide wheels were lowered front and rear and the steering locked simultaneously to keep the vehicle on the rails. We then had rubber/steel friction which made for good, standard braking – it didn't matter if the wheels locked. The speed was high, and any convenient place would do for turning the vehicle around. All the driver had to do was drive off the rails, turn round, drive on again, lock himself on the rails, and back he went! The vehicle could carry personnel, equipment for maintenance, elevating platforms, welders, compressors and electronic gear for signalling. The one big snag was the signalling system, as operated by British Rail and most other railways. This is based on a track circuiting system, whereby a low voltage current is passed down the railway line. When conventional engines or rolling stock are on the line, they form a connection between one rail and the other, and this operates the signal in the box controlling the relevant section, alerting the signalman. The system operates on a very low voltage, and depends for really good contact on the sheer weight of the engines pulling the trains, which may take up to 7 or 8 tons on each axle. Even then, they don't always make contact if the rail is very greasy or has not been used for some time, and has become rather rusty. Thus, with the Land-Rover and its rubber tyres, there was no hope of operating this system. The only other hope was that when the engineers were actually engaged on a major job of work on the railway, they would take possession of that section of track and control the traffic through it. If they were in control they could then bring their Land-Rovers up the point of work and get them off the line before letting any more traffic through. This seemed to offer a solution, but unfortunately, at the same time that all this work was going on, Dr Beeching was also going on, at British Rail – closing branch lines and small stations which would have been the very meat and drink for this Land-Rover operation. The prospects generally looked rather poor, and so our friends who were interested in marketing this equipment decided to withdraw.

Good as the cross-country ability of the Land-Rover is, there are always demands that it should be made to go further in even worse conditions. In this context, two special projects, quite different in scope, might be of interest: one was a tracked vehicle devised for conversion by the firm of Cuthbertson & Sons, at Biggar in Scotland, and the other a special big-wheel Land-Rover devised by the Forestry Commission Experimental Establishment at Alice Holt. The Cuthbertson conversion was really a sub-frame which carried track bogey wheels at each corner. The dimensions were so arranged that you could drop your Land-Rover on top of this sub-frame, remove all four wheels and then put a track round the bogeys and round a sprocket which replaced the road wheels on the Land-Rover. The front tracks were steerable in the conventional way, but with the aid of power-steering fitted to the sub-frame. With 4-wheel drive each track was powered at each corner but with differential motion, and there was no side to side scrubbing of tracks when turning as on a conventional tracked vehicle. The very nature of the conversion also meant high ground clearance, which (although not adding perhaps to the

The Cuthbertson conversion.

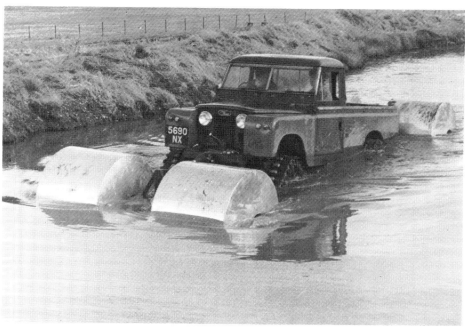

A Cuthbertson conversion used in Holland. The hollow drums are lowered hydraulically and support much of the vehicle's weight across the mud flats being surveyed. When the tide comes in, the vehicle floats on these drums and an outboard motor propels it back to hard ground.

The Roadless Traction conversion.

stability of the whole) at least made it more appropriate for operating in marshy and muddy ground, which was the intention. The Forest Rover, as it was called, had to have special axles made of considerably wider track so that they could carry the big wheels and tyres, 10 x 28, that were required, and also to give the vehicle a reasonable steering lock. The idea behind this was not so much the low ground pressures of the track vehicle, but rather what is known as step-climbing ability. The large diameter of the wheels really meant that with any luck the vehicle could climb a step the same height as the wheel radius. Thus, it could be driven over fallen logs up to a reasonable diameter, while its increased ground clearance meant that it could also straddle them and then carry on its way. The Forest Rover was made by a firm called Roadless Traction Ltd and proved to be an impressive performer on cross-country work, as did the Cuthbertson vehicle. However, they both had their drawbacks. With its 16 inch diameter track bogey, the tracked vehicle had poor step-climbing ability, so that if it was confronted with a bank to climb in marshy ground or in a river-bed, it was quite likely to mill its way straight ahead if it couldn't lift itself up. The Forest Rover, on the other hand, had such big wheels that it tended to become unbalanced and was not very controllable on the road, unless the speed was strictly limited. Accommodating the wheel arches also took up rather a lot of valuable load space.

During this period we were greatly preoccupied with extra-special cross-country equipment. One item we were asked to evaluate was the big, low-

A Land-Rover converted to accommodate Goodyear Terratyres.

The Vickers cushion craft conversion, fitted with crop-spraying equipment.

pressure tyre marketed by Goodyear, known as the Terratyre. Here again, its major function was to have the biggest possible ground area of tyre in contact with the ground, thereby improving flotation. One year we took it down to Romney Marshes where we thought we would find the sort of conditions that the operators required. Most of the operators were oil-field exploration companies who were gradually reaching out to find oil wells in more and more difficult terrain. The tests on Romney Marshes were very impressive, but again, because the tyre equipment was still at the pioneering stage, it was extremely expensive. Inevitably, it also made the Land-Rover a little less versatile and a little more cumbersome to handle, and so didn't find immediate favour. Today, of course, tyres of this nature are becoming increasingly commonplace on all-wheel-drive vehicles.

Perhaps the most bizarre application of all was the Hover Rover. This was developed in parallel with the hover-craft, an adaptation of a Land-Rover being carried out by Vickers, near Swindon, at the time they were building the first big hover-craft. Strictly speaking, the Land-Rover was more correctly termed a 'cushion craft'. The idea was to apply the hover-craft principles in such a manner that absolutely minimum ground pressures would be exerted by the vehicle's tyres on the surface, just sufficient for traction, steering and braking. The problem was that by the time the fans creating the air cushion had been fitted and another engine put in the back of the vehicle to supply the increased horse-power required, very little pay-load space was left, and really

A trailer or a boat on wheels? When traversing very marshy ground, the vehicle could proceed first and then winch the water-tight trailer across.

no pay-load capacity. The manufacturers claimed that as a lot of weight was taken by the air-cushions this was less important, and that in any case these things should be reassessed. However, the vehicle still had to be driven from depot to point of operation in the conventional way, and on many of the applications for which it was intended (for instance, one firm were interested in it for spraying purposes), it scattered so much stuff around the countryside due to the downward force of the air-cushion that it was rather impracticable. Vickers themselves said they wanted to use it simply as a means of publicizing their real hover-craft, and so it was left to private enterprise, in the form of Soil Fertility Ltd, to try it out on spraying jobs. Eventually, I believe the idea was abandoned.

Special Projects never became very involved with the military aspects of the Land-Rover business, chiefly because the military customer would usually complete the vehicle under his own auspices if the Rover Company was not building the vehicle to the full specification required by the military contract. However, two or three years ago Lairds of Anglesey approached us with the

The beacon and floodlight unit are supported on a mast which is coiled up into the roof box and does not intrude into the driving compartment. This is done using spring steel strips just exceeding semi-circular form so that, when pressed together, they interlock to form the column: a fall-out from the American space programme, in which the astronauts' probes were made in similar fashion.

A complete mobile cinema with public address and recording facilities – a popular unit with government eduation departments in African countries.

idea of manufacturing and marketing a half-track vehicle for military use. The stimulus was the imminent production of a Land-Rover with the V8 engine installed: the combination of this engine and the Land-Rover's other well-known features would give them a reasonably cheap half-track with a very good power/weight ratio, which would in fact be the first all-new half-track vehicle made since the Second World War. They encountered a spot of trouble with their initial approach to Leyland Cars (as we were then), as some of the newer young executives were unsure of how to handle such a request and whether it had any future. I at least had the advantage of having dabbled in the possibilities of selling the sawn-off front half of Land-Rovers in years gone by, and so when they came to see me I was very interested to see this idea cropping up again. Lairds set about the project in a very thorough-going way and did a superb job. Apart from day-to-day help on some aspects of specification, and details of design with transmission, I think all we did to steer them out of trouble was to help them obtain a Stage I prototype Land-Rover chassis frame and all the special components that went with it, to enable them to build up their prototype. They had originally intended to modify a Series III diesel engined vehicle that they had bought for the purpose before we suggested using the Stage I, and this would have involved an awful lot of time-consuming detail work before they could put everything together. We had to agree on a mutually acceptable test programme which would be appropriate for this unusual vehicle. A cross-country course in a worked-out ore mine in Anglesey, and high speed work on the nearby RAF airfield and on the ordinary roads were included to give a very searching test cycle.

In the mid-1960s I had a letter from a woman who said she had 'invented a device that would go very well with the Land-Rover', and could she come and talk about it? I was rather reluctant to spend time with a woman inventor (male chauvinist pig?!) but for the sake of our public image I asked her to let me know the next time she was in the Midlands, when I would be pleased to see her. Eventually the day came, and the good lady arrived. Far from being a battle-axe in a tweed skirt and flat-heeled shoes, with straw sticking out of her hair, she was a most charming and elegantly dressed young woman who breezed confidently into my office, sat down in the visitor's chair and proceeded to tell me about her invention. She lived on the East Coast and apparently had been much concerned with the problem of the disposal of manure from the many battery hen houses in farms round about. She had then conceived the idea of compressing this mixture into a form of fuel which could be used for heating the hen houses. To cut a long story short, she had talked to various authorities who agreed that there was some reasonable heat potential from this form of fuel, and she had subsequently processed some of this material through a rubber-extruding machine. At this stage in our discussion she dived down below the level of my desk top and reappeared with a sample from her briefcase. This took the form of a sausage-like affair of indeterminate length, some 2 inches in diameter . . . Her idea was that we should develop a compressing machine to sell as an attractive adjunct to the Land-Rover, which could then trail the machine from chicken farm to chicken farm, compressing their surplus manure for a reasonable profit. Though this idea was not up our street – no way could we spend time developing such a suggestion – our young lady was very determined. (It emerged later that she was the niece of Douglas Bader, the legless pilot; she was certainly imbued with the same degree of determination!) I spent a pleasant day chatting about the project, showing her round our new P6 assembly hall, and taking her out to lunch. I couldn't convince her that her plan just was not practical for us. She seemed determined that we should put it into development and even supply the machine as an optional extra in the back of Rover P6s – but we could not, alas, accede to this. Later that year, at the Royal Show at Stoneleigh, I happened to be walking past one of the Ministry of Agriculture stands, which was advertising 'Fuel Conservation on the Farm'. Out of curiosity, I looked in, and who should be lecturing to a group of young farmers, but my elegant friend of a few months ago! The young farmers seemed quite enthralled by what she was saying, or was it by how she looked? She came back to our house

To prepare the Land-Rover for wading in water up to seat level, a waterproof dynamo and ignition were fitted together with engine and transmission breathers, connected by plastic tubes to the carburettor 'snorkel' arrangement on the windscreen pillar. The fan belt was carefully adjusted so that the fan would slip if it became in any degree submerged.

Internally, the wipers and all instruments were raised except for the speedometer. This was left in its normal position for easy reading, and water-proofed.

for a meal that evening, and that was the end of that episode.

Special Projects was rather a sitting duck for way-out inventors, and we had our quota of them. One or two of them stand out as being exceptional, like the one just referred to. Another, also introduced by letter, was equally vague at the start. The letter just said, 'Dear Sir, I have invented an adaptation for the Land-Rover, are you interested?' This landed up on my desk, and I simply had to do something about it. It didn't give me much to go on, perhaps intentionally, so I was obliged to ask the chap to come to see us and tell us what he had got in mind. An afternoon was appointed, and I got back from lunch in time to be followed into my office by a young man who said he was The Inventor. It transpired that he had been developing a one-man forage harvester. This was an aspect of farming about which I knew very little, but events were to ensure that I learned quite a lot in the future months. Our inventor, by the name of Mike Fisher, had observed on his father's farm that cutting silage and taking it to the clamp was a very complicated operation. They used one tractor with a silage cutter in the field, cutting the grass for ensiling. Behind the silage cutter was towed a trailer specially adapted to catch the grass. When the trailer was filled, another tractor would come up, couple up an empty trailer to the cutting combination, and take the full trailer back to the place to be discharged. This process often employed two, if not three, tractors because they were running a shuttle service, plus two or three trailers, at least one silage cutter, and the labour force, plus a man on the clamp controlling the discharge and build-up of silage.

Our inventor's idea was to couple up a silage cutting machine to the front of a 4-wheel-drive vehicle and push it along in front, driving the cutter from the front. The discharged silage would be blown by duct over the top and into the body at the back of the driving cab (this body would replace the trailers). When it was full of ensiled grass, the driver would stop the cutting machine, lift it well clear of the ground, and then drive at high speed to the silage clamp – bearing in mind that he had all the advantages of a 4-wheel-drive suspended vehicle. Once at the clamp, he would reverse up, start up the moving floor of the body at the back – similar to that of a manure spreader, and discharge his load straight into the clamp. Mike Fisher was interested in developing something with the Land-Rover and, as far as I could judge, his system seemed to work quite well. However, it demanded a machine far bigger than any Land-Rovers we were making, and I could not see any future for it at that time, so we parted company.

A few weeks later, when I was considering a vacancy in our department, I thought of our young man again, and wondered whether he might like a job with us anyhow. Special Projects had just been made responsible for the maintenance of the adjoining 100 acres of Foredrove Farm, put in our charge when the farmers pulled out. Cutting the grass was a major problem, and I had in mind the development of some sort of super lawn mower from one of our old prototype Land-Rovers. He was well-trained in hydraulics and 4-wheel drive practices, and such a project would certainly benefit us while teaching him a bit more about his ideas. I dropped him a line, and he replied that he would like to take up the appointment. He hadn't been with us long when I realized that a particular prototype Land-Rover was about to be scrapped – this had been built originally for the Ministry of Defence, who did not require it in the end. It was a big machine of some 120 inch wheelbase, with forward control, rated by the Army as a 2-tonner but obviously capable of carrying a lot more, and fitted with a 5-litre Perkins diesel engine. I was able to stop it being scrapped, and we set to work to convert it into our Super Lawn Mower. (At this stage I should mention that Mike Fisher had conceived a name for his invention, which was SMOMOT, standing for Single Machine – One Man – One Team).

The super lawn mower which became SMOMOT.

With the wire cage removed, and spreaders fitted at the rear, the unit became an efficient manure spreader.

We obtained on loan nearly all the equipment we required: hydraulic drives, a forage harvester to go at the front, and a discharging body to go at the back. We put the machine together, fairly rapidly, and tried it out. It seemed to work well, but having got this far, we weren't quite sure what to do with our SMOMOT, apart from just mowing the Rover Company's 100 acres of farmland. One of the firms who had loaned us equipment pointed out that there was a Grassland Demonstration taking place at the Royal Show grounds in a few months' time, and that the organizers were asking for entries in the machinery section from anybody who had made a machine that contributed towards more efficient farming. He suggested we would be entitled to enter SMOMOT: even if we didn't get anywhere, at least we would get an expert panel of judges to tell us what they thought of it at no expense. This seemed a splendid idea and so we dispatched an entry form forthwith. In due course the area judging committee came along and we gave them a demonstration. They seemed to be pretty impressed, and later we heard that they had passed on a strong recommendation to the national judging committee, which meant that we were faced with a second demonstration before some very learned gentlemen. After this, we were asked to demonstrate the machine at the exhibition before the public, whereupon we won the machinery prize! Considering that all we had set out do was to make a lawn mower for the Rover Company's park, to end up winning a highly specialized agricultural machinery competition was quite a feather in our caps.

Auntie Rover's management was getting a bit nervous by this time, wondering if Special Projects was pushing them in a direction in which they were very reluctant to move. However, they need not have feared, because it was quite obvious to me that this SMOMOT machine was really the start of a whole new farming process. Even if there was money in it, it was going to be a very long-term plan, and other uses would have to be found for our 4-wheel drive lorry (which was virtually what it was) during those times of the year when it was not collecting silage. There were interesting possibilities here, such as swop bodies for liquid fertilizer, manure spreading, granulated fertilizers, cattle trucks, and so forth. But again, this was hardly up our street – it was all a bit too way out to graft onto the engineering base that we had available at that time. In due course Mike Fisher left us and went off to start his own company, which is very successfully manufacturing tankers for waste disposal, gully-emptying, and so on. The SMOMOT concept, although copied by two or three firms at later dates, never got off the ground. Maybe it is still lying around, waiting for someone with plenty of money behind him to develop it seriously.

Another inventor who came to see us with a likely idea was a chap by the name of Peter Moy, whose family had been much involved with the coal

The baggage loader with a 2-piece boom. The later model, with a 3-piece boom, was independently articulated at the forward end.

industry. His particular interest was to develop a continuous-belt loading machine which would have cross-country ability and be able to traverse open-cast coal sites and assist in loading coal lorries on site. He had got so far with his invention, and came to see us about adapting the Land-Rover power supply, hyraulics, axle-loads, brakes, and all the usual things that inventors want to know about when they are trying to make a Land-Rover do something that wasn't in the minds of the original inventors! During the course of our discussions, I mentioned that we had had approaches at various times for aircraft baggage loaders for use at aerodromes and that I thought his device could be equally well adapted for this purpose. In fact, as I recollect, Moy found this a more attractive proposition than his open-cast coal site loading, and henceforth concentrated his energies on developing a baggage loader.

We went through several stages with him, starting with a single boom which could be raised or lowered hydraulically, and finishing up with an articulated boom in three sections. The uppermost and forward section could actually be poked into the baggage hold and adjusted according the baggage loader's desires, then came the main belt with boom, while at the bottom a further small adjustable boom could be adjusted according to the discharging baggage from the trailer or truck on the ground. This was an interesting project, and Moy eventually sold several units to British Airways which were to be seen operating at Heathrow Airport. But I think it was a question of timing, here, because although certain aircraft were very suitable for Moy's loaders, the trend was towards containerization, and most new aircraft were being designed so that baggage could be loaded into a container, taken out to the aircraft and elevated to the cargo door level, thus giving the loader in the aircraft an opportunity to size up the whole load before deciding how to stow it. So, while this was a very interesting project, it eventually had to give way to changing demand.

There have been various attempts to develop the Land-Rover for deep wading and swimming, but the majority of these have been for military requirements, and are referred to in the Military chapter. However, we did receive a series of massive communications from an American who wanted to have his design for a swimming vehicle for leisure purposes built in the UK. We became involved because the basic components were to be Land-Rover as much as possible. The scheme was very ambitious and I could see that if we continued with it we would almost certainly find ourselves contributing to an expensive development exercise. I was unconvinced that there would be a worthwhile leisure market for what would surely be a very expensive form of transport. If there was a military requirement, then it was up to the designer to get the authorities to say so, and if they then approached us, it would be a job for the vehicle development sections. Also, my conservation conscience rather pricked me when I thought of such vehicles rolling out of the sand-dunes into the sea at otherwise peaceful seaside resorts. My impression is that such places

148

A mass radiography unit of the late 1950s ...

... and the power supply from the Land-Rover.

By the mid-1970s, miniaturization of much of the equipment made it possible to fit self-contained units on the Land-Rover.

already have enough problems controlling noisy in-shore speedboats without adding to their troubles!

Mass Radiography was another activity with which we became quite closely involved. It seemed that after the Second World War, the equipment available for mass radiography was rather unsuitable. The generators and some equipment and personnel were carried round in large, immediately post-war, if not ex-WD lorries towing a big caravan containing the X-ray equipment and records. All this equipment was gradually wearing out. Development had taken place resulting in a reduction in the size of the X-ray equipment, and there was a move to replace the old transport with something like a Land-Rover, which would be a mobile generator as well as being capable of towing a light caravan with all the X-ray equipment and accessories. One advantage of the Land-Rover was that, once on site, it could be moved away from the caravan, and parked where the noise of its engine operating the generator would not intrude. We co-operated with several firms on this activity, notably Siemens in Germany, Phillips in Holland, and one or two firms in the UK. The problem was that a local authority wishing to buy one of these units had to shop around a variety of different suppliers for the X-ray equipment, the caravan, the Land-Rover, the generator, and so on. What was really required was somebody to take over the rôle of main contractor, so that complete units could be specified and quoted for. This was an operation that Tooley Electro-Mechanical Ltd of Earl Shilton, Leicester, was prepared to undertake. However, although technically they did a very competent job, there were many branches of specialists involved: those concerned with caravans were jolly well going to continue to buy the caravans, those concerned with X-ray equipment were going to continue to buy the X-ray equipment, and so the problem of getting a main contractor to do the job remained. However, over the years, quite a few LandRovers were sold in this capacity. In some cases, particularly overseas and in out-of-the-way places, the units would consist of one caravan and two Land-Rovers, one carrying and driving the generator, and the other being a ferry vehicle, ferrying people in from the surrounding villages to be X-rayed.

As a mobile generator the Land-Rover has many uses, but one particular intended application gave us yet another slant on this aspect. A TV company, concerned with outside colour broadcasts, raised the problem of silent operation for their generators. They were anticipating a situation where an outside broadcast could be taking place at night or after working hours, possibly in a quiet suburban area, where they might not have access to mains supply electricity. In such a situation they visualized something highly mobile like a Land-Rover transporting a generator to its operating position and then driving it virtually silently. The unit would have to be capable of producing some 10-15 kva, which would in turn demand high output from the Land-Rover engine, requiring it to turn at nearly 3,000 rpm to meet peak demand – and at this rate, the noise output would also be at peak.

The boxy utilitarian shape of the vehicle does nothing much in the way of sound deadening, particularly in the engine area, and this had to be attended to as the first obvious source of improvement. Adding sound deadening material all round the engine bay produced some improvement but not nearly enough, as the TV company were asking for a unit that could not be heard at all at about 30 yards' distance. To cut down noise from beneath the vehicle's engine which bounced off the ground, we experimented with mattresses. This showed some improvement, but as so often in operations like this, as fast as you reduce one noise source another one, previously submerged, becomes prominent, and we now had clutch and gear noise at one end and cooling fan and air intake noise at the other. One means of reducing the latter, much more prominent noise, was to reverse the cooling air flow and use electric fans, situated low down at the rear of the compartment, to blow cool air over the engine and out through the radiator, with a baffled exit in place of the standard grille. This showed further improvement, but this time at the expense of engine temperatures which rose unacceptably because the air exiting through the radiator had been heated more than we expected after passing over the exhaust manifold and engine block.

The silent generator vehicle. Note the high level carburettor air intake made necessary by the partial sealing of the engine bay.

By this stage of development it was becoming fairly clear to us just how far we could reasonably go with adaptation, and the likely results in noise suppression. This led to our final specifiction which included –

1. Fibreglass undershield from No 2 cross member to No 5 completely sealing off the underside of the vehicle.
2. Special exhaust line routed through above.
3. Air intake baffle at front of vehicle to quieten air intake through radiator.
4. Sound deadening trim around engine bay, front wings, driving compartment.
5. Roll down 'skirts' of sound deadening material fitted all round vehicle's outer extremities, as further baffling of noise emanating from underneath the vehicle.

Although this wasn't quite sufficient to meet the TV company's standards, they realized that it was about as far as it was practical to go with the Land-Rover on a cost effective basis, and made arrangements to have several vehicles converted. Details were handed over to a small company experienced in this kind of work who would be capable of fulfilling any further orders likely to arise.

Although not much of a Land-Rover activity, a fascinating enterprise we became involved with was what was known as balloon photography. This was a system thought up by a photographer by the name of Conrad Nockolds, well-known for his *Motor Sport* photographs and others, and the brother of Harold Nockolds, the motoring correspondent for the *Times,* among other publications. Conrad Nockolds was obsessed with the problem of getting elevation for his cameras – not hundreds of feet up in the air, but just 50 to 100 feet or so. He devised a system of fitting up a small balloon, a miniature of the war-time ARP balloon, so that he could suspend a camera from it. The height of the whole assembly could be controlled from the ground while the camera could be controlled individually for traversing and elevation. I think he used a light-weight bicycle wheel rim with a little carriage on it, so that the camera could be rotated around for traversing and elevated or lowered accordingly. The system worked well, but he found the balloon was rather bulky. As he couldn't afford to spend time blowing it up when he got to a site, he had to take it already inflated on a trailer. I believe it measured something like 12 to 15 feet long by 6 feet in diameter, so it was quite cumbersome even on a trailer. Once he had arrived at a parking place, he found that by the time he had dismantled the balloon from the trailer, let it out a bit, fitted the camera gear, let it go up in the air, and then walked it along to the site he was photographing, he ended up rather like the Pied Piper, with all the small boys in the neighbourhood following him and making appropriate comments!

He wanted a less conspicuous method for carrying out his balloon photography, and his solution was to have a telescopic mast on the back of a Land-Rover which could be elevated and put into action quickly, and which would not excite the same attention during the course of its operation. He came to see us about masts and loading. He evantually found a chap who developed and built a mast that would go up to 100 feet and take his camera with it. When it was fully extended, this really was a most impressive sight. Conrad told me how, when he was first trying out his balloon photography, he once walked round the Bank of England on a Sunday afternoon, taking aerial photographs as he went. He couldn't help wondering what the Bank's security was and what they would say if they knew he had got photographs from the air of all their premises! He also showed me a most impressive aerial photograph of the Albert Hall, which I believe was taken with the mast and featured on the front cover of an early *Sunday Times* colour supplement. Masts for this and various other purposes are now made by Clark Masts Ltd in the Isle of Wight, and Land-Rovers are frequently equipped with them, though nowadays not so much for photography as for airfield work, radio communications, emergency landing strips and items of that nature.

It may be appropriate at this stage to make reference to various matters of policy which have affected the course of Special Projects over the years, to correct any impression that it has been one continuing saga of happy-go-lucky engineering playtime! The first important matter of policy was probably our transfer from the Sales Division to Engineering in the early days. When the department was first formed it was known as Technical Sales, and took into its orbit a few people, principally Robert Hudson and David Good, who had been operating Technical Sales as such, prior to our appearance on the scene. We linked up and formed a complete Technical Sales Department within the Sales Division. Our Sales Manager, and subsequent Director, Geoffrey Lloyd-Dixon, was never very happy about having us under his wing as he found himself having to deal with problems which seemed to be of an engineering nature, although they were in fact just problems peculiar to the Land-Rover which Sales should have been capable of dealing with. But Lloyd-Dixon, being a car-man, felt that it was engineering decisions that were required in many cases. He got fed-up with me badgering him, and – frankly – I was getting a little frustrated myself, being unable to get decisions when I wanted them. Then there was the other side of the coin: the Engineering Department was rather resentful that an engineering activity – or what was regarded as such – should be carried out under a Sales umbrella. So, inevitably, the crunch eventually came, and consideration had to be given as to whether or not we should be transferred to the Engineering Department. William Martin-Hurst took up the problems of this transfer, and we had a long talk together. He finally persuaded me that a move to the Engineering Division would be in everyone's best interests. I had a feeling that we might lose some of our freedom, but otherwise had no particular axe to grind, and the change-over, when it took place, presented no great problems. In due course we had as much freedom as we had enjoyed before, and in large measure this was thanks to Tom Barton (successor to Jack Pogmore as Chief Engineer, Land-Rovers). He recognized our role and allowed us to get on with it, and it has been like that ever since. In more recent years the problems have centred around top management never being quite sure whether a project that was put forward should be handled by the factory itself, or whether it could be left to Special Projects to sort out. From time to time I would be called to high-level meetings to discuss such projects, but I always felt that to involve me was a mistake: any job should either be carried out by Special Projects out of plant, or be done in plant. In certain cases, problems did overlap, and one instance of this concerned air-conditioning. Approved manufacturers had undertaken to supply and fit air-conditioning after production, but since it was almost mandatory for certain export markets, it had to be fitted and exported under the seal of factory approval, rather than that of the manufacturer/installer. I recall having to attend a meeting on behalf of Special Projects on this subject which was really convened to consider in-plant possibilities. As the 10 or 11 people sitting round the table discussed production problems – of which I had limited experience and with which I was not very concerned – I had very little to say for the duration of the meeting. It was chaired by Spen King, and I remember telling him afterwards, 'You know, Spen, that meeting reminded me of my school days: I joined the school orchestra and at our first concert had to play the triangle. In the first piece we played they had me counting through about 50 bars, then giving one beat on the triangle, and that was it – my total contribution!'

Another trend has been the move from the earlier, sometimes rather ad hoc planning committee decisions, to the creation of a full-time product planning department. I consider this to be an important move in the right direction, so long as the tendency to cramp Special Projects activities is resisted. A product planning executive once admitted in my hearing that had his department been in existence in 1948, there would probably have been no Land-Rover! So, by the same token, it is vital that Special Projects continues to retain some freedom for limited exploration in directions which at present produce no statistics to help and guide planning or market research.

The problem of special installations for the Land-Rover is one which has been steadily mounting since the early days. I have already mentioned the fact that Land-Rover is in itself almost a 'special project', and that once all the factory facilities are exhausted for supplying the different shapes, sizes and equipment for Land-Rovers, outside help is still needed to meet the demand. The vehicle is built to four very basic specifications, i.e. 88-inch wheelbase and 109-inch wheelbase pick-ups, 88-inch and 109-inch station wagons. From these basic specifications, a number of workable specifications are built up: petrol or diesel, 4-cylinder, 6-cylinder, or, latterly, V8, with varying wheel sizes, tyre sizes, etc, etc. When you have a basic working specification you can still go on and add extras, or E-numbers, which provide extra facilities over and above those required to make the vehicle work, such as heating and de-misting equipment, folding steps, fly screens, oil pressure gauges, heavy duty suspension, rear door instead of tail-board and flap on hard top vehicles, etc. Then further on there is a system of Specification numbers, or S-numbers, of which there are about a hundred. These are specifications built up principally for fleet-users (GPO, MoD, overseas armies, civil engineering firms, etc). Going on still further there is a Non-Standard Request Form, whereby we endeavour to supply customers with what they want according to our abilities. This very often takes the form of special paintwork, external holders for jerry cans in various forms, modified tool kits to suit customers' requirements, and additional fuel tanks. When all these resources are fully utilized, we still do not meet all our customer's demands, and some work has to be farmed out.

It struck me early on in the course of our operations that we could well do with a Special Installations Division, which could be set aside on a paying basis, and given the responsibility for looking after all this work. They would have facilities of their own for the majority of the work, but they would also be the main contractor in those instances where they might sub-contract to advantage for certain work to be done. Such things as winches, of which there is a great variety for diverse purposes, could come under this umbrella, and possibly complete front-end units, ie from the seat box forward, to be offered for front-wheel-drive, low-loading trucks or as a power-pack for other purposes, and powered-axle trailers and ordinary trailers. Customers using trailers with their Land-Rovers generally require auxiliary brakes to be fitted to the Land-Rover for operating the trailer brakes, and this was something else that a Special Installations Division could encompass. And then there was the awkward question of composite vehicles, eg a Simon elevating platform with a compressor fitted to operate compressed air tools. If Rover agreed to become the main agent for such vehicles, they would supply the Land-Rover but go to Simon Engineering, or Spencers, to fit the platform, and then go elsewhere to fit the compressor. By the time the vehicle had travelled between all the sub-contracting firms, it would have clocked up quite a mileage before the customer ever laid hands on it: nobody was fully responsible for the final entity, for its working efficiency, or for the quality of workmanship. This was a situation that a Special Installations Division could very well control, thus making sure that the customer got what he wanted. Such a division could also take over some of the production extras which did not fit in very well with the nature of the work at Solihull, such as supplying and fitting auxiliary fuel tanks (of which there are many variations), heaters and de-misters, air-conditioning and independent fuel-burning auxiliary heaters. Later on one could contemplate undertaking wheelbase extensions for special-purpose vehicles. The 1967 summary of the situation shows that in the preceding year, in the Non-Standard Extra business at Rover, 1,823 vehicles were painted with special colours, and this was spread over 69 different colours! There were 6,206 other vehicles all fitted with some form of the Non-Standard Extra or Extras, all adding up to quite a big problem which seemed to warrant a more orderly system of administration.

My first effort in this direction was made in the early 1960s, and again a fairly long period of lobbying was necessary for everyone concerned to see the problem and then agree to it. At long last I was able to convene a final meeting, to enable us to ratify the various agreements. We all sat round the table but five minutes later the whole thing was over. The Sales Director said that he didn't want to have anything to do with the scheme – he had completely changed his mind since I had last spoken to him – and so that was the end of that. Some years later I tried again, reinforcing my case by pointing out that a similar scheme had been highly successful with Bedford Trucks at Dunstable. The Manager there had very kindly showed me round all his facilities, and was quite happy to entertain a further party of visitors from Rover. After this visit, a massive and most interesting report was written by our then Production Director, WJ Robinson, which subsequently disappeared upstairs. Like so many reports, it then got itself pigeon-holed somewhere and I was never able to flush it out to get it discussed again. I think the reluctance was to some extent caused by a fear of industrial relations problems, particularly on the question of labour mobility/flexibility from a small unit operating within a union-dominated mass assembly plant. But, surely, with some firm management this was something which could have been overcome? A certain amount of disruption would also have been caused, as there were various little workshops situated around the site at Solihull undertaking bits and pieces of special work, some of which would have had to be eliminated, the others merging into an 'all-can-do' Special Installations Division. The other telling point – which could always be brought to bear when a decision had to be deferred – was that the plant was bursting at the seams with existing work, particularly with car assembly, and there wasn't the space to accommodate such an activity. This was very short-sighted, however, and I am sure that, today, had we pioneered such an activity in the late 1960s, we would have had a very useful adjunct to Land-Rovers at Solihull, operating smoothly and efficiently to Land-Rover's great advantage.

In the end, what Rover was reluctant to do turned into benefit for Spencer Abbott & Co Ltd, a company fairly well-known to Land-Rover users and sub-contractors. I had started to use them intermittently for such jobs as winch installation, and we eventually got this going quite well. This was in the late 1960s and early 1970s, when the Range Rover was about to come on the market, and, as I have related elsewhere, the prospect of using this chassis for a high-class ambulance became an attractive one. Since it was too short for a 4-wheel-drive ambulance, it was essential that we engineered a wheelbase extension. Tests of a prototype proved satisfactory, indicating that it would be of value to the ambulance field. Through the Product Planning Committee we made sure that the management was fully aware of the rather bigger than usual step taken by Special Projects, but the project was passed without any comment. We then decided that since it couldn't be done at Solihull, we must select one contractor to manufacture all the chassis extensions for us and for all our approved ambulance body builders. We got Spencer Abbott interested and trained up to carry out this work, but this was a job that could have slotted in very nicely had we had a Special Installations Divison functioning; as we hadn't, the work and profit had to go outside.

As already mentioned, when the Land-Rover came on the market one of the first customers for it was the War Office, who took away a quantity of vehicles to modify by installing 4-cylinder Rolls-Royce B-series engines. These were another wheeze of the War Office: Rolls-Royce built 4-cylinder, 6-cylinder and 8-cylinder engines for them, with many common features and maximum interchangeability of parts, so that they could then be used to power anything from Land-Rovers to heavy tanks and big transporters. I remember SB Wilks himself telling me, when we were discussing some Marauder problems, of his first reaction on seeing a little 80-inch Land-Rover fitted with a B-series engine. 'You went to drive the vehicle away, but found that the engine had got there first! There was scarcely room for anyone in the front driving compartment!' As a result of this policy, and the suggestion from the War Office that we should give them independent front suspension as well, we turned down military business at that time, deciding to stick to the commercial field. It was partly due to this that the Austin Champ came into being, as described elsewhere. I was always a little worried about the military business, as I felt that it would eventually become powerful enough to have a disproportionate influence on our production specifications, possibly to the detriment of the commercial world, apart from slowing it down. We can safely say that our military business has been both successful and profitable, but I would still maintain that it complicates life when we want to make specification changes to keep up to date with the demands of the commercial market. The 1-tonne, 101-inch vehicle was a good case in point: although extremely good for military purposes, it was so orientated in respect of size and overall weight, that we found no worthwhile civilian market application for it. Today, however, the complexity of international legislation in respect of safety, emission, noise, construction and use imposes a far greater burden on engineering resources.

One of the things I had always been interested in was the possibility of Land-Rover producing what might be called a 'Poor Man's Unimog'. The 4-wheel-drive Unimog produced by a subsidiary of Mercedes-Benz in Germany was an excellent vehicle which I had always admired, but it was very expensive. I believed that with the knowledge and expertise we had garnered over the years with Land-Rovers, and with the units available to us, we could have built a similar sort of vehicle but sold it for rather less money. In the early days, when we were looking at the front-wheel-drive low-loader previously referred to, known as the TempoWerke, and with the intermittent demand for a Land-Rover much bigger than anything we had contemplated, I felt that as a matter of policy we ought to develop an all-wheel-drive speciality, thereby ensuring that anybody wanting an all-wheel-drive vehicle would automatically think of coming to us first. Such vehicles, particularly those of the more expensive and exotic types, would use a high proportion of sub-contractors but would still be profitable. I touted this policy around without much hope of success and, indeed, it got scant consideration. Again, the perfect answer was that Solihull was bursting at the seams with present production and there was no room for it. There didn't seem to be much room for people who looked very far ahead either. Later on, at the time when SMOMOT came along, had we developed some kind of all-wheel-drive speciality, we could have looked at the proposals that SMOMOT seemed to offer rather more intelligently. If we had taken this route, it is hard to say whether we could have made it profitable, but the signs have been pretty positive. After all, there are several firms making a living from manufacturing all-wheel-drive vehicles to different and bigger specifications than the Land-Rover, and they seem to be making a go of it. A Special Installations Divison would have been just the right place in which to assemble the lower production volume of these machines.

Another very absorbing activity involving Special Projects is the transplanting of mature, or semi-mature trees. This idea is not, of course, a new one – it was employed by Capability Brown two hundred years ago, when he was altering the landscape on large estates throughout the country – but in those days it was horses and men that supplied the necessary power, while today it is all done mechanically, with a minimum of man-power. Without going into too many details, when we first became involved, the technique entailed the use of a trailer, specially developed for the purpose, which acted both as a lever to pull the tree out of the ground, and then as a transporter to take it to its new place of residence. To haul the tree out of the ground, the trailer was used as a pivot by means of winching on the extended drawbar, which stuck up in the air alongside the tree trunk, and then hauling on it by winch cable. Thus, when the trailer drawbar was eventually pulled down parallel to the ground, it pulled the tree and its trunk down and out of its hole. Then there is the question of hauling this heavy load out of the forest or away from the site. This usually involves a fair amount of all-wheel drive traction, and often the additional help of the winch to get away from the site, which is frequently in rough or boggy terrain. The process is more or less reversed for planting the tree at the planting site, and again involves some nifty work for the Land-Rover, or other form of traction. The trailer has to be backed up to the planting hole, with its tree clamped to it, and tree and trailer then have to be manoeuvred into a vertical position, again by judicious winching, so that the tree can be released and dropped into the hole. Amongst other things, this process was a good occupation for the Land-Rover as a demonstration for training people on the versatility of 4-wheel drive. When we started our Foredrove Farm Demonstration Site, we often had requests from the sales people to give a demonstration of Land-Rovers working off-the-road for visiting parties of salesmen, overseas

The special trailer is up-ended, attached to the tree through the collar around the trunk, and the telescopic draw bar is extended for greater leverage. A winch is used to haul in the draw bar which is then pulled down parallel to the ground. This action will lift the tree out of its previously excavated position ...

delegates and so forth. We had a tree at Foredrove Farm which we used for this demonstration, and in fact transplanted it at least half a dozen times. By all the laws of nature, this shouldn't have been very good for the tree, but it seemed to thrive on it! It was strong and growing well until they came along and plonked the Rover SD1 Car Plant on top of it; now that didn't do it any good at all!

When the Range Rover was first introduced, we made rather an administrative bungle of its air-conditioning system. During the development stage, our Managing Director, William Martin-Hurst, who was very keen on air-condi-

159

... and deposit the tightly wrapped soil ball over the trailer axle ready for transport.

160

The normal position for the roof-top air-conditioner.

The cold air ejection louvres are immediately beneath, inside.

Range Rover fitted with a roof-top air-conditioner.

High temperatures can build up in a closed security vehicle making air cooling essential. The unit on the roof of this vehicle is the self-contained Hubbard CT 140.

163

An air-conditioned security vehicle supplied by Glovers of Hamble. The additional petrol tank on the roof at the rear is a temporary fitting to make sure the long delivery mileage could be safely accomplished.

A radar surveillance vehicle also generates high internal temperatures. The vehicle is fitted with a roof-mounted refrigerant condenser and the cooling evaporator pack is fitted internally.

tioning, started a project to develop a system for the Range Rover which would cover the most extreme requirements the vehicle would ever be likely to meet. It was pretty massive, and as the units had to be specially made it was very expensive. Development progress did not keep pace with the launching of the vehicle, which had been speeded up by Leyland Cars as a matter of policy – I think we were told to announce it a whole year ahead of the original schedule. As soon as it was announced, several firms came along offering air-conditioning alternatives which they were prepared to supply and/or fit, and we had to have an audit to examine all these different systems. By this time William Martin-Hurst had retired and AB Smith was in command. We looked at systems which were fitted on the Range Rover roof, including our own, and those which were fitted inside the vehicle in various places, and AB Smith decreed that if we were going to have an air-conditioning system at all, it must be inside and not an external protrusion – which was fair enough. Anyhow, the Range Rover met with such an enthusiastic response that we were churning them out, in rather a halting fashion because of our premature start, which meant that we didn't have much time to devote to air-conditioning.

The Swedish ambulance conversion had a 1-meter wheelbase extension but did not increase the Range Rover rear overhang.

The specialist body builders welcomed the 10-inch wheelbase extension and added an additional 10 inches to the rear overhang.

Our 35-inch wheelbase extension was made up with two cross members joined to the 35-inch-long side members and positioned within the Range Rover frame, so that the central silencer and split propeller shaft mounting could be correctly located.

When we made a 35-inch wheelbase extension available, the specialist body builders welcomed this too but retained their 10-inch overhang! The Swedish vehicle (below), however, remained the same.

Besides fire appliances, Carmichaels produced a 6 x 4 personnel carrier.

The problem caught up with us all of a sudden, when the sales people said that we *must* have air-conditioning for certain developing export markets, principally those in the Middle East. As there was no factory-developed system, they turned to Special Projects and said, 'Can you find us a proprietary system for the vehicle to tide us over until we can get a fully fledged factory installation going?' The only quick solution was to take a system already in use on commercial vehicles in America, the main part of which consisted of a big box of components which sat on top of the cab roof – unsightly but efficient. This solved one problem worrying us at the time – that of having to place the condenser for cooling the refrigerant in front of the radiator. As the condenser in this unit was incorporated in the box, there could be no question of the engine over-heating due to obstructions in front of the radiator. So, rather ironically, and in spite of what AB Smith had decreed, we had no immediate alternative but to offer an externally fitted device. It kept us going for a few years and helped us along, but now of course fully engineered, internally fitted equipment can be obtained ex-works.

We introduced a 10-inch wheelbase extension principally for ambulance purposes and 10 inches was chosen as it appeared to be enough to get a standard stretcher into the compartment, while not requiring extra expenditure in the form of a lengthened and split propeller shaft: it only had to be lengthened. We noticed later on that a firm in Sweden, untroubled by our inhibitions, was producing a very fine ambulance on the Range Rover, to which they had given a wheelbase extension of 1 metre (about 39½ inches). We inspected one of these vehicles when it was over on a visit to the UK and a very fine-looking machine it was too. This gave us further thoughts about introducing a longer wheelbase extension than our modest 10 inches. Another reason was that while the original conception had been that an extra 10 inches was sufficient to convey a standard stretcher, it wasn't quite enough to satisfy the ambulance body-builders who wanted more space still, and they were therefore simply building the bodies with an extra 10 - 12 inch overhang at the back. This wasn't altogether satisfactory and we thought that to build an even longer wheelbase would get us back to a better balanced vehicle again. Our deliberations showed that a 35-inch wheelbase extension would be about right. Alas, plans didn't work out very well because some of the ambulance body-builders, once they got hold of the 35-inch extension, *still* went on and built a

Scottorn Trailers' 6 x 6 conversion.

10 - 12 inch extra overhang at the back, resulting in a rather monstrous vehicle. We also had to take into account the question of legislation over brake performance and such like with this larger, more heavily laden vehicle, and for this reason it had to be abandoned. However, this 35-inch extension was used by some body-building firms for luxury personnel carrying vehicles and, provided the rearmost extension did not exceed the standard Range Rover one, and the gross axle weight wasn't exceeded, it made quite a satisfactory vehicle for this purpose.

At the time of the vehicle's introduction, we were approached by Harry Carmichael of Carmichael's, a firm which builds fire appliances. He had conceived a scheme for converting the Range Rover into a 6-wheel vehicle, which he wanted to use as a first-rescue fire appliance. This struck us as a bit unusual, but once we had talked about it, and seen what practices of this nature were carried out in the commercial vehicle world, we felt quite happy about going along with him. Eventually we drew up a jointly agreed specification which was, basically, a Range Rover chassis with an additional trailing axle and frame extension added on at the back. This configuration then became known as a 6 x 4 chassis. We carried out comprehensive tests on this vehicle as it was a

All body conversions undergo a tilt test.

170

fairly fundamental chassis change, and ever since Carmichael's have had much success with this particular conversion. The next step was to make it into a 6 x 6 or all-wheel-drive chassis. Carmichael's studied the problem but I think we all came to the same conclusion, that such a conversion would really be very expensive and probably not cost-effective either to develop or for customers to purchase, so we let it lapse. To get the ball rolling again, it took the initiative of a young Frenchman who linked up with the Scottorn Trailer Company to develop such a configuration. This is now taking shape, and it will be interesting to see what sort of market it achieves.

Having become such a 'prestige' vehicle, the Range Rover has attracted a great many motor-car body-builders to the possibilities of restyling and making variations on the theme to suit certain customers. The first step was to have available a 4-door conversion, and the pioneers of this particular work were FLM (Panelcraft) in London. This company has been in the luxury end of the body conversion business for many years and has built up good contacts, not only in the UK but overseas – particularly in the Middle East. They found a ready market for the 4-door conversion, and other varieties, including special hunting vehicles for Middle East potentates. Their hunting entails the use of hawks for tracking down the prey, and as the hawk is a very valuable bird and takes a lot of training, they obviously don't want to lose it during the course of a hunting expedition. So everything on these special vehicles is designed to prevent this happening: perches are built in the back of the vehicle for the hawks to rest on, and in some cases, when they have been dispatched in pursuit of their quarry, the owner, sitting alongside the driver in the front, can elevate his seat up through the open roof and keep an eye on his valuable bird, making sure that in due course it can be safely recovered. There have even been vehicles made on the extended wheelbase with two elevating seats at the rear as well, so that the owner and observers can emerge through the Range Rover roof as it cruises along the desert, looking rather like a triple-headed Loch Ness Monster!

Automatic transmissions was another area we investigated, as we had been informed by the ambulance people that this would almost certainly be a requirement on the more de-luxe ambulances that they were contemplating making. We did the first installation ourselves, identified most of the problems and mastered many of them. But when the motoring journal *Autocar* published a road test of a Range Rover which had been converted by Automatic Transmission Services Ltd and wrote of it in glowing terms, it became clear to me that we should test and approve their installation rather than become involved ourselves. Automatic Transmission Services went ahead doing conversions mostly on basic vehicles. The call from the ambulance world never really materialized and only in a few special cases could the combined cost of lengthening the wheelbase and installing automatic transmission be justified.

With a span of over 30 years watching Land-Rover markets develop, it is interesting for me to see how the organization has changed. In 1948 we had

Our ill-fated post-hole borer.

hardly any Sales staff even for motor-cars, let alone Land-Rovers, and no clear identity within the Engineering Division, but such a lot has happened over the years that we have now passed through an over-kill situation, where we have had far too many jobs and people overlapping. These circumstances seem so often to beget complications in an organization. Organization charts for old *and new* departments proliferate and eventually lead to overmanning, then overlapping and confusion, and inevitably to loss of flexibility. Now that Land-Rover Limited has been formed as a separate entity with a bit more control of its own destiny, the situation should stabilize itself but – my goodness – we have had some peaks and troughs in the intervening years, with personnel and management changes.

S B Wilks was the first to see weaknesses in his staff and decided that we must have a Sales Director on the Board, and strengthen up the Sales Department. Then there was the merger with Leyland in the mid-1960s. At first all was quiet for us, as we were in what was called the Specialist Car Division which was profitable at that time; attention was given rather to building the Austin/Morris part of the organization into a more profitable concern. But, as history records, there were problems with Austin/Morris, and eventually along came Ryder, appointed by the Government, to put everything right. As far as I was concerned, for Special Projects and probably for Land-Rover Limited, this was not a good thing, because, amongst other things, a centralized accounting system was put into effect. Those of us who had had budgets to operate in the past and had taken pride in operating them, making sure that we ended the year well within budget, lost all control. My belief is that centralized budget control is generally a sign of weak or uncertain management. They may think that by doing this they are getting everything under their own control, but in reality they aren't, because in a large organization it is impossible to be all things to all men when it comes to authorizing expenditure: it has got to be devolved to some extent. Fortunately, people who have been around the organization for some time knew how to side-step some of the incompatible restrictions which appeared from time to time.

A good example of how centralized budget control can be self-defeating occurred over the development of a post-hole borer for the Land-Rover. Due to interest expressed in one or two overseas zones, we had developed and tested a post-hole borer specially for the Land-Rover. The unit was seen by a buyer of a well-known civil engineering firm who thought it would be suitable for a surveying contract they were about to embark on in Africa. On its arrival in Africa, the company had difficulty in getting the machine to function properly. They offered to accommodate our engineer free of charge, if we would release and fly him out there, to get the machine operational as it had been demonstrated to them at Solihull. The unexpected sale of the prototype unit for £1,000 was in my view a 'windfall' profit, as it would otherwise have been eventually written off. The cost of the engineer's return air fare was £300, so it seemed to me that we would merely be reducing our windfall by this amount, to £700. But since the engineering budget would have to finance the air fare while receiving no benefit from the sale, the customer's offer was refused. The net result was that:

1) We lost our machine. It could not be shipped back due to export restrictions in the African country.
2) We had to agree to cancel the sale and therefore lost £700.
3) We lost some goodwill with an important customer.
4) We lost the opportunity of further field experience in the development of a piece of equipment which could well have been very suitable for Land-Rovers and would have enhanced its work-horse image.

I am convinced that a strong management, which has real product knowledge and knows what it is doing, is much more likely to be effective if it devolves budget control as far as it possibly can, and then sets up an inspection team to go round monitoring the budget holders to find out what they are doing, what they are spending and why, and particularly whether they are within or over their budget. In this way, it will exercise much more control and find out much more about its business and what is going on at lower levels. I am sure that Land-Rover Limited will continue to improve as its new young management gains experience in handling what must surely be, in the context of the motor industry, a very odd-ball product – one which, after all, is sold as private transport, fleet transport, military and para-military hardware, industrial units, public utility vehicles, to all classes of people from heads of state downwards, and is one of the few vehicles that can be tolerated when seen operating in the dirtiest of workhorse conditions, or acting as a review vehicle to transport royalty past guards of honour or public displays.

My previous reference to the post-hole borer we devised for the Land-Rover reminds me of the circumstances connected with its first display. This was to be at an Earls Court Smithfield Show. Our exhibition section had submitted details of all the exhibits proposed for the Land-Rover stand to the Society of Motor Manufacturers and Traders, the organizers, as required by the regulations. I was surprised and not a little irritated when I was told that the exhibition secretary had objected to the post-hole borer on a technicality – when attached to a vehicle, the overall length of the combined unit was too long, or something like that. This prompted me to write a sharp reply, stressing the raison d'être of an exhibition to sell products, the aid to Land-Rover sales by the addition of a new implement to increase its versatility, and so forth. I also mentioned that post-hole borers were coming into use in some countries for grave digging, as they saved labour and with vertical burial saved ground. I concluded with the dire stricture that this might be the case when the exhibition secretary's turn came, and that he would surely like to think he had not in any way impeded development of such important conservation! In his reply the exhibition secretary conceded my arguments and gave his assent to the exhibit. He also

174

requested that, should I be officiating when the time came to lower him into his hole, would I make sure that he was facing in the direction of Earls Court!

During my career with Special Projects, I have often been asked if I thought that ideas for special equipment and conversions would ever dry up. I have never been able to foresee this happening and it is still the case today – so much so, that in writing these notes, I have had to leave out a great deal. Although, as I have said earlier, we sometimes seemed to be in danger of becoming a unit getting to know less and less about more and more, one could write again almost as many words as have been written on each of several of the conversions or equipment mentioned. In selecting items for discussion, I found the same problem intruding as when assessing the worth of some of the schemes put forward for approval. That was to resist the temptation to spend more time than sales potential seemed to justify on speculative projects with a high degree of engineering interest, and devote it instead to the sometimes more mundane sellers.

Changes for the eighties

The wind of change – and beneficial change – continues to blow, and for the Special Projects this brings about a rising status and better recognition of its function. Final cleavage from motor car activities has much to do with this new situation. What is this new situation? For conversions, the co-operation and approval of the converter/manufacturer is assuming more importance as it is realised to what extent he can become a strong arm of the overall sales promotion effort. Because, however, consumer legislation is gaining in complexity in so many markets, the obligation has increased of Special Projects to judge carefully the extent of approval tests required. This, of course, must be considered in the context of the number of extra Land-Rovers the conversion is going to sell.

A reorganisation within the Engineering Division has resulted in Special Projects, Military Contracts and Engineering liason with Spanish Land-Rover Manufacture being grouped together as 'Special Operations' under a Chief Engineer.

A procedure has been developed enabling the converter to carry out a large measure of self-certification towards his approval – a procedure that rightly throws a fair proportion of the testing cost onto the conversion firm. The proposed conversion is studied by a small vetting committee of members of the Marketing, Product Planning, and Special Operations departments before being accepted for self-certification. It can be seen that such a representative vetting committee has a very wide scan to bring to bear in assessing conversions. If the committee likes what it sees there follows, among other things, a very close appraisal of the converter's resources, financial standing and integrity. Finally, a programme is drawn up to cover all aspects for gaining Engineering Approval. Thus the handling of conversions by the Engineering

Back row: *basic vehicles – 88-in canvas hood, 88-in hard top, 88-in cab and ¾ hood, 109-in hard top, 110-in FC rear view, 110-in FC front view, 109-in canvas hood, 109-in cab and ¾ hood, 109-in Station Wagon.*
4th row: *elevating platform on 109-in, articulated trailer conversion on 88-in with trailer, belt conveyor on 109-in.*
3rd row: *mobile cinema on 109-in Station Wagon, Shorland armoured car, compressor unit on 110-in FC.*
2nd row: *mechanically driven drum winch, hydraulically driven drum winch and mobile compressor conversion on 109-in, emergency stretcher gear in standard Station Wagon body, ambulance-bodied 109-in, motor caravan conversion on 109-in Station-Wagon, fire appliance conversion on 110-in FC.*
Front row: *pto-driven saw bench at rear, cable storage drum of Plumett winch between seats on 88-in, snow blade on 88-in, crop sprayer 109-in, car recovery crane on 109-on, fire appliance conversion on 109-in, air-conditioner on 88-in Station Wagon.*

Division and Special Projects is now on a firm and recognised footing and is processed by one of two sections within the department, the second section concerning itself with the activities connected with factory-produced specials, optional extras, designing, and liason with all other relevant departments. A good example of this function is how refrigerated air-conditioning has moved from a proprietary, approved extra for the after market, to a factory option available ex-works. I do not think it would be entirely inaccurate to say that the

176

The last word in communications? This is CAP's 'Mobility '84' system which is equipped with a satellite earth station and provides round-the-world communications via voice telephone, VHF radio, facsimile, video text and slow scan video. In addition computer facilities allow data and word processing integrated with the communications equipment. The whole assembly is here mounted on a 110-inch crew cab.

advent of and demand for air-conditioning on Land-Rovers and Range Rovers precipitated, and *made* us solve this problem, as referred to on pages 159-168.

There seems a likelihood at the time of writing that a 6 x 6 chassis may be added to the Land-Rover model sales list, based on the new 110-inch. However there are some fairly expensive engineering hurdles to cross here – and how cost-effective would such a chassis be? One result of the advent of the 110-inch and 90-inch is that all the active approved conversions must now be re-assessed for adaptation and/or respecified for these vehicles, which is in itself quite a workload.

This is a good opportunity to mention that Special Operations now include a recognised function for correctly specifying Land-Rover units, engines, gearboxes, axles etc. for sale to other manufacturers. In the past this tended to be a sideline, supply being on an ad-hoc basis, which was understandable, in a way, as there was rarely any spare manufacturing capacity to cope with any

The Branbridge Mk. IV fire appliance from Pilcher-Greene Ltd.

significant demand that might arise. For a time the Gas Turbine Department became involved for no better reason than that, after the turbine car project had been shelved, they specialised in selling stationary engines.

It would be nice to think that a Special Installations Division (page 155) will be given further serious thought. When Special Projects was formed in 1957 our then Chairman told me that as long as I could convince him that Special Projects could cause the sale of an extra 200 vehicles per year he would feel the cost of the department justified. I went to great pains to do this, by circulating an annual report of our activities. In some years, when the company was desperately short of vehicles against the order book, it nearly had the opposite effect, with suggestions that our activities should be halted as we were diverting vehicles away from the main sales stream! This situation is unlikely to occur today, with more enlightened and integrated sales and marketing organisations, which haven't had to form their opinions only after dealing with apparently similar, but really diverging, problems affecting motor cars. Mind you, today we have computers and here is a temptation to let them produce lots of statistics in quite minute and idiotic detail. A close eye is required to be kept on the pendulum here, but the capability for assessing the value of a Special Installations Division is now much better.

Not long ago, I read Sir Michael Edwardes' book 'Back From the Brink' and what a much-needed and refreshing blast of common sense he caused to blow through BL. Even down at the level of Land-Rover Special Projects the benefits will be felt. I think of a conversation I had many years ago with one of our directors, the subject of which was the staff Christmas bonus, usually two weeks' extra salary. The year in question had been a poor one and profits were down. I suggested that it would be sensible and logical to reduce the bonus. All I got was a chilly nil response! From what Michael Edwardes said, I am confident No More Shall Confusion Reign when a MOD/Carmichael situation arises again (page 90). No More confusion for Sales Management having to grapple with car and Land-Rover problems, which are frequently far from compatible; this odd-ball product requires total commitment. No More of the situation that once occurred concerning the Engineering Department who were working against the clock to prepare two or three prototype vehicles, urgently required for submission to a foreign government who might award us a big contract. For the vehicles to be shipped on time some weekend overtime was required, but the union shop steward wouldn't budge. The situation was so desperate that Peter Wilks, then Technical Director and a persuasive speaker, offered to address the men. He was firmly discouraged by the management negotiator, such a move being considered 'improper' and creating an 'undesirable precedent'. The vehicles were delivered late. No More of the situation that I experienced more than once trying to put together a 'special', similar to the example quoted on page 78, with Rover as the main contractor. The sub-contractors had to give us their prices so that we could quote the customer for the whole package, as requested. A newly-arrived accountant of the Ryder régime flatly refused to do this: it was no business of his or mine, he said! Orders and requests such as this were sometimes quite incomprehensible to some of our transient masters from the car world. And No More post-hole borer situations please!

On a personal note, my feelings are that in work of this nature it is important to maintain the thread of product knowledge of the conversion, or special equipment, all the way through, for obvious reasons. What is not perhaps obvious is that this thread must also include practical experience, because theory and practice so often diverge. Product knowledge must include as much as possible of both. I felt strongly about this when I was actively engaged and I only hope that re-organisation, which so often elevates the importance of a tidy organisation chart above that of the flexibility of people and things, will not submerge this aspect.

Land-Rover can now recognise itself for what it is and it would even be fitting if it considered itself; **The World's Most Versatile Bespoke 4 x 4 Manufacturer.**

A final cautionary word though. In the 1960s the British motorcycle industry thought of itself as the makers of the world's superbikes, content to leave the manufacture of small bikes and scooters to the Japanese. Who makes the superbikes today? In the 4 x 4 world there seem to be a great many small Japanese vehicles about.

In this case, history is unlikely to repeat itself. Having met and talked to several of the new management team and had the opportunity of trying out the latest models – the 110 and 90 as well as the latest versions of the Range Rover – I am convinced Land Rover are now making, and are determined to continue making, the world's **Super 4 Wheel Drive Vehicles.**

Chapter 3
Land-Rover Conscripted

The Second World War shook the requirements for motorized transport to their very foundations. The complete havoc wrought by a handful of specially equipped desert vehicles in the North African Campaigns, under the command of Colonel David Stirling – founder of the SAS – against Rommel's 'Africa Corps', provided final proof of the necessity for Britain to build its own desert vehicle. A vehicle was needed that was capable of doing an even better job than the American machines – Willys Jeeps and Chevrolet trucks – that were being supplied to the British Armed Forces in large numbers from America on a loan/lease basis.

The war in North Africa created a new way of fighting. In terrain ideally suited to the use of armour but where the distances covered were immense, the objectives were to occupy remote oases, strike at the enemy well inside his rear flank and conduct long-range reconnaissance. Tanks and trucks had their vital function, and could travel virtually anywhere, but the fighting vehicles had to be able to embark on long-range reconnaissances covering several thousand miles in the space of a few forays and sometimes in convoys of only two or three vehicles. By making simple modifications to both the Chevrolet and the Jeep – fitting sand-tyres, larger fans and radiators, suitable filters, sand-shovels, jerry can holders, mounts for machine guns, and essential navigation tools such as the compass and sextant – they were equipped to go out and wage desert warfare with totally new efficiency.

The action during the latter stages of the Second World War accentuated Britain's need to develop a 4 x 4 vehicle of her own for military use. Unfortunately, the realization on the part of the British Government that such a vehicle was an economic necessity did not occur until it was too late for the product to be of use during that war, although its end did not mean that such development was unnecessary. Ironically the vehicle that was ultimately commissioned was to be superseded, on various levels, within a relatively short time by the Land-Rover.

181

The 'Pink Panther' was developed to meet the special needs of the SAS.

To achieve the British version of the Jeep, various manufacturers in the motor trade submitted tenders to the Fighting Vehicles Research and Development Establishment (FVRDE) for the supply of components for the new vehicle, which was not intended to be the product of one company. Rover was not asked to tender for any part as the company was considered too small scale and specialist, and Spencer Wilks was not impressed by the order potential, in any case, as the vehicle was destined for service exclusively by the British Army.

The project, entitled FV1800 ('Fighting Vehicle' for military use, but renamed 'Champ' for the civilian market) was inordinately slow in getting off the ground, initially because of the unrealistic proposal that competitors should collaborate over its construction. It was 1945 before the first prototype was built, by Nuffield, who were eventually offered the contract to assemble the vehicle subject to many modifications being incorporated. This caused more delays and it was therefore the start of the 1950s before production was realized, only after Nuffield and Austin had amalgamated and BMC had been formed.

Because of the protracted development of the Champ, by the time it was actually in production Land-Rover had been around for about five years and had already claimed part of the 4 x 4 market in the military sphere. The FVRDE had purchased 50 Land-Rovers in 1949 to assess their capability in the field, and time proved this to be the tip of the iceberg. Although the contract with the manufacturers of the Champ committed the military buyers to a massive bulk order, it was intended to be a one-off only, and despite this commitment the British Armed Forces were to place increasingly large orders for Land-Rovers from that time onwards. Initially the Land-Rover was used in conjunction with the Champ, as they were found to complement each other nicely working side by side. There were a number of ways in which the Land-Rover was the more attractive all-round solution for the forces – not least of which was the lower cost per unit, lower fuel consumption and lower weight – but the Champ had very impressive mobility, much more power, and was altogether better suited as a combat vehicle in the front-line, wherever the action was fiercest. In contrast the Land-Rover was fully occupied behind the lines as a general service vehicle, ideal for the transport of both personnel and freight – for which task the Champ was less appropriate as it was fitted with only four seats, and was protected only by a canvas hood. As the armed forces became increasingly familiar with the relative features of the two vehicles, it became generally accepted that, overall, the Land-Rover's versatility brought it out on top. Of course, it was constantly evolving, too, taking early criticisms

A Land-Rover being used by the 1st Battalion, the Royal Anglian Regiment, in Cyprus in 1973.

into account, so that when production of the Champ, FV1800, finally ceased some five years after it had begun, there was not much that could be done by a Champ that couldn't be done by a Land-Rover. The standard Land-Rover was never to venture into the front-line, though, in the way the Champ had, chiefly because the Army was now making use of armoured personnel carriers, and the Land-Rover has always been what is known as a soft-skin vehicle in the military world. Not unpredictably, therefore, it was only a matter of months after production of the Champ terminated before the Land-Rover was invited to become the official 'forward area' vehicle for the British Army in 1956.

With the ever-increasing demand for mobility in warfare, by the latter half of the 1960s it was becoming vital to have light-weight fighting vehicles on the spot for infantry and parachutists – and the obvious means of transporting them to the field of combat was by helicopter, once this new form of air transport was established. Before the advent of the helicopter, much experimentation had taken place over parachuting fighting vehicles to the battle front, but so many vehicles were wasted that the idea had to be abandoned. Apart from the risk of damage to the chassis on impact with the ground, even when mounted on special shock-absorbing platforms, there was the ever-present worry that the vehicle would land in such a position as to be impossible to drive off easily – a particularly pressing concern in wartime, when speed is often essential. With the invention of the helicopter, however, the situation altered significantly. The Westland Wessex machine was unprecedented for its weight-carrying ability, and the impressive precision with which it could land, or hover at a very low altitude over a given spot, meant that no longer need vehicles be dropped somewhat haphazardly out of the sky, to land within a vague radius of the intended position. Now, given that the vehicle to be transported was light enough (ie not much more than 2,500 lb), it could be suspended on a hook from the body of the helicopter by cable, and gently lowered down to earth.

But if this was going to work for the Land-Rover, it was going to have to lose a lot of weight to qualify! At first this seemed way below any reasonable target, even for the 88-inch Land-Rover, but as time went on Land-Rover engineers perceived that the only answer lay in a much more radical approach: removing not only obvious inessentials, but some of the less obvious, such as the upper body, doors, windscreen assembly and tailgate panels, while keeping the same basic chassis, engine, gearbox and axles as on the 88-inch commercial vehicle. As these body parts were designed to be built on to the machine on the production line, they could not be simply taken away. Instead, the machine itself had to be taken off before that stage and then built up to its own unique body specification, designed for maximum flexibility in detachable parts. By the time this process was complete, the minimum weight was still above the target weight, by 150 lb or so, but this was shown to be adequate if the helicopter reduced its cargo accordingly. The vehicle became known as the ½-ton Land-Rover, indicating the total payload, and is known as such today. It stands out from its fellow Land-Rovers by virtue of the austere appearance given by the

A ½-ton air-portable Land-Rover.

A ½-ton converted to carry the 106mm anti-tank gun.

peculiar styling that was necessary for the purpose of air-portability: flat panelled apart from a simple curve in the bonnet.

Nowadays the ½-ton is used to perform an impressive range of functions, including load and personnel carriers for the military, the police and civil defence; command vehicles for artillery, infantry, and other armed services; recovery vehicles; emergency two-stretcher carriers; towing light support weapons; specialist trailer towing and operation; signals communications, radio transmission and receiving centres, and of course special reconnaissance work. Its adaptability, and the fact that specific individual requirements can be accommodated, has won orders for the ½-ton from NATO countries and others, and it is currently available with 12-volt and 24-volt electrical systems – the latter with up to 90 amp alternators. All 24-volt vehicles are fully suppressed to meet military operational standards. The braking system is of the dual-line type with a warning light, activated by a pressure differential sensor, and a brake servo is fitted as standard. Thus, the ½-ton has indeed moved with the times, even though its appearance is still as 'naked' as ever. It can now be fitted with a full-length soft hood constructed of rot-proof, flame-retardant canvas, supported by galvanized hood sticks, and it is manufactured with both diesel and petrol engine. (In the early days of the ½-ton, there was little demand for the diesel because of the additional weight entailed, and because those first vehicles were unlikely to cover the miles necessary to counter-balance the extra cost of the unit.)

A later development of the ½-ton for military purposes was the Gunship Land-Rover. This was specially designed to meet a demand for fitment of the 106 mm light gun, and is known as the ½-ton Land-Rover 106 mm Anti-tank Gun. With all the high-mobility characteristics of the conventional Land-Rover, the added feature of air-portability renders it capable of operating in all conditions – sand, swamp and mountain – and makes it very versatile tactically. It differs from the original ½-ton in that its standard specification includes storage for both 160mm and sighting rifle ammunition, seats for the gun crew, blast shield for front bonnet and wings, barrel clamp mounted to the dashboard, stowage for pick and shovel, spare wheel positioned at right-hand side incorporating running board, stowage for cleaning rods, provision of loading ramp for gun, split windscreen, and provision for two jerry cans. It has a cruising range of 600 km and a maximum road speed of 90 kph, allowing it to assume a strategic position both quickly and inconspicuously.

A very significant vehicle on the military scene was the 101 inch 1-tonne Forward Control Land-Rover, which was announced at the 1972 Commercial Motor Show. It was specifically designed for military use, with a payload capacity for towing a 1½-ton powered-axle trailer. In fact, one of the prime factors behind its development was the British Army's requirement for a vehicle capable of towing loads of up to 4,000 lb, and in particular the Light Gun (as opposed to having it mounted, as on the ½-ton unit described above), which was too heavy to be towed by any existing Land-Rover. The priority was power, and durability.

186

The 101-inch 1-tonne Land-Rover was developed to meet a British Army requirement for a 1-ton payload 4 x 4 vehicle.

Luckily the design team didn't have far to look for the right engine – the V8 was already being used in Rover's newest product, the Range Rover. This engine/gearbox/transfer box assembly, combined with the most sturdy Salisbury axles, was married to a new design of chassis frame to provide the basis of the revolutionary new forward-control military Land-Rover – though with its snub-nosed, bonnetless front, 7 foot height and 6 foot width, it was not readily identifiable as part of the Land-Rover stable! The V8 engine – a military version of the light-weight Rover 3.5 litre unit – was positioned more or less between the seats in the cab, rendering it uncomfortably noisy and hot most of the time. With half-elliptic spring suspension and the 1-ton 109 inch brakes, this new military Land-Rover was designed to have as many detachable parts as possible – like the ½-ton Land-Rover. This simultaneously increased its versatility while reducing its weight for the purposes of air-portability by the later generation of helicopters, now capable of carrying loads of up to 3,500 lb – 1,000 lb up on the ½-ton Land-Rover requirement some five years earlier.

In 1975, Squadron-Leader Tom Sheppard, one of Britain's most able explorers at the present time, led a Joint Services' Expedition across Africa from west to east – the Atlantic to the Red Sea, using four new 1-tonne 101 inch Land-Rovers, all featuring constant 4-wheel drive with differential lock. Three of the vehicles were fitted with the optional trailer drive and all were equipped with 9.00 x 16 Michelin XS tyres. The lead vehicle in the convoy was the very first production model off the line, and the subsequent report on the expedition amply illustrated the versatility and worth of these unique machines. Two of the vehicles were towing prototype 1-ton powered axle trailers, built in 1967 and 1971 respectively, and refurbished for the purposes of the expedition by the manufacturers, Rubery Owen. The Special Projects chapter of this book

The Joint Services' Expedition with four 101-inch 1-tonne Land-Rovers pausing to recce the best route over some dunes in the Mauritanian 'Empty Quarter'.

describes the development of a special powered-axle trailer for use with the Land-Rover. This was started by the Special Projects Department in 1959 using, for test purposes, the simple method of a sawn-off back half of a 109-inch Land-Rover incorporating a newly designed drive-line, coupling, brake gear, etc. The project was taken on by Scottorns who were endeavouring to produce a powered-axle military trailer for the New Zealand Army at the time, and since then the evolution of the trailer has been a joint effort. The Ministry of Defence version, made by Rubery Owen and the kind used on the Joint Services' Expedition, achieved excellent traction with its 6 x 6 capability in different extremes of terrain, but ultimately has been proved too costly and complicated to be a commercially viable product. These trailers were also fitted with the 9.00 x 16 Michelin XS tyres. The following table gives an idea of the weights both Land-Rovers and trailers had to carry at certain points of the expedition:

	Front Axle	Rear Axle	Vehicle Total	Trailer	Gross inc Trailer
Solo Vehicles:	3,826 lb	3,640 lb	7,466 lb	–	–
	3,868 lb	4,046 lb	7,914 lb	–	–
Trailer Vehicles:	3,472 lb	3,766 lb	7,238 lb	4,032 lb	11,200 lb
	3,572 lb	3,398 lb	7,070 lb	4,088 lb	11,193 lb

These were the maximum weights carried and were by no means constant, the total weight of the convoy being reduced by about 750 lb per day. The Expedition Report details the most important modifications to the vehicles, for the specific requirements of the project, as follows:

a) installation of air compressors and reservoirs on two vehicles for tyre inflation.

b) repositioning of the carburettor air intake from the wheel arch to the battery box to minimize the induction of dust.

c) removal of tilts, hoodrails, windscreens and windows to save weight and allow the fitting of the Coles Mk II sun compass on the dash between driver and passenger.

d) removal of the spare wheel from behind the driver's seat to improve storage space and rearward visibility. (Spare wheels were carried lashed on drums or in the trailers.)

e) fitting of venting pipes on all four corners of the fuel tank to preclude the possibility of air locks when refuelling.

f) installation of electric car clock to assist DR sun compass navigation.

g) fitting of kph speedometers with trip odometers for accurate navigation and fuel consumption calculation.

h) door mirrors were replaced by larger (10 x 6) convex type for adequate rear view.

j) fitting of a 12v DC/230v AC transistorized inverter to one vehicle to supply sine-wave 50 cps AC current for various pieces of film and sound equipment. Ni-Cad battery charging.

Aerial shot of the four 101-inch 1-tonne Land-Rovers, two with trailers, in the Sahara on the Joint Services' Expedition.

VEHICLE/TRAILER LOAD PLAN

2 x SHOVELS

SUN COMPASS

DELICATE KIT,
RADIO, CAMERAS ETC
PERSONAL KIT,
SCIENTIFIC GEAR

FUEL
2 x 4 gall
drums

SAND LADDERS
EACH SIDE

WATER
1 x 45 gall drum
8 x 4½ gall cans

STORAGE BOX
Spares, film etc
cooking gear

RATION BOXES

LUBE OIL

FUEL
4 x 45 gall
drums

FUEL
10 x 4½ gall
cans

SPARE TYRES

These modifications were carried out by Rover at Solihull and by the RAF at Uxbridge. The Report goes on to say:

'During the expedition the vehicles seemed to stabilize after an early rash of faults, apparently inevitable in new vehicles, and were very reliable considering the nature of the terrain crossed and loads carried . . . The overall reliability and performance of the four vehicles improved steadily throughout the expedition . . . The main considerations throughout the expedition were logistics and weight; vehicle selection was influenced primarily by these considerations – the best combination of payload and agility was required, and with so much payload devoted to fuel and water, strict weight limitations had to be placed on other equipment. Preliminary calculations showed that four 1-tonne Land-Rovers, two with 1-ton powered-axle trailers, was the minimum – and maximum – complement of the convoy.'

This expedition covered a total of 12,054 km (7,494 miles) and took 100 days. It was the first ever major user-trial of a production 1-tonne Land-Rover and was considered entirely successful. However, while the whole team was unanimous in its admiration for the overall performance of the vehicle, they did have the following criticisms to offer, as listed in the Report:

a) leg-room cramped for passenger and tall drivers.
b) accessibility of rear spark plugs difficult and all plugs required a very thin plug spanner to remove.
c) hot starting occasionally difficult.
d) shovel carrying brackets very flimsy, affording no firm support to blade or handle.
e) getting in and out of the vehicle requires practice.
f) the engine cover catches are small and fiddly and the rubber surround prone to distortion and splitting unless great care is taken when replacing the engine cover. Harness fixings tend to interfere with replacement also.
g) reverse gear frequently difficult to engage without 'crunching' the gears.
h) contact breaker points' life seemed very short and after only 3,000 miles all showed bad burning and pitting.
j) the brake light operating switch jams readily through dust and grit ingress and is very difficult to set up satisfactorily.
k) the diff lock warning light switches were all unreliable, refused to work at all, or flashed on and off. As it is a sealed unit, replacement is the only solution but no guarantee of better performance.
l) steering, though satisfactory cross country, was rather vague and heavy on tarmac roads.

m) brakes became somewhat ineffective on one or two vehicles and demanded very high pedal pressures. Oil seal failures caused lining contamination and subsequent severe pulling to the left on one vehicle. It is relevant to note that the brakes were little used during the expedition due to terrain and the need for extreme fuel economy in the purely desert areas; linings may therefore not have received a normal bedding-in en route.

n) rollover bars were obtrusive to passenger and driver due to the danger of bumping their heads on it when in rough going. Rubber padding was used on all vehicles and was found necessary. (The mounting of the rollover bar was also criticized.)

o) oil coolers were very effective overseas but over-cooled the oil in the UK. Aluminium foil was used to cover them in the UK. In service on normal units, however, excessive oil cooling will shorten engine life. An oil thermostat may well be the solution.

p) though doubtless due to the constraints of the specification, the ergonomics of the driver's compartment were poor, namely: the windscreen washer bottle (removed on expedition vehicles) invites foot damage: the door strikers are exposed and leave oily marks on passengers: the door handles (internal) can catch in the passenger or driver's trouser pocket and allow the door to open: elbow room is restricted and the steering wheel too small: there is no parcel shelf or oddments stowage: the rifle clips (removed) are lethal: the spare wheel when normally stowed severely restricts rearward vision: the 'flying buttress' rear compartment heater duct, the outrigged hydraulic reservoirs and general internal appearance is crude and untidy: the radiator cap is very awkward to remove and is likely to be incorrectly replaced by careless or inexperienced drivers: oil dipstick access door is too small: the normal rear view mirrors are flat and too small (10 x 6 convex proved ideal): heater output was negligible without booster fan and there were no fresh air ducts. The high/low ratio and trailer-drive levers are easily confused and led to some mistakes en route; they should be transposed (ie trailer-drive, the less frequently used, should be farthest away from the driver) and each knob be a distinctly different shape from the other.

The Report then continues with its conclusions regarding the 1-tonne Land-Rover:

'The many small points of criticism above on detail design should not be allowed to convey the impression that the overall verdict on the vehicle is poor. It was felt in fact that the 101-inch Land-Rover was possibly the only vehicle in its class in the world that could have performed so well and as easily over the wide variety of terrain encountered. Possibly the most

A Boeing CH47 Chinook of the U.S. Army makes light work of lifting a 109" Land-Rover. (Land-Rover Ltd)

A Centaur V8-powered half-track on trial in the Middle East. (Land-Rover Ltd)

One of our testing expeditions in the Sahara Desert.

An encounter between "Ships of the Desert"!

A silhouette now familiar in the Third World.

The relaxed elegance of the Range Rover still takes a lot of beating.

A 110 during The Camel Rally in Brazil sponsored by the 'Camel' cigarette company. (Land-Rover Ltd)

outstanding attribute was the flexibility and tractability of the engine and it was possible to pinpoint, as the expedition progressed, many occasions when the comparative inflexibility of, for example, the 4-cylinder Land-Rover engine, would have resulted in a bogging. Other notable factors contributing to the very effective performance of the vehicle, and general conclusions are:

a) excellent power-weight ratio. This is combined with satisfactory choice of gear ratios and has been achieved without the penalty of high fuel consumption.

b) relatively short wheel-base and 9.00 x 16 tyres achieves excellent underbelly obstacle clearance.

c) weight distribution in laden condition is close to 50/50 front/rear and makes negotiation of marginally soft going notably better than in any previous Land-Rover.

d) more compliant suspension and larger wheel movement than in other Land-Rovers makes articulation and traction in rough and marginal terrain exceptionally good.

e) forward and downward visibility could hardly be improved and was a definite and tangible aid to safe and quick cross-country performance, frequently eliminating the need for on-foot recce of severe obstacles.

f) the large footprint, radial construction, braced tread and unique tread-pattern of the Michelin XS 9.00 x 16 contributed very considerably to the overall high level of agility and flotation in desert conditions, both sand and rock.

g) of the modifications fitted to expedition vehicles, the repositioned air intake to reduce dust induction and the larger door mirrors are considered worth embodying on production machines.

h) without knowledge of or reference to the specifications there is considerable room for improvement in the ergonomics of the vehicle that would make it easier and safer to operate.

j) despite taking some time to settle down, overall serviceability was very good.'

After all these comments and findings in favour of the 1-tonne Land-Rover, the great pity is that the vehicle is no longer in production. As we pointed out in the Special Projects Chapter, while the vehicle was excellent for military use, it was so orientated in respect of size and overall weight that no civilian outlet was ever established for it. As a vehicle for the military the 1-tonne was sold overseas as well as to the British Armed Forces: in Cairo, Egypt, in 1980, at the Annual Military Parade the Anti-Tank Missile Swing Fire was, for the second time, seen fitted to the 101-inch. Thus, the demand still exists in these circles, and it is not unreasonable to suppose that a non-military application could also have been found for it. After all, companies such as Stonefield and Daimler have

The Joint Services' Expedition reaching the Red Sea.

Equally at home in desert or water, this is a 101-inch 1-tonne Land-Rover proving its wading ability at the Ministry Wading Establishment at Instow in Devon.

developed similar vehicles with a successful outcome, but probably costing a lot more than a civilian 1-tonne Land-Rover would cost. During a recent discussion with Tom Barton, who officially retired from Land-Rover Limited two years ago but who continues to work as a consultant on a part-time basis, still promoting Land-Rovers all over the world, he confirmed that Land-Rover's best policy was:

> 'to keep the top end of the market, weight-wise and capacity-wise, where we can beat the others. We have looked at the small vehicle market, Daihatsu, Subaru, Mini-Moke, etc, and talked to our confederates, and we have all decided that there is no way we could compete with the prices of the Japanese and other countries. We have been forced to go up, build stronger and more durable vehicles with greater load-carrying capacity and this is the field in which we excel.'

The more's the pity that the life-span of the 101-inch was so short in terms of production. After its announcement in 1972, even though the sole concept behind it had been its military function, it found an unaccountable lack of popularity in overseas forces and failed to attract large orders. At home it was steadily fed into the Army's military machinery during the period between 1975 and 1978, when production was halted, probably permanently. It is fervently hoped by many, however, that some day it will be revived. (A few weeks ago, when the Rover car plant at Solihull had to be shut down, the ears of the hopeful pricked up: could this be the second chance for the 101-inch to get off the ground?) If that day comes, and if a civilian market is to be found for it, a lot more attention will have to be paid to driver and passenger comfort – a point that clearly emerges from the critical comments of the trial expedition. It would seem that when the vehicle was developed in the early 1970s, this aspect of its design was a low priority! One thing is sure about this strange extinct beast: we shall not be alone in watching with interest for its hoped-for reappearance on the scene.

In 1979 most people in Britain would not have been able to avoid noticing the fact that there was a full-scale military defence exercise going on. Called Crusader-80, this was probably the most important exercise held by NATO, and in particular the British Forces, to date. It was certainly by far the largest exercise yet held in Europe, and anyone who saw the large movement of troops heading towards the coastal ports in the south of England, at the end of August and beginning of September 1979, could not have failed to be astonished at the range of military vehicles employed in the operation, including of course a whole array of Land-Rovers in one form or another. One of these Land-Rovers, which could be described as the big sister of the ½-ton machine discussed earlier, is the ¾-ton, based on the standard commercial 109-inch vehicle. This ¾-ton development is available in two guises, tactical and non-tactical, and of the tactical vehicles there are a number of interesting variations, which give us a clue as to why Land-Rovers are now so numerous in the military sphere.

There is, for example, the Ambulance 2/4 Stretcher, specifically designed to provide casualty evacuation in forward areas, with accommodation for up to four stretcher-cases as well as a medical attendant (the body on this vehicle is fitted by Marshalls of Cambridge). An armoured patrol car and an armoured personnel carrier based on the ¾-ton Land-Rover heavy-duty chassis has been developed by Short Bros of Belfast. Especially useful as a cost-effective solution to urban or rural terrorist activity, it has become an all too familiar sight on our television screens, on duty in Northern Ireland. Another conversion, by Shorland, offers protection for up to eight men against NATO 7.62 mm rifle or machine gun fire, and also has special features to protect them against nail, pipe or petrol bombs. As a support vehicle, fitted with the 24 volt electrical system, the ¾-ton Land-Rover is capable of being used with the British Aerospace 'Rapier' Blindfire low-level surface-to-air missile system, as a tow vehicle or as a mobile launcher for the Blindfire radar tracker and 'Rapier', while also carrying four 'Rapier' missiles, the 'Rapier' optical tracker, and other ancillary weapon system equipment. The vehicle can also be used for transporting and launching the British Aerospace 'Swingfire' wire-guided anti-tank missile system; the pallet-mounted 'Beeswing' launcher is installed in the rear of the vehicle and fired using a remote controller. The ¾-ton Land-Rover is also capable of being used as a command post for the Marconi Field Artillery Computer Equipment system (FACE). Finally, Land-Rover has worked very closely with Racal-Tacticom (of the Racal Electronics Group) to produce the most comprehensive range of communications systems available anywhere in the world today. Thus, all in all, the tactical usefulness of this Land-Rover doesn't leave much to be desired. It has certainly come a long way since the early days of competing against the Austin Champ, and has thoroughly earned its 'Jack of All Trades' role within the forces at home and overseas.

Enter the V8 Land-Rover ... We have mentioned the V8 engine in the context of the Range Rover and the 101-inch 1-tonne forward control Land-Rover, but it was not until 1979 that it eventually became available in the standard 109-inch wheelbase Land-Rover. In military terms, it can be adapted to many of the conversions and variations already mentioned, but one notable conversion specially developed to utilize the greater power of the V8 is the Centaur Multi-Role Military Half-Tracked range of vehicles. The underlying concept of the Centaur range is to combine the easy operation and road performance of a well-tried wheeled vehicle with the excellent traction, off-road capability and high load-carrying capacity of a tracked vehicle. This 'compromise' has been so successfully worked out as to deserve some attention. The resultant high road speed combined with accurate steering allow the half-tracked Centaur variants to be deployed with standard road vehicles, while their cross-country ability enables them to be used with equal facility in company with fully tracked fighting vehicles. The V8 petrol engine drives both the front wheels and the track through a manually operated gearbox. The vehicle has eight forward speeds and two reverse speeds, which are provided by a high and low ratio transfer facility in

196

Standard military ambulance body on the 109-inch Land-Rover built by Marshalls of Cambridge.

The Centaur multi-role vehicle undergoing successful trials.

197

the four-speed gearbox. Simultaneous track and front wheel drive is arranged through a differential unit built into the gearbox which transmits equal power to the track and the wheels. This differential can be locked when required. The half-tracked concept has been battle-proved in many parts of the world and, owing to its extreme mobility on almost any terrain, its road speed and its ability to transport almost any combination of armour, weapon systems, bodies, equipment fits, cargo and personnel up to a total of 3 tonnes, it is now recognized as the most adaptable form of fighting and logistic vehicle. It is the result of intensive engineering development by Laird (Anglesey) Limited, combining the combat-proven Land-Rover and the Ministry of Defence-designed Scorpion light tank track. The resultant half-tracked vehicle offers unique advantages in both performance and cost-effectiveness. In addition, maintenance and spares support can be based on existing arrangements, and both maintenance and driver training requirements are minimal, servicing for the vehicle being no more than that which is usually associated with a standard Land-Rover. All routine maintenance points are easily accessible and major items such as the engine and gearbox can be readily removed and replaced in the event of major overhaul. The driving controls, too, are identical to those on a standard Land-Rover, so there is virtually no retraining requirement for drivers.

The Centaur is currently in service with government troops in Oman. It is an ideal vehicle for desert work but the competition is strengthening all the time:

The Centaur combines the proven Land-Rover and the Ministry of Defence Scorpion Light Tank Track.

Hotspur have developed a 139-inch 6-wheel version of the Sandringham 6 as a sequel to their 125-inch model, using the V8 Land-Rover as a conversion base for its stable ride characteristics and high power. The 139-inch has been specifically designed for military (and commercial) applications where extra body capacity is necessary. The French designed the ACMAT as a 4 x 4 to meet the requirements of the French Foreign Legion, and subsequently produced a 6-wheel-drive version which is now sold in large numbers. Britain and France, probably because of their imperial past, are supreme in the design of desert vehicles, and another new British military machine is the Tuareg – aptly named after the resilient tribespeople of the Sahara Desert, renowned in their heyday for their warrior instincts. Manufactured by Glover, Webb & Liversage, it has a simple body with the excellent Mercedes-Benz 6-cylinder 8-litre gasoline engine, and with its three armoured fuel tanks (giving it a range of 1,200 - 1,500 miles) and pressurized water-cooling system, it is a truly formidable piece of machinery. The price is almost equally formidable, however – a factor that can never be overlooked now that armed forces everywhere are controlled more than ever before by the economy of their governments.

Standard Land-Rovers have been traversing the desert in times of war and peace for many years now without too many modifications. The more recent arrival on the scene of the V8 Land-Rover has provided a unit which could almost have been tailor-made for this purpose, requiring very little modification to meet the military needs of the Third World in particular, in terms of both cost

The Centaur multi-role vehicle (metal body version) during trials, fitted with Plessey artillery sound ranging equipment.

The Hotspur 139-inch Sandringham 6.

and performance. It has the advantage over a 4-cylinder Land-Rover in being far faster both on tarmac roads and in off-road conditions, as well as providing greater mobility, less fatigue, greater ordnance carrying capacity, lower fuel consumption and improved flexibility on all terrains, all of which makes it highly suitable for operating behind enemy lines. The best form of defence in a desert war being attack, this vehicle at long last offers the capability of mobile defence in very compact units.

The V8 could also be used with NATO forces in Europe. We are constantly being told that, should war ever break out in Europe, the first few days will be critical, due to the massive superiority, in terms of quantity, of Russian units over those of the West. While reinforcements and materials are being rushed to Europe, the V8 could play a vital role alongside other anti-tank and specialized vehicles, its superb mobility enabling units such as the SAS to move rapidly from one defensive position to another.

All this gives rise to further speculation about the future use of the factory facilities recently vacated by the Rover car – whether, for instance, Land-Rover could produce a military version of the V8 at Solihull. With the Royal Air Force about to take delivery of the huge new heavy helicopter, the Chinook, the V8 could possibly even be adapted for air-portability – a very remote prospect in the 1960s, when the 88-inch Land-Rover was being redesigned to meet the 2,500 lb

A Land-Rover fitted with a Helio machine-gun hatch.

requirement of the Wessex lifting capability. Again, the passage of time has presented Land-Rover with a new, far more sophisticated military field to explore, and, cash permitting, we feel sure they will.

Chapter 4
The Range Rover Story

The advent of the Range Rover stems more from the vehement and consistent resistance to 'tarting up' the Land-Rover on the part of its management than from any other single factor. Time and time again, proposals have been submitted for modifying the Land-Rover design, to make it more stylish, more comfortable, and more luxurious, to cushion the ride and widen its appeal. However, with the wisdom of long experience, the management have always dug their toes in and maintained that the function of the Land-Rover is well-defined and clear cut: it is a utility vehicle, and no more than that. Too much styling and softening could only detract from what has made it so universally useful, and successful. It has often been aptly described as 'the workhorse of the world' – and no one vehicle can be all things to all men. If the Land-Rover team were to bend their ideas towards a more prestigious vehicle it could never be called a Land-Rover, and could certainly not resemble a Land-Rover in appearance. The resemblance would be concentrated entirely on performance, toughness and versatility – the invisible assets, but the crucial ones.

Within the organization there were many who were single-mindedly loyal to Land-Rover, and so committed to its utilitarian, functional features that they were unable to view a revolutionary new design of 4 x 4 vehicle – aimed at a different sector of the market altogether – with anything but pessimism and scepticism. One of the main arguments was that the combination of power and speed in a 4-wheel-drive cross-country vehicle was courting disaster: it could only be a danger off the road as it would be driven too fast, and would most likely fall to pieces anyway ...

Fortunately, there were those enthusiasts who predicted the emerging trend for multi-role 4 x 4s, and doggedly worked away at the design of a vehicle that would be quite unlike anything yet produced. Serious research into the design of a car-type Land-Rover vehicle had already taken place in the 1950s when Maurice Wilks had encouraged Gordon Bashford and his team to explore the

203

The first Road Rover prototype.

potential of producing such a machine – but the concept was not sufficiently far-reaching. At the time, funds were limited and the only chassis available on which to base the new vehicle's design was that of the Rover saloon car, known as the P4 chassis, apart from that of the Land-Rover itself. Economy required that this be used. The expense of an entirely new body would have to be met, and this was as far as funds would stretch: the rest had to be an inspired jigsaw puzzle of existing components. Although the first complete prototype was with 4-wheel drive, the demand at the time seemed to indicate that conventional 2-wheel drive would be preferred. Thus the vehicle that evolved, which was known as the Road Rover, did not have 4-wheel drive, which of course immediately curtailed any cross-country ability. Based on the P4 chassis, it was fitted with a 2-litre Land-Rover engine, but its styling was far from satisfactory or aesthetic, quickly earning it the nickname of 'The Greenhouse', for its angularity and flat-sided clumsiness. The difficult balance between an all-purpose off-road vehicle, and one that handled well on the highway had not been struck, and – to cut a long story short – it died a natural death in 1958 before it had been launched. Its relevance here is that it illustrated that the much later Range Rover idea was by no means totally innovative, even if the end product turned out to be just that.

The time lapse between the two projects was to provide a clearer definition of the requirement for such an entity, and of course vehicle body styling in the meantime had progressed by leaps and bounds. Peter Wilks, who was the nephew of Spencer and Maurice Wilks, took charge of engineering during the early 1960s, and had long believed that the time for a 'luxury Land-Rover' would, in due course, come. A design for a '100-inch Station Wagon', with the 6-cylinder 3-litre engine, had been undergoing development about this time – but the fillip that the project needed came with the discovery, quite by chance, of the

V8 3½-litre engine, which was to elevate this new vehicle into a category of its own. As always, the success of the new scheme depended on the climate being right at the time – and it so happened that discussion on the ideal engine for the 100-inch Station Wagon was in the air when the Managing Director, William Martin-Hurst, had to go off to the United States for a business trip to General Motors in 1963. One of General Motors' engines had recently been abandoned as too expensive to produce, though it lacked nothing in respect of performance, dependability and engineering, having been thoroughly proven. It was the V8 3½-litre and when Martin-Hurst came across it during his visit he was at once struck by its supreme suitability for the 100-inch Station Wagon project, being lighter (it was constructed of aluminium alloy), more compact and more powerful than any Rover engine to date. It produced tremendous torque at low speeds which increased reliability and engine life while ensuring excellent pulling power throughout its entire rev range. After the usual formalities, Martin-Hurst secured the rights to take over manufacture of the unit from General Motors in 1965, and it was this that provided the heart of the vehicle that was to become the Range Rover. It has since become the most important single power unit used by Rover.

Because no similar vehicle existed, the designers had to be sure of the basic aims of their product, having no yardstick to help them along their way. What the brief boiled down to was that the vehicle must be faster, larger, more

A 1972 Range Rover. Its off-the-road capabilities were soon appreciated.

An expedition-equipped Range Rover with roof-mounted air-conditioning.

'civilized' than a regular Land-Rover, but quite as practical, and recognizably a Rover product. In designing the new transmission system, 4-wheel drive was the jumping-off point. The vehicle had to have the versatility that this would engender (and therefore the high ground clearance, wheel mobility and ruggedness it entailed), but it was only later on that permanent 4-wheel drive was decided upon, making it completely different to the Land-Rover, rather than merely a smartened-up version of it. A transfer box was located behind the new main gearbox, giving high and low ratios on all main gearbox speeds. Front and rear drive was permanently engaged via a third differential, lockable by a vacuum control switch. The third differential was incorporated on to a system that was in other respects similar to that of the Land-Rover, to obviate transmission 'wind-up' between front and rear. This increase in traction gave it an even greater cross-country ability – which in itself demanded vastly improved suspension design. Long-travel vertical coil spring suspension was devised, with axle location by radius front and rear, with Panhard rod (front), and support rods and central wishbone assembly (rear), controlled by long-stroke hydraulic telescopic dampers. The rear suspension incorporated a self-energizing ride-levelling unit.

The changeover from the 6-cylinder 3-litre to the V8 3½-litre engine was warmly welcomed by Peter Wilks, Spen King and Gordon Bashford who were the mainstays of the enterprise. They considerably developed and modified it, and most of the engineering details and design of the vehicle had been adjusted to accommodate it by 1966. By this time the project was being called after the first Road Rover, and no longer the 100-inch Station Wagon (though the 100-inch chassis was about the only original dimension to remain constant

A Range Rover chassis.

throughout the execution of the design). The last big hurdle was still to be overcome, however – that of styling. While the precise market for the machine was still rather vague, it was generally accepted that it had to look good. The engineers who had laboured so long over it had their own notions of body style. Spen King and Gordon Bashford worked out the lay-out and built a mock-up themselves rather than waiting until the Styling Department could undertake it. The decision to make it a 2-door vehicle was made early on in the design stage, because of doubts about the strength of the body structure on a 4-door model, especially for cross-country work. A 2-door vehicle was also a lot cheaper to produce, which would be reflected in the final cost price – even though the 2-door design finally necessitated the inclusion of expensively designed and manufactured seat belts. The usual seat belts, anchored to the BC posts, proved awkward and hazardous when the front seats were tilted forward for access to and from the rear seats, so it was decided that they be incorporated in the back of the front seats. Although successful, this was a costly development, and tended to reduce the 2-door cost saving. However, Spen King and Gordon Bashford achieved a body style in their own prototype which even then was recognizable as the Range Rover of today.

In 1967 Rover was to merge with Leyland (the latter becoming the dominant partner) and it was anyone's guess how the new management would view the production of a vehicle like the one Rover was now offering, the actual outlet for which was still fairly indeterminate. Luckily, they seized upon it enthusiastically and couldn't wait to get it out. They may have thought it would represent the auspicious start they all hoped for. Whatever its shortcomings, it would be a product of the Land-Rover stable which could only stand the company in good stead – even though it shared practically no common component with the Land-Rover vehicle. The prototype already in existence, therefore, was immediately passed to the Styling Department, to be professionally assessed and modified under the eye of David Bache. He must take the credit for the overall styling detail that has made the Range Rover, bulky as it is, into such an elegant

207

machine. Its graceful proportions and pleasing lines conceal its ruggedness and its power, as well as the fact that, unlike so many commodities these days, it is designed and built to last, and to withstand punishment. It was subsequently exhibited at the Louvre in Paris as an outstanding example of modern sculpture – an unusual accolade for a motor car!

By now, the vehicle had been retitled the Range Rover. Production was aimed to begin before the close of the 1960s – but there was an enormous amount of detail to be finished off on the design and styling side, alternatives to be considered and tested, as well as the physical problem of where it was going to be built. Space had to be made available somehow, since although many parts of the vehicle had been contracted out to be manufactured by other firms (springs, dampers, self-levelling strut, some of the axle components, even the frame itself, and some of the alloy body shell panels), factory space was required for building the transmissions: of the major components, only the engine was already established. Right alongside the existing Land-Rover tracks, Range Rover assembly commenced, and it was eventually six months after the start of the 1970s before the new machine was launched on to the home market. Range Rovers began to appear in public at last in June 1970, but even then it had been something of a rush job in the end, to the chagrin of the men behind the scenes who were indoctrinated with very high Rover standards, and would have liked another year in which to iron out the final wrinkles.

Not surprisingly, production was initially very low key. Teething troubles in assembly were inevitable at the beginning and it was months before a realistic number could be seen to emerge from the factory gates at Solihull. In the first 10 weeks or so, the average was less than 10 vehicles a week, building up gradually to more like a 100 a week by the beginning of 1972 compared with 250 a week by 1975. The first Range Rovers cost about £2,000, but not for long. The rate of price escalation has been sharp, as can be appreciated by the fact that a 1984 Range Rover (2-door) fetches in the region of £16,000 on the home market. But back in 1970, a £2,000 price tag was still placing the vehicle amongst the élite, which in itself probably contributed to its instant popularity: it was not only essentially practical, but it had snob value. Within weeks of its release, the public was clamouring for Range Rovers, and all previous speculation on the strongest potential outlets had been proved to be wildly below the mark. Far from appealing only to land-owners, horse-racers and gentleman farmers, it found favour with the many and diverse Land-Rover fans who needed additional performance, comfort and space for certain purposes. The Police Force was a case in point: they could hardly clock a sports car exceeding the motorway speed limit with a Land-Rover, but the Range Rover's maximum speed was only fractionally below 100 mph – quite remarkable in a 4-wheel drive vehicle. The sheer height of the vehicle when compared to any conventional saloon car also proved to be an attraction. Suddenly people could get above the rest of the traffic in towns, not to mention their improved vantage point when driving cross-country, allowing them to observe obstacles more easily and see beyond the usual obstructions of walls and hedges, while still feeling perfectly safe: for, despite its increased elevation, the vehicle remained stable because of the low centre of gravity ensured by the solid steel chassis and low mounting of axles, gearbox and engine. Ground clearance was, nevertheless, still exceptionally high (12.6ins – except below the axles where it was 7.5ins), allowing the vehicle to negotiate muddy, snowy, rocky, sandy, marshy or any kind of uneven ground with ease, and to ford rivers – for which reason all electrical components were specifically positioned at the top of the engine to avoid swamping of the ignition system.

Unlike the Land-Rover, whose post-war development precluded the use of much steel in its construction, the Range Rover's inner skin was built up from pressed steel sub-assemblies bolted together, clad in a body of light aluminium alloy similar to that used on the Land-Rover. The steel structure was much stronger than pure aluminium and in effect provided a safety cage for the occupants. One of the initial faults in the Range Rover was insufficient anti-corrosion treatment of the steel, which inevitably resulted in evidence of rusting before very long. This had to be rectified in all subsequent models by comprehensive protection against corrosion both of the steel body panels, and of the welded, deep box section chassis. Nowadays, the chassis undergoes two galvanizing dips and an electrophoretic paint dip. The steel body components

This 2-door Range Rover was specially converted by Spencer Abbot for Sir Alfred McAlpine.

An unusual crew-cab cum pick-up based on a standard Range Rover.

are also electroprimed and dipped twice in acrylic paint. All downward facing surfaces are undersealed, and steel and aluminium surfaces are separated by sealant. One other early amendment was the elimination of the limited-slip feature from the centre differential: with permanent 4-wheel drive, the vehicle's traction proved to be adequate for most off-road conditions without this additional feature, which was dropped only months after production got under way.

One of the Range Rover's most impressive built-in features has always been its towing ability. With a specially strengthened rear cross member on the chassis, it is ideally suited to pulling trailors, caravans, horse boxes or boats, which again broadened its appeal from the outset. The following gives an idea of its capability in this area:

	Trailer Weight	*(+ Vehicle)*
Off-road trailer:	1,000 kg	(3,504 kg)
On-road 2-wheel trailer:	2,000 kg	(4,504 kg)
On-road 4-wheel trailer with power brakes:	4,000 kg	(6,504 kg)
For emergency purposes:	6,000 kg	(8,504 kg)

In the early stages – apart from a hiccough at the disclosure that fuel consumption was as high as 15 mpg – the demand for the Range Rover grew steadily, far in excess of supply, and once it became available overseas orders began flooding in from all corners of the earth. The production volume couldn't hope to match the order books, and the frustrations of long delays in delivery eventually gave rise to a flourishing black market in Britain, where purchasers were known to pay well over £1,000 above the list price of a new vehicle. This was revealed in a television documentary exposé in the mid-1970s, which specifically investigated the Range Rover market. It is interesting to note that, whereas it was one of the hardest vehicles to buy before the start of the recession, in the early 1980s the company was having to dangle carrots to tempt potential Range Rover customers, with a selection of up-market 'prizes' for purchasers ranging from salmon fishing and golfing, to tickets for Wimbledon, Badminton or the British Grand Prix!

No sooner had Range Rovers become an accepted part of the landscape – or the cityscape – than a tendency amongst certain Range Rover owners began to manifest itself: a desire to convert the vehicle into something even more special. The inspired blend of engine, transmission and suspension that provided its unique performance, coupled with its hardiness and style, had without doubt caught the imagination of the appreciative motorist – but some of them wanted more. The Special Projects chapter of this book describes some of the elaborate conversions – citing for instance the exotic Falconry Range Rover with elevating seats – but the most obvious inclination was towards building in two more side doors, to avoid all that clambering in and out of the rear seats. While 1981 at last heralded the introduction of Land-Rover's own version of the 4-door Range Rover, it is worth looking back at some of the earlier, independent findings on the subject.

Although firms like FLM (Panelcraft) were converting 2-door Range Rovers to 4-door models on the existing wheelbase, there was a minority firmly in favour of extending the wheelbase at the same time, to increase passenger comfort and interior spaciousness: a constant criticism had been that leg room is restricted on standard models for the rear seat passengers. Without fitting a new, smaller front door, the existing dimensions demanded an undersized, narrow rear door which detracted from the advantages of the conversion, whereas by extending the chassis the rear seat passengers should be amply accommodated. During the late 1970s, our organization was approached to develop an extended, 4-door Range Rover for a Middle Eastern client, regardless of the fact that it would almost treble the cost. The concept was simple enough, but the execution was a lot more laborious: the idea was to insert 35 inches into the chassis between the wheel arches, and we have our design to the coach-builders, Smiths, of Kettering. The finished product looked well, was streamlined and capacious, but had it retained its versatility as a cross-country vehicle? Or could, perhaps, a 2-wheel-drive limousine do the same job? Too much tampering with the original only dilutes its basic attributes in the end – which is why so many of us welcomed Land-Rover's own design of the 4-door with relief. Here was a trustworthy, practical, integrated version that had lost none of its flexibility or innate good looks in the process of development.

211

This Glenfrome Falcon is typical of the highly specialised sporting vehicles demanded by the Middle Eastern market.

Although this new availability would have been welcome years earlier, as it happened it was timed perfectly to give the Range Rover a new sales boost when most needed, when the market was showing signs of flagging. The small but significant demand continues to exist for special Range Rover conversions by firms such as Wood & Pickett (who have produced their own exotic and stylish range, named Sheer Rovers, with a wide variety of well-thought out and unusual features), FLM (Panelcraft), and Monteverdi (of Switzerland). They were able to capitalize on BL's long overdue 4-door development by producing some interesting and exotic Range Rover versions of their own. FLM (Panelcraft), whose own version of the 4-door has been approved by BL since 1974, carry out approximately 50 special conversions a year, the majority of which go to Middle Eastern states and include variations on the existing 100-inch wheelbase, the 118-inch extended wheelbase, and 12-inch rear body extension. The most popular requirement is for the 118-inch 4-door conversion. Apart from the hunting Range Rover, which can be fitted with gun racks, falcon perches, refrigerators, supplementary fuel tanks, refreshment cabinets, drinking water containers, stone guards, dust deflectors, search lamps and winches, as well as the unique elevating seats (rising up to 23 inches) and folding roofs, other special conversions carried out by this firm are a power-operated convertible 2-door Range Rover, a 4-door open model with

212

The FLM (Panelcraft) 110-inch Range Rover conversion.

The Vogue Range Rover for 1984.

fold-flat windscreen, a 2-door open model with side-facing seats, detachable canvas top, roll-top side curtains and fold-flat windshield, while a further option is a power-operated metal roof, and automatic transmission.

Another interesting coach-builder/converter is the Bristol-based firm, Glenfrome Engineering Ltd, who started as a small family business a few years ago and now employ 65 people. While they concentrate on Range Rover conversions, producing in the region of 500 "specials" a year, they have also started playing with Land-Rovers.

Of existing Range Rover conversions, the vast majority have always gone to the Middle East, but in-roads are now being made into the Far East and certain European countries. No two end-products are alike but the basis of their range is about 10 different models, including four extended wheelbase models, the Filton extended by 9 inches, the Clifton by 24 inches, and the Westbury, and Portway by 36 inches, each unit being cut and reassembled on their own manufactured jig. Another popular model is the very strange-looking Facet sports coupé, the basis for which is a wedge-shaped glass-reinforced polyester shell dropped onto the Range Rover chassis, which boasts the most comprehensive equipment of any all-terrain vehicle in the world, and is specifically designed for the more aggressive Middle East market so that it in no way resembles the Range Rover as we know it. It sells for about £55,000. There is

Power-operated convertible Range Rover, converted by FLM (Panelcraft).

The same Range Rover is equally at home in the city or in the desert.

215

The interior of the Range Rover has become increasingly luxurious. This is the 1984 model.

an opulent-looking convertible model up there at the top of the range too, the Ashton, at £48,000, which is all Range Rover from the waist-down but fully modified above (except the windscreen) the end result being a spacious and elegant soft-top saloon car with top quality finish, which is the hallmark of Glenfrome's products, (as their prices reflect!). The Glenfrome Six is an ingenious 6-wheeler, either pick-up or saloon, with widened wheels for even better road-holding, the price of which starts at £24,000.

Glenfrome has not been slow to supply the demand in certain Arab countries for hunting vehicles, and have developed two basic options: the Falcon, an open-top adaption with two doors or four doors, and the Hawk which has a closed cab.

The various optional extras available include a Hawk perch, with adjustable tail support, leash clips and dirt tray, and also dashboard-mounted or portable falconry radar equipment complete with aerial (hand held or vehicle-mounted). This latter seems to us grossly unsporting as it locates the direction of the falcon and indicates whether it is in the air or on the ground, leaving the poor prey with dismally low odds. One wonders why the 'huntsmen' don't stay at home and play video-games then they would have no grounds for complaining that the birds are being over-hunted and populations declining. However, that's another issue: the Falcon and the Hawk vehicles are very practical for their purpose, and can also be fitted with such refinements as long range fuel tanks and fresh-water tanks and elevated rear seats (the Falcon only). This company is certainly one worth watching, for the originality and perfectionism of its products.

There is no reduction in the load space of a 4-door Range Rover when the rear seats are folded forward.

4-star fuel only in the 4-door Range Rover.

Range Rover with in-dash air-conditioning by ARA of Texas. Note new steering wheel design.

A 4-door Range Rover, built by Range Rover, had seemed a logical step for a long time when it was introduced in 1981, after the 2-door model had been on the market for 11 years. The Chairman of BL at the time, Sir Michael Edwardes, succeeded in securing the necessary government funds to implement the full-scale investment plan demanded by such a step. BL estimated that, with the vastly improved production facilities in the Midlands, the 4-door would account for four out of every five Range Rover sales, and rightly so: by 1984, on the home market, the 4-door had taken over 90% of Range Rover sales. Having been assembled for so long on a split track in cramped conditions alongside Land-Rovers, the Range Rover's move into its own premises meant that, for the first time in its history, supply would have a chance to catch up with demand. All of this tied in with the massive £200 million investment programme which was instigated by Sir Michael Edwardes, and was the cornerstone of the BL recovery plan of the early eighties.

The site – North Works – is based on the old Rover 2000 factory which was totally gutted, renovated and extended to house the new complex, of 1 million square feet – or the equivalent of 10 football pitches. The high-technology plant cost £85 million to build and is effectively two factories under one roof, as it accommodates the Land-Rover, in part, as well as the Range Rover.

Interior of the 4-door Range Rover, with left-hand side doors removed for the photograph.

The 4-door Range Rover was expected to account for 80 per cent of Range Rover sales.

The objectives were to up-date and improve their products, invest in new machinery for higher standards of quality and increased productivity, and also to improve the working environment. Originally the investment plan included development of facilities at Canley, not far from Solihull, but Mike Hodgkinson managed to convince the BL board of the advantages and good sense in keeping Range Rover and Land-Rover together at Solihull – hence the blossoming of the North Works. Credit was also largely due to Mike Hodgkinson for the development that took place on both vehicles during his period as Managing Director of Land-Rover Limited – before this, the emphasis was chiefly on increased output, rather than product refinement and development.

The move into North Works was effected early in 1981, giving 2-door and 4-door Range Rovers their own separate, self-contained assembly plant and paint shop, covering 565,000 square feet, divided up into six main areas: body and engine assembly; final assembly and trim; storage, panel preparation and paint; rectification and paint inspection; rolling road testing; and customer assurance line and final quality clearance. The manufacture of Range Rovers is by advanced mechanical handling systems, and stringently applied quality controls. The area of the plant assigned to Range Rover manufacture cost £15 million to complete and equip; it offers a capability of producing up to 600 vehicles a week, on two work shifts. The rate of production of each model is flexible according to market demand. This is a built-in feature of the plant, allowing variants to be accommodated readily.

This philosophy of meeting as many sectors of the market as possible, without detracting from the integral performance or quality of the product, led not only to the introduction of the 4-door Range Rover, but to the up-dating and refining of the 2-door model. This was first carried out in 1979, about six months after the introduction of the V8 engined Land-Rover. By then improvements were long overdue, but the 1970s had not been a time for expansion of product development. Until Mike Hodgkinson took up the reins, and had access to the kind of funds that enabled progress in this direction, the Range Rover had quite simply failed to evolve and keep pace with the times. Having arrived on the scene with an impact and opened up an entirely new, dual-purpose, 4-wheel-drive market in 1970, by 1979 it was badly needing a face-lift. Many details of interior trim were up-graded, the air-conditioning unit was at last incorporated in the dashboard instead of on the cab roof, and the external lettering of RANGE ROVER was altered to adhesive plastic strip, easily applied and eliminating the rust-factor of the former individually mounted letters, as well as making cleaning more practical on the bonnet and tailgate. In 1981 further-reaching modifications were carried out so there were then two different basic versions of the vehicle assembled in Solihull: the standard improved model, and the 'Fleetline', which evolved in accordance with the requirements of a specific outlet, namely fleet-users (and the police in particular), and those wanting the Range Rover's combination of load-

A picnic hamper is included with the In-Vogue Range Rover.

A lockable console unit is standard on the 4-door Range Rover.

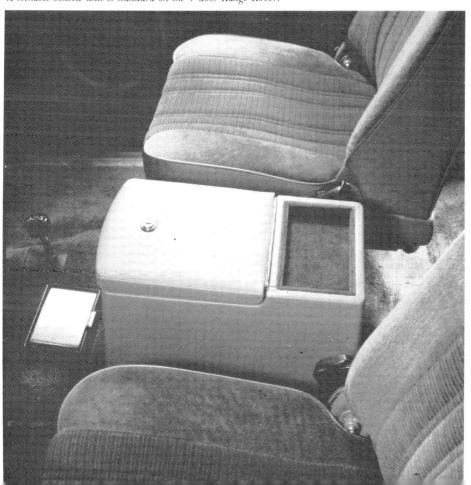

carrying capacity and speed, without the de-luxe fittings. In 1984, some three years after the introduction of the 4-door model, the original Fleetline model started to be phased out because by then over 90% of the UK market was using the 4-door unit. While a 2-door unit is still manufactured in limited quantity, the rather down-market vinyl seats, manual steering and uncarpeted floor of the Fleetline have gone forever: upholstered seats, power-assisted steering, and carpets are obviously a necessary part of the Range Rover, for fleet-users as well as the private owner.

As part of its efforts to widen the vehicle's appeal to the fleet market, Land-Rover Limited has authorized a liquified petroleum gas conversion to be carried out by Landi-Hartog Limited, either on existing vehicles or to be ordered as a built-in feature. Liquified petroleum gas (LPG) is considerably cheaper than petrol for a VAT-registered company: currently, it costs about £1.41 a gallon as opposed to £1.85 or thereabouts for a gallon of petrol. Even though fuel consumption is higher, it is possible to make significant savings if mileages are sufficiently high. In the Landi-Hartog installation the normal fuel tank is reduced from 18 to 7½ gallons, and two LPG cylinders of a 6¾ gallon capacity give a total fuel capacity of 21 gallons. The LPG tanks are fixed below the floor of the vehicle, so that the load space is not affected. The fuel source can be changed while on the move by operating a simple rocker switch on the fascia, and the

The 4-door Range Rover from the rear.

difference in performance between LPG and petrol is slight. LPG is a cleaner fuel than petrol and reduces pollution from exhaust emission, while it is also supposed to prolong engine life. In Holland – the base of the parent company of Landi-Hartog – 600,000 cars and vans are using it. With the introduction of the 110-inch V8 engine Land-Rover, the same application can also of course be made to the Land-Rover.

The conversion of the 2-door Range Rover to a 4-door model was executed by shortening the existing doors, converting the B-posts to BC-posts and inserting the D-posts to marry-up with the trailing edge of the rear doors. At the same time the rear seat was moved back 3 inches and the heelboard was realigned, retaining its original base-line and sloping backwards to meet the rear seat pan. These modifications resulted in good access to the rear of the car while also giving increased leg room for rear seat passengers. To increase fuel economy and reduce noise, the compression ratio was raised and a low lift camshaft was introduced. This gave revised valve timing and lift, and meant that maximum power was achieved at 4,000 rpm instead of 5,000 rpm. The crankcase was stiffened, also with a view to reducing noise, by the use of lasers. The combination of higher compression ratio and revised valve timing increased torque – both maximum values and at lower speeds, which enabled the transfer ratio to be changed from 1.113 to 1 to 0.9962 to 1, increasing the overall vehicle gearing from 21.23 mph to 23.72 mph at 1,000 rpm in top gear, with consequent improved fuel economy but without affecting performance. The carburettors and ignition distributor were retuned to meet the changed engine characteristics, and sliding contact breakers were incorporated in the distributor, greatly improving contact breaker point life and maintaining more consistent ignition timing over higher mileages.

The most common criticisms of the old Range Rover tended to revolve around the inconvenience of access to the rear seats, the lack of legroom in the rear seats, the weight of the wide front doors when being opened or closed, the inconvenience of the wide front doors when opened in a restricted parking space, and the noise. The new 4-door conversion set out to rectify all of these points as neatly and efficiently as possible. By repositioning the rear seat 3 inches further back, the space behind the rear seats was reduced, but when the rear seats were folded down the interior load space was just the same as it always had been. In effect, therefore, better and more practical use was made of the interior space, without any alteration to the length of the wheelbase or any external dimensions. Now that there were two doors to do the job of one, the front door came down to a manageable scale in terms of weight and size, while the noise problem was tackled by revising the machining of the helix gears in the transfer box. This combined with the revised gate layout introduced in 1980, not only reduced the internal mechanical noise but made gear changes a great deal smoother. The compression ratio was increased from 8.13 to 9.35 to 1 (4-star petrol became a standard requirement, as opposed to the former 2-star requirement). Other refinements in 4-door models included a new

More power to your elbow! The adequately powerful standard 3.5 litre V8 of the Range Rover here given twin-turbocharger treatment by Janspeed.

windscreen wash/wipe system which was probably the most comprehensive ever developed. Mounted on a single stalk from the steering column, it combined a 2-speed wiper, single flick wipe, delayed interval wipe and an adjustable wipe cycle after windscreen washing. The interior light now remained on automatically while the ignition key was inserted, on a delay system – and if the key was already in place but a passenger was alighting, it stayed on for a shorter period. There were two lamps to light up the engine bay when the bonnet was lifted, and every model was fitted with twin door-mounted stereo speakers, wing-mounted aerial and full wiring (though not the radio/stereo equipment itself, obviously). The interior detail of the vehicle received considerable attention, and the result went a long way towards elevating the Range Rover to the luxury limousine category, with its vanity mirror on the passenger sun visor, lockable centre console with ashtray for rear seat passengers, elasticated map pockets on the back of both front seats, carpeted spare wheel cover, tool box cover and rear wheel arches, a ticket pocket on the driver's sun visor, and childproof locks on the rear doors (of the 4-door model). In addition to all these new standard fittings, there was a special option pack available for the 4-door vehicle – at a cost of £750 extra, or £1,575 including air-conditioning – to raise the image still further. This consisted of alloy wheels, wood veneer door cappings, metallic paint, and fully carpeted loadspace and interior of tailgate. One thousand 2-door Range Rovers were built to incorporate these de-luxe extras as a limited edition, fulfilling a demand which was sparked off after one had been produced as a promotion for *Vogue* Magazine, for a photographic session in the South of France. It went by the name of 'In Vogue Range Rover', and was available in pale metallic Vogue Blue, or metallic Silver Birch. The price included air-conditioning and a matching picnic hamper, as well as the luxury optional extras.

A variety of amendments and alterations have been made to the Range Rover from time to time over the years. One of these was the inevitable inclusion of power-assisted steering, several years after its introduction, without which it was almost impossibly heavy to handle in traffic, or to park, although adequate for cross-country purposes. The main reason this feature wasn't incorporated in the original Range Rover package was the attitude of the old Land-Rover die-hards, whose firm belief was that unless it was hefty and cumbersome to drive, it would be a danger to humanity. Even the puritans eventually had to admit that its success was largely attributable to its curious mixture of characteristics – a tough performer, but smooth to handle and a pleasure to ride in – and began to recognize that ease of handling, speed and comfort need not necessarily be synonymous with fashionable, flimsily built, short-life cars. It is perhaps worth mentioning here that another argument in favour of four doors on the Range Rover came from certain sectors of the overseas market. In areas where security has to be a priority, potential customers would decline to buy a Range Rover for fear of being trapped in the back seats in the event of an ambush. It was rugged enough and fast enough, but the 2-door aspect was a definite deterrent. This also applies to the military market to a certain extent, where no real place for the Range Rover has been found. As a field car, the Land-Rover still meets most of the cross-country demands, and less specialized 2-wheel-drive vehicles are considered adequate for the transport of officers and higher-ranking personnel on the road. So far, what the Range Rover has to offer has been beyond the requirements of the military user – thought it is rumoured that they as used by the SAS on special operations.

When the Range Rover was announced in 1970 its market was, as has been said, somewhat vague, but it was a very short time before it attracted overseas attention. By 1975, two-thirds of the Range Rovers that were being produced were being exported, and this figure has never diminished. The up-grading of the Range Rover has become an integral part of its survival, and in 1983 it was the turn of the transmission to come under scrutiny. The end result was a two-fold development: the purpose-designed 5-speed manual gearbox, of great benefit to the long distance motorist, and the option of a fully automatic gearbox, with all the advantages of a high and low range transfer box. On its release, Land-Rover gave us the loan of an automatic Range Rover for a couple of weeks to try it out. Dubious about the off-road handling, we determined to put it through its paces on hills, fields, rough tracks and beaches; a thousand miles later we had to admit to being impressed. The machine looked after itself very nicely, minimising the gap in the gear-change in dicey conditions, and generally saving on transmission wear-and-tear (not to mention driver wear-and-tear!). Up to now the Range Rover market has not extended to the United States, partly because in the past it failed to reach the necessary regulation standards, but the demand for 4 x 4 vehicles in America being what it is, this is surely a market worth attaining. Jaguar have already set a fine example by showing with what kind of success the British product can be received, but the potential for a top-quality all-terrain motor in America, with such vast tracts of rugged country and open desert to utilize, is without doubt a great deal more significant. The quality-conscious Managing Director of Land-Rover Ltd, Tony Gilroy, ought now to be able to reap the benefits of his philosophy.

At the same time as the launch of the 90-inch Land-Rover in 1984, Range Rover was ready to announce its latest series of refinements and design improvements, aimed to give greater value-for-money. In 1982 it had won the Design Council's award for "excellence in design and in recognition of an outstanding product from British industry", and in the same year the automatic transmission option was introduced. In 1983 the 5-speed manual gearbox option arrived and also in that year Range Rover production exceeded 12,000 vehicles; sales at home and in Europe were the best-ever. When the latest improvements were announced, Land-Rover proudly boasted that over 400 changes had been made to the vehicle, all with the customer in mind. Be that as it may, the net result is unquestionably superior to all former models, and the list of modifications includes, internally, an entirely new instrument binnacle (with 15 warning lights), illuminated switches to operate all the lights and the rear window heater, an intermittent wipe-facility on the rear wash/wipe, a fascia-mounted clock, a 20-fuse fuse panel, side window demisting vents, new door trim (changing the position of handles and speakers), improved heater (with pipes to rear-seat passengers on the top-of-the-range models), and reclining front seats (not on 2-door models) which are also height-adjustable, as are the new seat belts. Externally, improvements include one-piece windows on the front doors to enhance visibility and reduce wind noise, aerodynamic mirrors, and easier-to-close upper tail gate (which also operates a new courtesy light).

The 'In-Vogue' limited edition of Range Rovers proved so popular that an equivalent super-deluxe model is now standard at the top of the range, known simply as the 'Vogue'. This model, launched concurrently with the improved standard 4-door and 2-door Range Rover, features such nice touches as electrically heated and remote controlled mirrors, electrically operated windows front and rear, headlight pressure washers, wooden door trims, front and rear headrests (as well as rear seat belts which were already standard on the 'In-Vogue' version), digital stereophonic audio system with four speakers, sumptuous grey upholstery and a clever cover for the rear load space which can be conveniently stowed when not required. Power-assisted steering is standard on all Range Rovers, as are servo-assisted disc brakes on all four wheels. We had the privilege of driving a Vogue model off-the-road just prior to its coming onto the market, and with automatic transmission as well as all the comfort and convenience elements, of superb seat-support, electric windows, mirrors, top quality sound system and so forth, it was genuinely impossible to make driving over fields and up rutted lanes, or through squelching muddy swamps and rocky streams, the least bit uncomfortable! All in all, the Range Rover has reached the stage of development where to drive it, no matter where, is to be instantly convinced of its supremacy in its class.

The following gives a resumé of the basic specification and the vital statistics of the 4-door and improved 2-door Range Rovers:

Engine: High compression 'economy' engine: eight cylinders in V formation, aluminium alloy construction with five bearing crankshaft and self-adjusting hydraulic tappets. Bore 88.9mm (3.5in). Stroke 71.1mm (2.8in). Cubic capacity 3,528cc (215 cu in). Compression ratio 9.35:1. Max power 93.2kW (125 DIN bhp) at 4,000 rpm. Max torque 258 Nm (190 lb/ft) at 2,500 rpm.

Transmission: Main gearbox incorporating four forward and one reverse speeds, manually operated with synchromesh on all forward gears. Transfer box on main gearbox output giving high and low ratios on all main gearbox speeds. Front and rear drive permanently engaged via a third differential which may be locked by a vacuum control switch. Overall ratios (final drive):

	High Transfer	Low Transfer
Top:	3.52:1	11.76:1
Third:	5.31:1	17.69:1
Second:	8.63:1	28.78:1
First:	14.34:1	47.84:1
Reverse:	12.92:1	43.07:1

Axles: Beam type axles front and rear incorporating hypoid spiral-bevel type differentials and fully floating axle shafts. Differential ratio 3.54:1. Front axle incorporates enclosed constant velocity joints.

Suspension: Long travel coil spring suspension. Axle location by radius arms (front and rear) with Panhard rod (front) and support rods and central wishbone assembly (rear). Control by long-stroke hydraulic telescopic dampers. Rear suspension incorporates self-energizing ride-levelling unit.

Brakes: Lockheed hydraulic disc brakes on all four wheels with servo-assistance and dual circuit piping. Drum-type handbrake operating on transfer box rear output shaft.

Steering: Adwest Varamatic power-assisted steering with damper and safety column, 3.5 turns lock to lock; or manual steering employing Burman recirculating ball, worm and nut system, 4.75 turns lock to lock.

Wheels and tyres: Styled pressed steel wheels, five stud fixing, size 6.00JK x 16, fitted with 205 x 16 tube type dual purpose radial tyres. Optional cast aluminium alloy wheels, size 7.00K x 16.

Fuel system: 82 litre (18 imp gallon) fuel tank, located between rear chassis frame members, feeding two Zenith-Stromberg carburettors via a Bendix electric pump.

Basic construction: Welded box section chassis protected by two galvanizing dips and an electrophoretic paint dip. Pressed steel body frame fitted with bolt-on body panels, most of which are of lightweight, corrosion-resistant aluminium alloy.

Heating and ventilation: Through-flow heating and ventilation system with two-speed fan providing fresh or recirculated air. Adjustable individual face level vents and rear quarter panel extracter grilles.

Windscreen wipers and washers: Single steering-column-mounted stalk operates two wiper speeds, flick wipe, intermittent wipe and programmed wash and wipe sequence. Single speed rear wash and wipe system operates from dashboard mounted rocker switch.

Seating: Individual orthopaedically designed front seats incorporating integral inertia-reel safety harnesses. 2-door vehicles are fitted with a mechanism allowing seat to tip and slide forward for ease of access to rear seat. Rear seat accommodates three passengers and may be folded to increase payload area.

Instrumentation: Main binnacle incorporates speedometer, fuel gauge, water temperature gauge, odometer, trip recorder and twelve warning lights. Supplementary instruments consist of battery voltmeter, oil pressure gauge, oil temperature gauge and electric lock. Soft green instrument illumination is switchable.

Electrical supply: 12-volt negative earth system incorporating 65 amp output alternator and 60 amp-hour battery.

Lighting: Quartz-halogen headlamps (60 watt main beam, 55 watt dipped beam), sidelamps, indicator lamps with hazard warning system, stop/tail lamps, reversing lamps, rear fog-guard lamps, number plate lamps, twin interior courtesy lamps with delay system, automatic underbonnet inspection lamps (except the Fleetline model).

Miscellaneous: Padded sun-visors with vanity mirror (passenger's side) and ticket pocket (driver's side), tinted glass with laminated windscreen, child safety locks on rear door (4-door model), integral parcel tray/passenger grab handle, spacious glovebox (except with air-conditioning option), provision for radio installation, opening quarter vents, two exterior rear view mirrors (door mounted), cigar lighter, heated rear window, lockable fuel filler cap, rear mud flaps.

Chapter 5
The Expedition Workhorse

Britain has always had a strong tradition of exploration – history books abound with tales of intrepid adventurers embarking on devastating journeys, in earlier times by sea, on foot, on elephant-, horse- or camel-back, across deserts, through jungles, up mountains, over glaciers. The challenge was there to be met, and that incorrigible streak of curiosity common to many island-dwellers provoked potential pioneers to seek far-off lands, eventually to build empires. Our more recent attainments have been inescapably linked with technology, for as the undiscovered world was being discovered, science was forging forwards and machines were being developed: sailing ships were fitted with engines, and horse-power was rated in terms of internal combustion. The advent of the Land-Rover – with its rugged versatility and robust utilitarian construction – was soon recognized as the passport to new horizons. Designed to withstand the wear and tear of the farmers' demanding off-road tasks, it was the first light-weight vehicle equipped to cope with arduous cross-country driving, and available at the right sort of price. Before it was barely three years old, someone had entered it for the Cape Rally, in 1951, and achieved first placing along with a Jeep and a Delahaye – there were no British entrants apart from Land-Rover. It has never looked back. By the 1960s, the overland routes to India, Africa, even Australia, were well-known to Land-Rovers which, in various forms, were turning up everywhere. Primitive people, with scarcely a word of English, could readily identify a Land-Rover by name – for now amateur adventurers felt that they could indulge their fancies: get a Land-Rover, and away we go!

For several years towards the end of the 1960s, we worked for a firm operating foreign tours in Land-Rovers, then a rapidly expanding business. Although many of the trekking routes we covered could well have been tackled by regular cars, vans or buses, it was the Land-Rovers that sold the tours, for fashions were changing and there was something definitely daring about a holiday 'roughing it' in a Land-Rover. At the same time, the vehicle was asking to be put through its paces, and the trekking routes were becoming more adventurous, more remote, and more attractive. Fleets of 'safari prepared' 12-seaters would leave Britain every autumn to spend the winter in the desert, the sites of Morocco by now being far too tame, meeting successive batches of tourists at their airport of arrival and duly depositing them back there again three weeks later. During this era, a lot of expensive lessons were learnt about how to get the best out of a Land-Rover in these conditions – or rather how not to abuse it, for the average lifespan of these redoubtable machines was about six months! The reasons were obvious enough: to ensure profits, the vehicles were filled to capacity with passengers, who had luggage, who needed tents, who needed feeding, not to mention the tools, spares, fuel and water that had to be carried to keep the show moving. Some of the drivers had never driven off the road, some had never driven a Land-Rover, some had never driven in convoy, and while all these skills were being acquired the vehicle took a pounding. The full-length roof-racks were both ill-designed and over-laden, causing the windscreen to shatter, starting with a crack appearing at the top outer corners, and the same thing occurred with the rear side windows which took the strain of the roof. Cracked chassis frames, split bulkheads, snapped bonnet locks, non-closing doors, tropical roof separating from body, rear wheels sheering off – none of these were uncommon and all were usually attributable to over-loading in one way or another. Since the

An example of an overloaded Land-Rover being driven too fast in Algeria.

arrival of the Range Rover on the expedition scene, it too has suffered equally from excessive loading.

At one time, Land-Rover was able to test the vehicle's expedition-worthiness through the efforts of Colonel Leblanc, who organized a variety of projects using Land-Rovers in the Middle East. It was he in fact who first started the Land-Rover expedition tradition, by taking his brand new 80-inch model to Abyssinia, as long ago as 1949, when the Land-Rover was scarcely one year old and completely untried. The son of a French-Canadian (who was one of the chief engineers involved in the construction of the Paris metro), Colonel Leblanc was a colourful adventurer, whose independent efforts to sell Land-Rovers overseas were producing orders for the Rover company even before it had an export department. Leblanc loved expeditions, and he loved deserts: having been a pilot in the Royal Flying Corps in the First World War, he had spent much of the Second World War in North-East Africa with the Sudan Defence Force, and in the Western Desert.

By 1951 he regarded Land-Rovers as his old friends, and as production was by then well up, and the company was keen to widen its market, Rover offered him a job as a sort of travelling salesman, demonstrating his Land-Rovers wherever he went, for a basic retainer fee. He accepted the job, but turned down the fee: his terms would be no salary, no expenses, but 0.5 per cent of all future sales to the Middle East – a far-sighted policy indeed! At that time such sales were negligible and his terms were met; he received a letter of confirmation from one of the Wilks, and away he went. For his first sales-expedition he planned an impressive manoeuvre all round Africa with half-a-dozen Land-Rovers, bi-lingual salesmen, specialists and service engineers. Roger McCahey, who is now Manager of UK Government and Military Sales at Solihull, was on that expedition, and takes up the story:

'The Rover company wanted to announce the Rover 75 car that same year, so instead of all that, Leblanc got one Land-Rover, one car, and me! We set off on 27 February 1952 and went from Algiers to Nairobi, and back up the other side. We would stop outside the towns to wash the vehicles down, put on clean shorts and clean shirts and polish our shoes, before going in to see the local police chief, army, oil companies, or whoever might be interested, then on we would go. Leblanc drove the car – a P4, or Post-War Model No 4 – and, thanks to his desert driving experience and dogged determination ("I'll get this car back to Solihull even if I have to dismantle it and load it onto a camel!"), the Rover lasted the round trip, faring nothing worse than multiple punctures and broken springs. To my astonishment, Leblanc was a great believer in string, a huge ball of which he carried everywhere; his cure for a broken spring was to bind it copiously with string which as a temporary repair often lasted up to a thousand miles so was hardly to be scoffed at! The tyres were Dunlop "Forts" and when we got home we were still using the original ones we set off with, much patched, of course.

Colonel Leblanc (far right) before setting out on one of his Land-Rover expeditions.

Leblanc had filmed the tyres in action, spewing sand all over the place, and from this piece of film Dunlop was able to start developing its first-ever sand-tyre. Travelling around in this way, he gradually formed the basis of a network of local dealers for Land-Rovers in the most unlikely places – and Leblanc was tireless: I remember once we were travelling from Beirut to Baghdad in a hurry – this was in 1956 – and we drove without a proper rest for 22 hours. I was dropping with exhaustion but Leblanc only said "Must press on, dear boy!" and it was only the fact that he was in his sixties, and me in my twenties that kept me going! He organized countless expeditions with Land-Rovers; another African trip we did together was in 1958-9 from Cairo to Addis Ababa and back again, through Anglo-Egyptian Sudan (the Nubian Desert in those days), taking eight weeks or so. By this time he knew that part of Africa like the palm of his hand ...'

But he also knew the Middle East – he had been sent to Baghdad in the war, where he became a Senior British Officer – and of course his gamble was to pay off. Middle East sales hit the jack pot within a very few years, and Leblanc soon saw the returns on his 'investment'. He died at the age of 78, in 1966, having made a significant contribution both to the Land-Rover and to expeditions as a whole.

Opposite: A Station Wagon with fitted roof tents.

Over the years Land-Rovers have carried scientists and explorers through jungle and desert, swamp and snow, demonstrating unparalleled endurance and reliability for vehicles of their class. Other early Land-Rover exploits were the Oxford and Cambridge Universities Expeditions to such remote places as Cape Town, Singapore and South America, while a more recent achievement is the British Trans-Globe expedition which is circumnavigating the world through the North and South Poles, using Land-Rovers loaned by the company. In 1980 the Royal Geographical Society celebrated its 150th Anniversary, and the occasion was marked by the initiation and sponsorship of an important exploratory and scientific project in the Karakoram range, which embraces Afghanistan, Pakistan, China and India. The international expedition was a tribute to the Society's long history of service to worldwide geographical studies, and to honour the event, Land-Rover saw fit to lend three V8 Land-Rovers to the project. Roger Ball, Land-Rover's Product Marketing Manager, liaised closely with the expedition in order that the vehicles should render maximum support. In times of such economic restraint, an expedition has to be a bit special to attract that extent of sponsorship, but if the Royal Geographical Society itself does not qualify, what could?

Before the Range Rover was launched in 1970, the Rover Company hired the services of the company we were with to guide two Range Rovers and a 1-ton 109-inch Land-Rover, with technical development staff from Solihull, across the Sahara with a 109-inch Station Wagon for support services. Our first sight of the Range Rovers is described in the introduction to this book. The 1-ton Land-Rover, soon to become dubbed 'Lulubelle' by the Rover crew, was a test-bed model fitted with the Range Rover V8 engine and transmission. Unlike the V8 Land-Rovers of today, it thus had equivalent power to the Range Rover –and greater payload, which caused us to realize that here was an ideal combination of power and size for many expedition purposes. We were to wait nine years, however, before the V8 became a standard Land-Rover engine.

The Range Rover testing trip was an unusual departure from the norm, and none of the Solihull staff knew really what to expect. Early on, Alf was heard to remark to Dennis, as our convoy startled a group of ostriches in the middle of nowhere, 'Bloody big budgies here, mate!' – but it only took the familiar sight of a Land-Rover-in-distress to make them feel quite at home. As ambassadors for the company, they could not have worked harder: wherever, whenever a Land-Rover of any age or condition was encountered, it was treated to their loving ministrations. One early morning, driving towards the sunrise over empty desert, we met two Land-Rovers, one carrying the Governor of the oasis for which we were heading. He was disconsolate at having had to abandon one of the Land-Rovers from his fleet a few kilometres back, so imagine his delight at running into a band of Land-Rover experts! Naturally, they repaired the offending vehicle's carburettor (diagnosis took place instantly), passing a happy couple of hours with heads bent over engine, while the Governor praised the spanking new Range Rovers with overt envy. His gratitude for the repair to his

Extra long-range fuel tank designed by Ken Slavin, fitted by AE Smiths.

ancient Land-Rover was expressed in his invitation to have breakfast with him and his entourage, where one egg (ostrich) made enough omelet to feed everyone! Later that same day we had to check in at an army outpost: well and good, until our party discovered a yard full of Land-Rovers at the back of the barracks. Here many hours had to be spent examining, explaining and adjusting – all in the cause of Public Relations and the famous Rover goodwill!

This expedition was something of a milestone for us because it was our first close contact with personnel from Land-Rover. During the course of the subsequent 15 years or so, we were to become increasingly involved with the use of Land-Rovers on expeditions, finally becoming advisers to Land-Rover Limited in the expeditionary field in 1979. The findings from the expedition, as an exercise to see how capable the Range Rover was going to prove, were generally highly favourable. One complaint at the time, though, was that it was impossible to get it stuck in the sand, normally the commonest of desert-driving hazards, without digging it in deliberately – and then it was too easy to get out! But on the Darien Gap expedition, in 1972, it was a different story. Totally different and much worse conditions played havoc with the vehicles, and at one point both Range Rovers had broken differentials, believed to be due partly to overloading of the axles, partly to the fact that they were fitted with 'swamp' tyres, which increases the risk of a broken differential by about 500 per cent, and partly to the drivers' lack of experience in driving and handling Range Rovers.

Eventually a cry of help reached Solihull, whence an expert on Range Rovers was despatched, and a Land-Rover was tracked down in Panama and flown in to join the somewhat crippled expedition and save the day. Thereafter, the Land-Rover was to act as 'scout car', but the expedition still attracted a lot of publicity for the Range Rover, being relatively new at that time, for tackling such formidable terrain.

If it was easy to overload a Land-Rover, it is even easier to overload a Range Rover, and this factor cannot be overlooked when working on expeditions. If a Range Rover is to be given its full rein and used extensively it needs to be backed-up by a load-carrying vehicle, as we were able to prove on a recent venture. In the first months of 1979, we mounted an expedition in the Western Sahara with the World Wildlife Fund and London Zoo, to research the potential of certain tracts of desert as National Parks, and to ascertain whether or not certain species of antelope still survived in those areas. We were offered the loan of a brand new V8 Land-Rover to test on the project, prior to the vehicle being launched (initially on the Export Market only), and so decided to commonize engines and spares on all vehicles taken. We took a Rover 1-tonne V8 101-inch ex-military Land-Rover as the principal load-carrier, carrying food, water, fuel reserve, spares and tools, baggage, and one passenger; the V8 109-inch Station Wagon also carried spares and tools, as well as camping equipment and the more delicate scientific and photographic equipment, samples, etc, and one or two passengers; while the Range Rover was lightly loaded, to be used as a reconnaissance vehicle and for path-finding, carrying three or four passengers and extraneous equipment. This combination was the closest to the ideal that we have ever achieved as the line-up for a very hard-pushed expedition, but getting it off the ground was fraught with snags. The prototype V8 Land-Rover wasn't ready to leave the factory in time to set off with the 101-inch and the Range Rover,which meant that once the technical development department were finally prepared to release it, our own modifications and equipping had to be effected with alacrity – between tea-time on a Saturday and breakfast-time the next day. The following preparation was carried out during the night:

Roof rack – full length, clamped to roof gutters
Side jerry can holders
Internal tie bars, behind rear seat
External reinforcing bars, over rear side windows
Internal storage boxes, behind rear seat
Extra windscreen mounting brackets
Extra pop rivets into body side panels and rear door post
Rear side-facing seats and internal trim removed
Mud flaps removed (these cause obstruction in sand)
Pop rivets added to various known weak points of body

Prototype V8 Land-Rover being driven by Ken Slavin in Africa.

The channel crossing, the drive across France, the Mediterranean crossing to Algiers, and the drive down through Algeria and Niger can take upwards of a fortnight – given delays at border crossings, and officialdom generally – but thanks to the increased mobility, power and comfort of the V8 (not to mention the interest it stimulated wherever we took it, which helped to persuade officials to 'make an exception'), we arrived at Zinder, our first destination, two days earlier than the other two vehicles, within nine days of leaving home. The fuel consumption was better than anticipated, at 18 mpg, and the constant 4-wheel-drive made light of the usually treacherous tracts of soft sand to be crossed, while the passengers could enjoy a far more comfortable ride than would ever have been possible in the 4-cylinder over such terrain. At one point it had looked as if we might be marooned in Southern Algeria for two days, but the V8 stepped in (indirectly) to speed us on our way. While parked on the outskirts of an oasis, to do routine maintenance to the vehicle before heading south, a chap wandered over to have a look under the bonnet, and ask questions. We gave him a demonstration, and were invited back to his office to meet a friend of his: it turned out that he was the Governor of the oasis, while his friend was the Military Commander for the area. We talked about V8s in particular and Land-Rovers in general for an hour (their greatest requirement was for Land-Rover buses and Range Rover ambulances), then made our exit, impatient to get back on the road. Outside the town, at the Customs Post, we found we were forbidden to leave. They had run out of documents and by the time replacement stocks were due, the Customs Office would be closed – for two days! This, we gathered, was 'final', so we went quickly back to the Town Hall, where the Governor told his secretary to type out new documents for the Customs then and there, and go with us to ensure that we had no further delays. Subsequently, we heard that the Algerian Army had a V8 Land-Rover for assessment, so perhaps the precedent set by Colonel Leblanc back in 1949 still holds good: Land-Rovers will sell themselves if you can get them to where the need is.

Once established at a base camp, the Land-Rover and the Range Rover were stripped down to minimal weight and used daily for local exploration and research. Because of the improvement in fuel consumption and in speed, it was possible to cover greater areas each day than predicted, and to devote more time to working in the field, completing that stage of the survey sooner than it would otherwise have been feasible to contemplate. The Range Rover had had to have its wheel arches cut back to allow Michelin XS tyres to be fitted (more commonization between the fleet) and was light enough to glide over the dunes like a ski champion on the snow, faltering at nothing. The V8 Land-Rover still lacks the sheer smoothness of the Range Rover's suspension, and the view from the front seats certainly does not equal that of the Range Rover since like all Land-Rovers, it lacks the windscreen height that makes Range Rover driving such a pleasure. Because it is relatively dependent on another vehicle for carrying weight, the Range Rover will never be able to match the Land-Rover's suitability as an expedition workhorse, however; and what the Land-Rover used to lack in terms of performance has now been recitified by the introduction of the Stage I V8, from which departure only exciting improvements can emerge.

(Since this was written, we have of course had the 110-inch Land-Rover enter the scene, with its superior coil suspension, and increased windscreen height, answering the above criticisms of the V8. Though we haven't yet had the opportunity of using the new model on expeditions, judging from its performance off-the-road at home we suspect it will come pretty close to the ideal expedition vehicle: more useful as a load-carrier than a Range Rover, and a lot more comfortable than all former Land-Rovers).

Some years ago, Land-Rover Limited asked us to amend and revise the *Guide to Land-Rover Expeditions* that they had found necessary to compile in answer to the quantity of enquiries and requests for information – and, inevitably, sponsorship – regarding the use of Land-Rovers on expeditions. As it contains a great many points of general interest, we have seen fit to include this Guide here.

A GUIDE TO LAND-ROVER EXPEDITIONS:
The number of overland journeys and expeditions using Land-Rovers, and now Range Rovers, increases every year, and the scope of projects tackled in difficult terrain is ever-widening, but to successfully achieve their objectives these

projects require meticulous preparation and planning: the more knowledge that is gathered beforehand, the greater the economy will be in expense, time and effort, not to mention the safety factor. The purpose of this Guide is to help expedition-planners to avoid some of the pitfalls and to protect their vehicle investment.

Body Style: The closed Land-Rover is generally considered to be more suitable for long-distance travel. A Station Wagon, or hard-top, on either short or long wheelbase, is not only more dust-proof but when fitted with proper locks and security catches is also more burglar-proof. However, if a hard-top purchased in Britain is fitted with windows, VAT and Car Tax must be paid, unless the vehicle is to remain out of the country for at least 12 months. Tax is also payable if the vehicle is sold within 24 months of its return to Britain, irrespective of the age of the vehicle. Full information on this subject can be obtained from HM Customs and Excise, at VAT Office, Northgate House, 1 Remnant Street, Lincoln's Inn Fields, London WC2A 3JH.

General: There is always a tendency to take too much equipment, thereby over-loading the vehicle. The recommended maximum axle loading, as specified in the Land-Rover Manual, should be taken seriously: it is important to remember that the lighter the vehicle is, the faster and more economical it will be to run, and the longer it will last. It is not recommended that a trailer be taken but, if considered necessary and cross-country driving is anticipated, the trailer should be fitted with wheels as large as possible to reduce rolling resistance. It is a good idea to use the same size wheels and tyres as fitted to the vehicle. If consideration is given to a roof rack, it should only be used for carrying light-weight, bulky items, evenly dispersed, the normal maximum loading for a Land-Rover being 150 lb (inclusive of the roof rack). A Land-Rover Station Wagon can be modified to take a heavy-duty roof rack by strengthening the bulkhead and windscreen, and fitting internal tie-bars at top and bottom of rear seats; external reinforcing bars should be fitted from roof rack to side body panels or side jerry can holders. In this way fuel can be transported on the roof in jerry cans secured in specially constructed, lockable compartments. For extra storage inside, rear seats can be removed, and a plastic mesh partition can be fitted behind rear seats to prevent the load in the rear from being thrown forward over uneven ground.

If the expedition is to a hot climate with a hard-top Land-Rover, a tropical roof is highly recommended to shield the vehicle roof from direct sunlight in daytime, and retain heat during cold nights. Alternatively, a complete Station Wagon roof assembly comprising roof (with Alpine lights and ventilators), tropical roof panel, trim and interior light can be fitted to hard-top models. There is no cost difference between left-hand and right-hand steering if purchased in Britain, so if the vehicle is returning to Britain it is advisable to purchase a right-hand drive model, while if the vehicle is to remain overseas it is advisable to purchase a vehicle with steering on the appropriate side.

It is recommended that two, or possibly three, people should travel in a short-wheelbase, and four, or possibly five (if baggage is not excessive,) in a long-wheelbase Land-Rover. The more people per vehicle the less comfort, and with the numbers advised the payload should be near maximum including the personal baggage. These considerations, however, will be governed by the itinerary of the expedition and the distances to be covered on it.

Engines:

Land-Rover engines in standard form can operate over an extremely wide temperature range, and for most expeditions modifications need not be considered. Contrary to popular belief, oil coolers are not required on 4-cylinder Land-Rover models, unless the vehicle is to be used to drive ancillary equipment whilst stationary. The following ambient temperatures at which the standard Land-Rover can normally be started and operated are given for guidance:

Minimum: Petrol models: $-30°C$ ($-22°F$)
Diesel models: $-30°C$ ($-22°F$) (subject to low temperature fuel availability)

Maximum: 2.25 litre petrol engine: $48°C$ ($118°F$)
2.6 litre petrol engine: $45°C$ ($113°F$)
2.25 litre diesel engine: $40°C$ ($104°F$)

Note: These maximum temperatures are for a vehicle operating continuously at peak torque second gear high transfer (ie representative of a vehicle working in soft sand or towing a heavy trailer up a hill). Under lighter load conditions the Land-Rover can operate in ambients of about $50+°C$ ($122+°F$).

When driving in high ambients the driver must always keep a close watch on engine temperature and coolant levels, and if the vehicle is to be used for driving ancillary equipment the 4 x 4 Special Projects Department, at Solihull, should be consulted.

In areas which have higher ambient temperatures than Europe, oil coolers should be considered for 6-cylinder and diesel Land-Rovers.

A heavy-duty cooling specification is available ex-works for 2.25 litre petrol engined Land-Rovers for use in ambient temperatures above $48°C$ ($118°F$), comprised of fan, radiator cowl and shroud as fitted to 2.25 litre diesel units. It is essential to use only high grade fan belts with this feature.

Advantages of the Petrol Engine Versus the Diesel Engine
1. Higher power and torque output
2. Higher maximum speed
3. Quieter (can be relevant when travelling in areas such as wildlife parks to reduce disturbance of wildlife)
4. Lighter
5. Generally more easily understood
6. Less expensive to purchase

240

7.   As a fuel, petrol is cleaner and less pungent to handle
8.   Petrol is usually easier to obtain

Advantages of the Diesel Engine Versus the Petrol Engine
1.   No ignition system (beneficial when wading or when fire risk exists)
2.   Fuel generally less expensive
3.   Fuel consumption considerably better
4.   Better low-speed torque, good in soft sand

   Government Tourist Offices and Embassies can usually supply a list of petrol and oil prices appertaining to most parts of the world, and also indicate where fuel is difficult to obtain. In some countries fuel coupons are available.

Preparation
Expeditions and long-distance journeys are best undertaken in new Land-Rovers or Range Rovers, but if a second-hand vehicle is used it is essential that it be thoroughly overhauled and serviced by reliable mechanics before the outset: time and money is well spent on thorough pre-expedition servicing. Although there are Rover Distributors and Dealers throughout the world it cannot be over-emphasized that the more remote the location the more difficult and expensive it is to obtain spares, therefore a comprehensive spares kit should be taken.
   Particular attention should be given to suspension and engine performance. Faulty suspension may, in the course of time, and depending on the nature of the terrain traversed, cause structural and mechanical damage. Reduced engine performance and poor compression may lead to other defects besides loss of power. Tell-tale oil leaks should be examined and rectified and all nuts and bolts securely tightened at the earliest opportunity.
   It is most desirable that drivers should possess sufficient mechanical aptitude and knowledge of their vehicle to perform servicing and repairs, often to be carried out in adverse conditions. A vehicle handbook and workshop manual are *essential* and can be obtained from Rover Dealers and Distributors. A list of overseas Rover Dealers and Distributors can be obtained from:
   Land-Rover Limited,
   Lode Lane,
   Solihull,
   W. Midlands,
   B92 8NW.

Vehicle Extras: When preparing a vehicle for an expedition the following items are desirable (those items marked * are required only for arduous off-road conditions):
   9½-inch diaphragm spring clutch (standard on current models)*
   Door locks
   Bonnet lock

Locks for spare wheel on bonnet
Lock for fuel filler
De-luxe seats
Spare wheel carrier on bonnet
Deluxe trim for doors and floors
Capstan winch with 50ft of rope (preferably manilla, but keep it dry so that it does not rot)*
Covers for propeller shaft universal joints (for use in grassland)
Fire extinguisher
Reverse lamp kit
Seat belts
Sun visors
Wire mesh guards for all lights
Laminated windscreens
Extra fuel tanks (available on special order only)

Fuelling up Range Rover jerry cans. Fuel should be carried in this way only when absolutely necessary.

A full list of Optional and Proprietary Equipment and Specialist Conversions can be obtained from Land-Rover Limited.

Extra containers for petrol and water may be carried. Metal or plastic jerry cans containing water can be fitted in the radiator recess (not on V8 model) although this may interfere with the fitting of other equipment (chaff guards etc). (Front-mounted jerry cans should not be used to carry fuel due to fire hazard in the event of front-end collisions.) Jerry cans cause a restriction in air flow to the radiator which may result in overheating in very hot climates; drivers must watch the engine temperature closely, particularly with diesel and 6-cylinder petrol models. Jerry cans carried inside the vehicle should be properly secured, care being taken with regard to fire hazard. In some countries it is illegal to carry fuel inside the vehicle. Plastic cans should never be used for carrying fuel. (The usual place for carrying extra fuel is either in roof-mounted jerry cans or in side-mounted jerry cans, but it should be noted that each jerry can full of petrol weighs approximately 50 lb.) Provision should also be made for carrying adequate supplies of oils, distilled water, brake fluid, etc.

Non-Rover Equipment:
    Roof rack
    Side jerry can holders
    Front jerry can holders
    Sand ladders for desert use
    Internal load nets
    Reinforcement of chassis, windscreen frame and bulkhead*
    Internal reinforcing bars*
    External reinforcing bars*

When extensive cross-country usage is contemplated with permanent pay-loads in excess of 500 lb (88-inch models) or 1,500 lb (109-inch models) heavy duty suspension is advisable. Under normal circumstances, with a high proportion of light-load duty on metalled roads, heavy duty suspension gives a harsh ride, so on the return of the expedition it may be considered more suitable to refit standard springs.

A hydraulic steering damper is available to reduce 'steering kick' and is advisable for long distances on rough roads. A propeller shaft universal joint cover should be fitted for use in long grass. After wading in mud or muddy water, cleaning out the brake-drums will prolong brake-lining life.

Chaff-guards restrict air flow to the radiator, so should only be fitted where essential, eg for operating in long grass where seeds may clog the radiator.

All vehicles should be fitted with safety harnesses, though for cross-country driving the lap-and-diagonal type harness may be uncomfortable; using just a lap-strap type gives greater mobility and comfort.

A loud and penetrating horn is necessary in many countries.

Flyscreens on dash vents are essential in tropical climates, and come as standard on Series III and V8 models.

Locks on doors, spare wheels, petrol cap, jerry can holders and bonnet deter pilfering.

External mirrors, of the 'springback' boomerang type, are advisable when visibility through rear view mirror is obscured by baggage inside.

De-luxe seats greatly increase comfort, improve support for the driver, and are strongly recommended for long journeys.

2¼ petrol-engined vehicles have alternative carburetter jets available for prolonged use above altitudes of 5,000 ft, while for low altitudes it is essential to refit the standard jet to prevent engine damage due to the weak fuel/air mixture.

Painting the bonnet and top of the wings matt black reduces dazzle in bright sunlight, but also increases absorbtion of solar radiation thus increasing under-bonnet temperature.

In 1983 Land-Rover gave their seal of approval to a new bull bar (nudge bar, kangaroo bar, cow catcher, or what you will) which was produced in Australia by Harry Brown whose company, Durbar Pty Ltd, now has a branch in this country. The main difference between this and all previous designs is that it is made in aluminium and is therefore much lighter, which is especially relevant to expeditions where weight is necessarily an important factor. An aluminium roof rack is scheduled from the same firm and this could have an enormous effect on weight carrying capacities for Land-Rovers and Range Rovers, again of particular interest for expedition purposes.

Tyres: As an all-purpose tyre does not exist, the tyres must be selected for the predominant terrain. Information regarding some Land-Rover approved tyres is given below:

Standard tyres,	Suitable for all road and track
Dunlop RK3 or	usage and cross country terrain
Avon Ranger:	in favourable conditions.
Michelin XZY:	Road and track use together with rough terrain.
Dunlop T28 or	Rugged rough terrain, mud and
T29A (Trakgrip):	other difficult conditions.
Michelin XS:	Desert of all types – soft sand, scrub or rock.
	(Grip on wet tarmac not outstanding.)
Michelin XL:	Available in 6.50 x 16-inch size, for mud conditions.

On 88-inch models, fitting the 109-inch type 7.50 x 16 inch tyres and wheels can be advantageous, giving higher overall gearing and increased ground clearance (subject to Rover approval).

A spare wheel – weight approx 75 lbs – can be carried on the bonnet, or on a roof rack, but for rough cross-country driving a spare wheel mounted on the rear door is not recommended as its weight damages the efficiency of the door catch and lock and distributes weight unevenly.

An extra inner tube and self-vulcanizing puncture repair outfit with a clamp is recommended. For emergencies, sleeve patches are useful for making temporary repairs in case cracks develop in the tyre wall. Always use metal dust caps as, unlike the plastic type, these will form an air seal. Other useful items available from Schrader Ltd are:

    5-in-1 valve repair tool
    Valve core kit
    Spark plug air pump (petrol models only)
    Electric pump (essential for diesel models)

The latter two are extremely useful, as manually inflating large tyres in hot conditions can be very exhausting.

If driving in conditions where night temperatures are low and midday temperatures are high, correct tyre pressures should be set before starting in the morning, and not bled during the day, as damage could result. Pressures return to normal when the temperature drops at night.

Lowering tyre pressures to 75 per cent of normal can give superior traction and flotation in soft sand or mud, but it is essential that only very slow speeds are used in these conditions, that great care is taken around obstacles, and that tyres are re-inflated after the soft patch is past. Failure to re-inflate will result in tyre overheating and blow out. A 20 per cent overload can reduce tyre life by as much as one-third!

General: A tow rope (tested to at least 2 tons) and shovel are recommended. The rope should be at least 100 ft long so that the towing vehicle can maintain a reasonable distance between it and the vehicle to be recovered. An extra fold-up trenching tool is light and takes up little room. Military-type shovels are recommended for serious recovery work. Towing points on the front and rear of the vehicle can be useful.

Some expeditions have found a hand throttle useful. This is standard on diesel Land-Rovers.

A winch is most useful in an emergency. Some form of anchorage, such as trees or rocks, is of course a necessary adjunct in winching. The front Capstan winch, with 3,000 lb pull, is generally satisfactory for self-recovery, obstacle removal, etc. The winch is protected by a sheer pin to prevent damage through overload, and several should be taken. A drum winch is easier to use, but dearer and heavier than the Capstan winch, and usually has limited cable length. When fitting a winch it is also advisable to fit diesel front springs because of the extra front end load.

A fire extinguisher of at least 1 kg capacity, preferably larger, is essential and should be stowed in an easily accessible place.

For improved ventilation the top half of each front door can be removed by undoing two nuts.

For long distances on good road surfaces free-wheeling hubs may be considered. The function of these is to reduce the rolling resistance of the vehicle when 4-wheel drive is not required. They isolate the front wheels from their drive shafts and transmissions both in forward and reverse directions.

If severe sand storms are encountered the radiator grille should be covered when stationary to prevent blockage by sand. The windscreen should also be covered to avoid sand abrasion which could render it opaque and the vehicle should be positioned with its back to the wind, also to protect the screen.

Tools
Land-Rovers have the following tool kit:
 Licence holder
 Wheel brace
 Double lifting jack, shaft and handle
 Tyre pump – hand operated
 Tyre pressure gauge
 Grease and oil gun
 Starting handle
 Tool roll
 Combination pliers
 Screwdriver ⅜-inch blade, 9⅜-inch long standard and Phillips
 Spanner 3/16-inch x ¼-inch Whitworth
 Spanner 5/16-inch x 7/16-inch Whitworth
 Spanner single-ended ⅜-inch Whitworth
 Spanner 5/16-inch x ⅜-inch AF (bleed screw for DPA pump, diesel only)
 Spanner 7/16-inch x ½-inch AF
 Spanner 11/16-inch x ¾-inch AF
 Spanner ⅝-inch x 9/16-inch AF
 6-inch adjustable spanner, large, 1½-inch adjustment
 Sparking plug spanner and extension (petrol models only)
 Box spanner
 Tommy bar
For travelling 'off the beaten track' the following extra equipment is worth taking:
 Set of socket spanners
 Electrical screwdriver
 Valve lifter or spring compressor
 Pin punch
 Feeler gauges, 0.0015-inch to 0.025-inch
 Hammer, 1 lb
 Large mole grips
 Chisel
 Small magnet with bar
 Hand drill with bits
 Brake bleeding kit
 Inspection lamp and extension lead
 Steel tape (metric and imperial)

Hacksaw and spare blades
Flat file, smooth and rough
Round file
Box spanner, 1⅛-inch x 1¼-inch Whitworth
Oil can
Box of assorted nuts and bolts, screws and hose clips
Length of electrical wire and electrical connecters
Large flat metal drip tray for mechanical repairs
Long nose pliers
Roll of electrical insulation tape
Roll of masking tape
Tyre levers
Puncture repair outfit and spare inner tubes
Radiator sealer (emergency use only)
Fibreglass repair kit and filler for repairing tanks, sumps etc
Assorted strands of welding wire
A hydraulic jack may be substituted for the standard jack
Flat plates to support jack on soft ground
An axe
Length of flexible petrol pipe
Penknife

Spares
Spare parts will depend on the age and type of Land-Rover. For more ambitious journeys Land-Rover Ltd will provide a suggested list of spares on receipt of the following information:
Engine number
Chassis number
Date of first registration
Type of Land-Rover
Destination
Duration of expedition

For touring, the following may be of assistance:

Petrol Touring Pack

Description:	Quantity:
Decarbonizing gasket set	1
Spark plugs	1 set
Spark plug covers	2
Spark plug cover seals	2
Distributor contact set	1
Distributor cover	1

Rotor arm	1
Condenser	1
Coil	1
Petrol pump (electrical or mechanical)	1
Fan belt	1
Flexible petrol pipe	1
Brake fluid	1 can
Bulbs	1 set
Wiper blade	1
Exhaust valve	1
Puncture outfit	1
Schrader valves	1
Fuses	1 set
Set of water hoses	1
Oil filter and joint washer	1
Front and rear main spring leaves	1 of each
Spring bushes	3

Diesel Touring Pack

Description:	Quantity:
Decarbonizing gasket set	1
Fuel lift pump	1
Fan belt	1
Flexible fuel pipe	1
Brake fluid	1 can
Wiper blade	1
Bulbs	1 set
Exhaust valve	1
Puncture outfit	1
Schrader valves	2
Fuses	1 set
Set of water hoses	1
Oil filter and joint washer	1
Injector	1
Heater plugs	2
Fuel filter element	1

Tyres: It is essential to start the expedition with good quality tyres – and to exercise great care in traversing rocky ground (see also remarks on tyre pressure). With this proviso it is not necessary to burden the vehicle with more than one spare wheel and cover. An extra spare inner tube, a comprehensive tube and cover repair kit and a set of long tyre levers is essential. If the vehicle is old, it is worth having the covers removed before departure (to break the grip of a rusty rim) and put back using tyre lubricant: the benefit will be felt the first time you have to repair a puncture in the field.

Maintenance

Routine inspection of the vehicle should be carried out right from the start. Daily checks are imperative: a few minutes spent checking for oil leaks and the tightness of nuts and bolts can prevent a major break-down later. It is advisable to stop for the evening early enough to complete the end-of-day inspection before dusk.

The Handbook for the appropriate model of Land-Rover indicates the full scope of routine checks and lubrication to be carried out and these should be adhered to. More frequent inspection of sparking plugs is recommended in countries where only inferior grade fuel is available. In such countries it may be necessary to retard the ignition in accordance with the details given in the Instruction or Workshop Manuals. Lubrication checks must be scrupulously observed – failure to do this may cause irreparable damage. In sandy conditions more frequent oil changes are recommended. Fuel obtained in these areas is frequently dirty; extra filtering may be necessary when filling the tank.

Garage and service facilities in most under-developed countries usually fall short of British standards. Although mechanics are often quite good, it is advisable to supervise all repairs. In many countries the village blacksmith is the only person who can undertake structural repairs, but it is surprising how effective they can be. Since spare parts may be hard to come by, improvisation is often necessary.

Hints on cross-country driving

When a Land-Rover is used cross-country, regular inspection and maintenance is vital. Wear and tear is greater than on normal roads, and although the increase can be kept to a minimum by a good driver, special attention must be paid to ensure that the vehicle is operating correctly.

The following notes are intended as guidance on some of the more important aspects of driving technique which in the end, of course, only experience can perfect.

1. Adopt a relaxed, upright sitting position ensuring that the safety belts are correctly adjusted. Maintain a firm grip on the steering-wheel but do not attempt to 'fight' violent steering-wheel movements: allow the wheel to slip through your fingers.

2. Never wrap your thumbs around the steering-wheel rim. If the vehicle hits an obstacle the steering-wheel could be jerked so hard that the spokes could catch and break your thumbs. This lesson has often been learnt the hard way!

3. It is generally desirable to use 4-wheel drive in conditions of poor adhesion. When on rocky corrugated surfaces, 4-wheel drive can sometimes be useful even in high range. It will halve the shock-loading on the rear half shafts and also give surer grip. It should be borne in mind that transmission 'wind-up' can occur between front and rear axles resulting in excessive tyre-wear. When the low range of gears is selected, 4-wheel drive is automatically engaged.

249

Contact between the right foot and the adjacent body (side) panel will improve accelerator pedal control.

4. Where the conditions are soft, ie marsh or sand, reduced tyre pressure will increase the contact area of the tyres with the ground, which helps to improve traction and to reduce the tendency to sink. Tyre pressures should, of course, be brought back to standard when such situations have passed.

5. Where conditions appear particularly difficult, the shape of the ground surface with possible obstacles should be determined by a preliminary survey on foot, and a path selected, thus reducing risk of damage, or 'bogging-down'.

6. Before attempting a difficult section, select a suitable gear and remain in it whilst crossing. For most purposes second gear, low range, is very practicable.

7. Keep the application of the clutch and brake pedals to a minimum. For descending steep and slippery slopes select the same gear as you would use to go up; allow the engine to provide the braking retardation, which it will do easily without the assistance of the brakes. Braking on slopes, or selecting too low a gear, can induce sliding and loss of control.

A bogged-down Land Rover on the beach where the Sahara meets the Atlantic. Shovels have been judiciously placed to denote the position of sand-ladders beneath the surface.

8. Apply the accelerator pedal cautiously as sudden power surges may induce wheel spin.

9. The momentum of a fast moving vehicle will overcome drag and reduce the traction needed from the wheels. When it is clear that no obstacle is in the way to cause damage, a fast approach to steep slopes, soft sand, waterlogged sections etc is often the most effective, but even a Land-Rover will break if grossly overstressed.

10. Bearing in mind the action of differentials, select a path so that the condition under each wheel of the same axle is similar. The same applies in determining the correct angle of approach to an obstacle to avoid wheels being lifted off the ground.

11. Be aware of the need to maintain ground clearance under the chassis, and a clear approach and departure angle. Avoid existing deep wheel ruts, sudden changes in slope, obstacles etc, which may interfere with the chassis and/or differentials. If there is any danger of under-vehicle damage in severe sections, have your passengers get out and marshall you through; they can see all parts of the vehicle and clear you over rocks.

12. The maximum advisable fording depth is 1½ feet (0.45 metres). Before fording make sure the clutch housing drain plug is in position and, if the water is deep, remove the fan belt and avoid overspeeding of the engine to prevent saturation of the electrical system, although if the exhaust pipe is submerged engine speed should be high enough to prevent stalling. Sometimes a sack over the engine (well clear of the fan belt) will keep it dry enough to survive bad spray. There are many water repellent agents on the market which are extremely effective in protecting the ignition system.

13. After being in water, make sure the brakes are dried out immediately, so that they are fully effective when needed again. This can be accomplished by driving a short distance with the foot brake applied. Also remove the clutch housing drain plug. If the ford has been unexpectedly deep, check the air cleaner for water ingress. Bear in mind that deep or prolonged fording in cold water can cool the air space above the axle oil enough to suck in water through the breather. A subsequent check of the oil condition is worthwhile.

14. Should it be found that the vehicle is immobile due to loss of wheel grip, careful thought and practical experience will usually provide the solution to this problem, but improved driving technique will in itself ensure that such instances are kept to a minimum or avoided completely. Driving practice in 'impossible' conditions is highly desirable before leaving on a journey.

The following hints will be useful:

Where the vehicle is fitted with a winch, recovery becomes relatively straightforward. Avoid prolonged wheel spin as it only makes matters worse. Additional resistance to the spinning wheels must be provided by some means. Attempt the removal of any obstacles, ie rocks, parts of trees, etc, which may also involve the clearing of earth piled in front of the wheels, bumper or chassis. Resist the temptation to skimp the digging in a recovery situation! A few minutes extra work will ensure a 'first time' recovery. Part or complete removal of the payload, or the equalizing of front and rear axle loads, can improve traction.

If the ground condition is very soft, reduced tyre pressures will give an improvement in adhesion.

Clogged tyre treads should be cleared.

Reverse as far as possible; the momentum gained in going forward again may get the vehicle over the obstacle.

Brushwood, sacking, or any similar 'mat' material placed in front of the tyres will help in procuring tyre grip. If necessary, jack up the vehicle to place material under the wheels. Avoid the exhaust when placing brushwood, as heat can start up a fire.

15. In soft sand or marsh conditions avoid following the tracks of the preceding vehicle; the crust of extra load bearing ground will have been broken.

16. When sand-ladders are required for traction to free a vehicle from being bogged down in soft sand, the following should be borne in mind: (a) with Series II Land-Rovers, care should be taken not to damage the exhaust system with the ladder; (b) removing the sills from the sides of the Land-Rover facilitates use of sand-ladders; (c) note where the ladders are placed in the sand, as once the vehicle is clear they can be well submerged and time can be wasted in searching for them.

Sand ladders facilitate progress up soft dunes.

17. In sand dunes always recce on foot if in doubt. Dangerous surface angles can be obscured from view when the sun is overhead. Steep slopes should be avoided.

18. When negotiating difficult terrain two vehicles are better than one, as they can assist each other, particularly if one or both are fitted with winches. Always get one vehicle across an obstacle before attempting it with the second.

General Information

Visas: In some countries travel and visas are restricted. If you have doubts you should check with the Embassy concerned *well in advance* of your departure date. Vehicle customs carnets are required before entry is permitted to some countries. Up to 100 per cent of the value of the vehicle may have to be guaranteed by the carnet issuing agency. This is payable as customs duty in the event of the vehicle being sold or otherwise disposed of in the territory. Carnets are obtainable through the RAC or AA or your local Chamber of Commerce. Also make enquiries regarding unusual local entry regulations.

Information concerning visas, health and currency regulations, customs and climates, etc, can be obtained from a booklet entitled *Guide To International Travel* available from:

ABC Travel Guides Ltd,
33-40 Bowling Green Lane,
London EC1.

Routes: Transcontinental routes are many and varied. Seasonal weather changes will influence which route to choose, eg some roads are impassable during the rainy season. Delays due to predictable weather conditions are most frustrating. A compass is a useful item to carry.

International road information can be obtained from:

The Royal Automobile Club,   The Automobile Association,
Touring Services,   Overseas Touring,
PO Box 92,   Fanum House,
Croydon,   Basingstoke,
Surrey CR9 6HN.   Hants.

Local permission is occasionally required to follow certain routes, variable according to season, eg the north-south route across the Sahara.

All expedition drivers should learn the basic motoring laws of the host countries, otherwise an offence can be unwittingly committed, for which the penalties are sometimes very severe.

Maps etc: The RAC and AA can also advise on appropriate maps, but the following are especially recommended:

Bartholomew's World Series, scale 1:4,000,000

GSGS Map, scale 1:1,000,000

Carte Michelin

Embassies, Consulates and High Commissions often issue tourist maps and supplementary useful information.

Photography: Most expeditions take at least one good camera. A photographic dealer can advise on equipment, but the following tips may be helpful.

1. Be fully conversant with all your equipment and correct any faults before you leave. Read the instruction book before you leave (not when you come back!).

2. Insure your equipment adequately.

3. For 35mm users, a 36 exposure cassette is no larger than a 20 exposure cassette.

4. Excessive heat, sand, dust, and water (particularly sea-water) can quickly damage your camera and films. A polythene bag offers general protection, but remember that changes in temperature may cause moisture to condense on the inside of the bag. This danger may be eliminated by use of silicagel crystal sachets which absorb the moisture, but the best precaution is meticulous care with blower and brush every night, as well as the use of polythene bags.

5. Have exposed film processed as soon as possible to prevent deterioration, particularly in humid conditions. Films purchased abroad can be of a different process rating to that supplied in Great Britain, so before developing, ensure that the correct rating is used for development.

6. When exposing a large amount of film without being able to have it processed on your travels, it is advisable to see the results of one early reel to confirm that the camera is working properly and the exposure is being judged correctly.

7. Keep sensitized materials in the manufacturer's containers as long as possible. Some customs checks use infra-red/X-ray detectors, and these can damage film negatives, so care must be taken.

8. Films and cameras must be kept cool; do not store in the footwells, parcel shelf nor leave on the seats in sunlight.

9. Particular care should be taken of lenses, since they are more likely to be contaminated with airborne grit in tropical conditions. A lens cap should be used when not filming. Plain glass in a filter mount is a permanent lens protector.

10. To get the best use out of your camera, take plenty of pictures. The more you take the more proficient you become, and you may never be there again.

11. Remember, in some countries even the most innocent of buildings or structures can be classed as 'of strategic importance', and respect the fact that

some people object to having their photographs taken.

12. It may be cheaper to purchase photographic supplies in some foreign countries rather than in the United Kingdom. They can however sometimes be delivered free to ports of exit.

Domestic: Land-Rover travellers are usually campers, and adequate equipment is therefore necessary, but as the equipment will naturally depend upon both the size of the party and its field of operation, to suggest an exhaustive inventory for all possible contingencies here would involve too long a list. However, weight and space are the most important factors – especially weight – so if in doubt, don't take it.

Care should be taken when loading the Land-Rover to ensure correct balance, aiming for an even weight distribution. Stowage should be carefully planned to avoid rattles and clanks, unnecessary wear and tear on equipment and extra work involved in looking for mislaid items. A well packed rattle-free vehicle tends to encourage better driving.

Some suggestions are as follows:

A gas cooker of adequate size is probably the best type to use. A large gas reservoir will last for weeks with normal use. Petrol stoves are almost as convenient and fuel is readily available if commonized with the vehicle supply, but safety precautions must be scrupulously observed – accidents happen all too easily with petrol stoves. Unbreakable, light plastic containers with screw top lids and polythene utensils should be carried, avoiding glassware and breakable crockery. Mugs and bowls that stack into each other save space when packed.

An inflatable or Dunlopillo mattress, and a light camp (Safari) bed are comfortable and demand little storage space. Beware of sharp thorns with inflatable mattresses and pillows. Polythene closed-cell foam mats, such as Kampamats, are extremely light and surprisingly effective if weight is a problem. The better the quality of a sleeping bag, the greater the comfort – but select with a view to climate. Avoid sleeping bags with zips in deserts (ie sandy or dusty conditions). Washable bags are available, but cotton sleeping bag liners are recommended for reasons of hygiene. 'Space blankets' are efficient: light yet warm. Sleeping bags should be checked for spiders, scorpions, etc, before each use, as should shoes and boots.

A canvas groundsheet is very useful: for repairs under the vehicle in adverse ground conditions; as a sunshade or windbreak; to lash down stores on the roof; and to provide a clean floor for sorting out equipment, etc. A mosquito net that tucks under the sleeping mat keeps mosquitoes as well as other unwelcome insects at bay, and allows less covering up in warm temperatures.

Creaseless and non-iron clothes are a great boon, but they must be tough enough to withstand really hard wear and be appropriate to all climatic conditions expected.

Paper towels are more disposable and more hygienic than cloth towels

255

where laundry facilities are limited. They have a hundred uses, from washing-up, to face flannels and washing cloths. Take plenty. Don't forget toilet paper, preferably flat-pack tissues.

A length of clothes line and pegs should be carried, and elastic straps for lashing down equipment inside the vehicle. A ball of strong string is also very useful.

Large Thermos containers for hot or cold food and drinks are most useful, but secure them properly.

A lockable container bolted securely to the inside of the vehicle can be used to carry valuables and documents.

A convenient way of washing clothes whilst travelling is to put them in a waterproof, sealed container in the back of the vehicle with a suitable amount of water and washing powder. After 100 miles they should be clean! Water for rinsing must of course then be available.

Food and Health: The following information is for the guidance only, and more specific details should be obtained from your own doctor, or from one of the Schools of Tropical Medicine, or specialized units in the country.

Foresight in equipping your medical chest sensibly can allay anxiety about health whilst you are abroad, and thereby add appreciably to your enjoyment of the trip.

Any left-over food at the end of the expedition is always gratefully accepted by local people. Spare medical supplies can be handed to any doctor or hospital.

Water: As a guide to the quantity to take, well-organized expeditions in hot desert areas allow approximately 2 gallons of water per person per day. Ambient temperatures above 105°F and/or prolonged exertion such as digging or climbing can cause consumption to rise alarmingly to 3 or 4 gallons per head. Cut usage in any other way but do drink all you need; the human body just will not work without enough water. Halazone, Aqua Clene, Sterotabs, or other water purifying tablets should be used if there is any doubt abut purity. Metal jerry cans should be treated before carrying water.

Food: There is no need to be unduly squeamish about eating strange dishes as they are usually prepared from the staple food of vast populations and can be eaten with enjoyment and benefit, provided certain precautions are observed. Generally all hot, well-cooked food is harmless; on the other hand cold food should be viewed with suspicion in hot countries, especially such things as shellfish, salads, and ice cream. Make sure that all food is fresh when purchased and cleaned before being eaten. In hot climates take additional salt.

Only a limited quantity of tinned food should be carried as an emergency supply because of the weight involved. There is an increasingly wide range of

AFD (accelerated freeze dried), and dehydrated foods on the market these days; ready meals, vegetables, fruit, milk, desserts, etc. Provided adequate water is available en route, dried food is strongly recommended for weight-economy. Dried fruit should be included regardless of water supply as it can be eaten without re-hydration and contains vital vitamins.

An insulated box can be used to carry some foods or keep drinks cool, and portable 12-volt refrigerators are available for those who like 'Scotch on the Rocks'!

Health: Bowel upset: however much care is taken, this remains one of the commonest hazards of foreign travel. If in doubt, water should be boiled before drinking and the same applies to milk. One tablet of Streptotriad taken twice a day is a useful precaution, increasing the dose to three tablets three times a day if trouble arises.

Immunization: As soon as your travel plans are definite, you should consider your state of immunization in relation to the countries that you plan to visit. Try not to leave it to the last minute, thereby avoiding the risk of a strong reaction to a vaccine occuring during the early stages of the expedition. Time should also be allowed for a course of vaccinations prior to departure, eg a second cholera vaccination may need to follow the first after a two-week interval. Consult your doctor, the RAC, the AA, shipping companies, airlines, or the Embassy of the country concerned for information on compulsory immunization. If you are likely to travel overseas unexpectedly, it is worth adhering to a regular schedule to keep your immunization levels at a peak, and avoid last minute panic. Immunizations may generally be divided into the compulsory and the optional, but the latter may be regarded as a good investment, especially for the seasoned traveller. Your International Certificates should be presented to the doctor for signature, and should be countersigned by the local Medical Officer of Health.

Sunburn: Beware of the sun, particularly if you have a fair skin, until you have had time to acquire a protective tan. Reflected sunlight from water, sand or snow can burn the skin, and even if one is beneath an awning the sun's rays can penetrate.

There are many skin preparations on the market for the prevention and treatment of sunburn, and of these Skol or Sol Tan cream for application before exposure, and After-Sun lotion later, are probably as good as any. Considerable work has been done in recent years on the use of oral preparations to combat sunburn and for anyone who is especially susceptible, Sylvasun (a vitamin A compound) can be taken in a dose of two tablets at night for prevention, increasing if necessary to two tablets hourly until relief is obtained. For the highly sensitive, a barrier cream such as Uvistat is indicated. A good pair of polarized sun glasses, or well-fitting skiing goggles are advisable

257

for driving in desert zones or in any bright or dazzling atmosphere. It is worth taking a spare pair.

Malaria: This disease is still epidemic in many parts of the world and if your journey is to involve even a transient stay in a malarial zone you should take a tablet of Paludrine 24 hours before you are due to arrive and then continue with one daily for a month after leaving the area. The usual anti-malarial precautions such as mosquito-proofing and the use of insect repellent should be observed at night.

Snake Bite: The danger of snake bite tends to be exaggerated. First aid treatment consists of reassurance and aspirin, while covering the bite with a cloth. It should be neither cut nor sucked, as there is a risk of infection and incisions may produce bleeding and damage to important tissues. The amount of venom injected can be judged by the swelling 10 minutes after the bite. If local swelling has appeared and medical treatment cannot be started within the hour, a firm but not tight (repeat not tight) ligature should be applied a few centimetres above the swelling using a cloth or handkerchief, and left on until the victim reaches the nearest hospital. The affected limb should be moved as little as possible to inhibit the spread of venom. Try to identify the snake to help the doctor find the appropriate antidote. Do not give the patient alcohol.

Heat Exhaustion: See 'water'. Thirst, headache, vomiting, cessation of sweating, increasing body temperature and, eventually, unconsciousness, mark the progression of heat exhaustion. Be alert to the symptoms. Regular and copious drinking of water will avert more serious problems. If body temperature rises, soak the patient's clothes to benefit from evaporative cooling. If vomiting precludes absorbtion of water, a saline drip and/or hospital treatment –quickly – will be necessary. Avoidance by drinking plenty is far better than the cure.

First Aid Kit: Take a small but adequate kit including a supply of sealed sterile dressings of various sizes, eye pads, Micropore Tape, several tins of 3-inch Elastoplast (which should be kept in as cool a place as possible), triangular bandages for use as slings, and an antibiotic preparation such as Fucidin ointment. A book on First Aid should be kept handy.
NB: It is generally advisable to take an extra supply of Aspirins to meet local demand.

General Comments: When travelling in remote areas where good medical care is unlikely to be near at hand, if you are prone to any particular ailment that responds to a specific drug, make sure that you take an adequate supply as it may be difficult to obtain, or sold in an unrecognizable form. If any illness develops after returning from abroad tell your doctor where you have been, as this may give a clue to the diagnosis.

258

Finance: Adequate currency should, obviously, be carried. American Express or Cook's cheques are commonly recognized by most foreign banks, and sterling bank notes or dollar bills command ready acceptance. Always make a note of travel cheque serial numbers and keep this separately, revising it as cheques are used, so that if cheques are lost the appropriate company can be notified immediately. In a few remote areas, only hard cash is acceptable. The overseas department of your bank will be able to offer advice on finance generally. The free market rate of exchange in some countries often differs appreciably from the official bank rate. Although profit can be made through dealing in this market, it is illegal and can lead to serious consequences. You should always find out the official bank rate of countries to be visited as it is often more advantageous to buy foreign currency in some countries than others.

For costing purposes it can be taken that the fuel consumption of the 4-cylinder and 6-cylinder petrol Land-Rover should be about 12 mpg, of the V8 about 18 mpg, and of the diesel about 20 mpg. These figures include an allowance for any arduous conditions the expedition might encounter. Oil consumption for an engine in good condition should be at least 250 miles per pint.

Embassies and Consulates: While British representatives abroad will always assist in an emergency, this does NOT extend to lending money to disorganized travellers who cannot afford the return fare to the UK. Adequate funds must always be reserved to get you home from wherever you are in case you have to return in a hurry.

Documents: Particulars of insurance and documentation of the vehicle can be supplied by the AA or the RAC who can also advise concerning visas. Having all papers in order before starting the journey is highly recommended to avoid subsequent inconveniences and delays.

Where any doubt exists concerning visas, the appropriate Consular Authorities should be consulted.

Passport Photographs: Take some spare passport photographs since various countries, eg Afghanistan, require travellers to fill in supplementary forms on arrival for circulation and route permits, and possession of photographs of the right size will forestall possible delays.

Vehicle Purchase: Land-Rovers are available through the Personal Export Department at Solihull, or from a Land-Rover dealer. Home or Export dealer address books are available from the Technical Service Department.

A limited number of second-hand Land-Rovers and Range Rovers become available from time to time through the company's Used Vehicle Sales Department.

For expeditions with low vehicle budgets it is well worth contacting both L. Jackson & Co, Rocket Site, Misson, Bawtry, Doncaster, DN10 6ET, and P. F. Foley, 74, Mandeville Road, Freezywater, Enfield, Middlesex, EN3 6SL, tel. 0992-718366, who supply ex-military (and other) vehicles that include Land-Rovers of all ages. We have purchased Land-Rovers from them over many years and have always received excellent value. When buying an ex-military vehicle, remember that it might have been unused for quite a time, so it's well worth allowing plenty of time to go over it and sort out any unseen problems before it is taken abroad. If wavering between purchasing a Land-Rover with a 12-volt system and a 24-volt system, opt for the 12-volt because parts are much more readily available.

Insurance: Arranging Land-Rover insurance outside Europe is a complicated business. It is advisable to consult an insurance broker, as few insurance companies offer cover.

Comprehensive cover, if obtainable, would be exorbitant but third party excluding passenger liability need not prove too expensive. Passengers and valuables can be covered under separate policies.

Sponsorship: The Land-Rover has been associated with expeditions for many years and the publicity to be gained from these and similar ventures is now minimal. Consequently, as a rule, any request for monetary or material assistance will not be considered.

Finally, it is worth mentioning here that in order to put your Land-Rover through its paces, you don't *have* to go to the other end of the earth, for Rover enthusiasts in Britain have now organized themselves into 'The Association of Rover Clubs', known under the title of 'Rover Owners' Association' since 1955, and before that as 'The Land-Rover Owners' Club' – formed as early as 1949. While this incorporates all types of Rover vehicles, some specialist clubs concentrate on certain models, such as 'The Rover Sports Register' who include all Rover cars built since 1904, and 'The Land-Rover Register: 1947 to 1951' whose members are specially interested in the renovation and historical development of 4 wheel-drive vehicles. Meetings are held regularly at Solihull, and close links maintained with Land-Rover Limited who support the club in various ways. For further information on this see the list of affiliated clubs in the appendices, which includes the address of the Honorary Secretary. The association is beginning to foster links with overseas clubs, and information is exchanged with about thirty clubs throughout the world including Germany, Australia and the United States.

Chapter 6
As It Is Now

So much for the Wilks brothers' stop-gap agricultural Rover for the farmer, intended only to tide the company over until more favourable conditions prevailed and they could look again to the serious and lucrative business of manufacturing their prestigious motor cars ... The intervening years have shown that, from the beginning, the Land-Rover was here to stay. Having existed as a mere off-shoot of Rover cars for so long, Land-Rover and Range Rover finally became a company in their own right in 1978, as Land-Rover Limited. Under the umbrella of BL, it has its own sales and marketing team, a workforce of over 12,500 and an annual turnover of £380 million. To run the company, Sir Michael Edwardes – the BL Chairman – chose Mike Hodgkinson as Managing Director, whose 5 year era saw dramatic improvements. In 1983 when Hodgkinson left he was replaced by Tony Gilroy, a man known to have a sharp concern for quality, especially in engineering, whereas his predecessor had been more of a finance man.

Ever since the late 1960s, Land-Rovers had been losing ground through lack of capital, at a time when the value of the pound was low and the demand for 4 x 4s was rising fast. Mike Hodgkinson has said since that, 'if we hadn't had a 10 year sabbatical on product development, the overall picture of Land-Rover might be looking altogether different.' But during these years, Land-Rover and Range Rover production was fluctuating at between 50,000 and 60,000, and although a major investment was proposed in 1975 by Lord Ryder and his team, it was not to be implemented until 1978 after the massive shake-up of the management, when Mike Hodgkinson arrived on the scene. With his background of industrial economics and his enthusiasm for the product, he took the bull by the horns and started to make changes, recognizing at once that Land-Rover was going to have to make up for lost time and step into the world of aggressive marketing, to counter the increasing threat of competition from overseas manufacturers. He managed to get final approval of the

The Land Rover 110 assembly line.

investment programme within a few months. The facilities available were largely directed towards product development, manifest in such strides forward as the 110-inch, the 2.5 litre diesel engine, the brand new 90-inch, not to mention the 4-door, automatic Range Rover, but productivity was also undergoing a shake-up. Since moving into the stream-lined, up-to-date North Works Plant productivity has doubled. The stream-lining hasn't stopped there either, as further 'centralisation' has since taken place with the re-opening of the former Rover Saloon car plant at Solihull, built in 1976 at a cost of 30 million pounds, at the time the most modern car assembly plant in Europe. Land-Rover's management reckon that by getting the whole of its manufacturing operation on one site, closing down satellite sites in Cardiff and Birmingham (with an eventual loss of over 1500 jobs), the cost savings will amount to about 14 million pounds a year, while also radically improving efficiency. Current MD Tony Gilroy says, "it is a once-in-a-lifetime opportunity... to replace a series of mainly very old, small, uneconomic plants with a single, integrated modern facility. It will improve our competitiveness significantly...".

It is reckoned that if Land-Rover Limited had to stand alone it could not only survive but could finance its own development on normal commercial terms, since – apart from Unipart – it is the only self-contained business within BL to make a profit. Instead however, the Land-Rover management has constantly to look over its shoulder to the parent company. Recent speculation has even suggested the possibility of the Land-Rover company being sold separately, which indicates that whatever the destiny of BL proves to be, Land-Rover Limited is destined to survive and grow, come what may.

Since the formation of Land-Rover as a separate entity from BL, the workforce has seemed to identify more strongly with their product, and the old Land-Rover loyalty is apparent throughout every department. Younger men now hold some of the key positions, but Mike Hodgkinson maintains that they have achieved the right blend of experience and youth, with a strong emphasis on teamwork, to which he attributes Land-Rover's survival through the 1970s. This enthusiasm is reflected far less, unfortunately, in some of the larger Land-Rover franchise holders in Britain. The under-developed countries benefit by

The ex-military Series II 88-inch Land-Rover belonging to Norman Barrett (secretary of the Association of Rover Clubs), on a competitive safari course at Leighton Buzzard in 1978.

The aims of the Association of Rover Clubs include development of interest in all new Rover products, whether vehicles or optional extras, together with the organization of caravan rallies and 4-wheel-drive motor sport, ranging from gymkhanas and family vehicle trials through to full cross-country trials and speed events.

having Land-Rover personnel on the spot to manage the sales for their specific region, bringing with them the commitment to the vehicle that the firm generates, but the off-hand and often ill-informed approach of many local agents does little to boost sales at home. In some cases their hands are tied, by having to handle diverse models of which Land-Rover and Range Rover are but two, but as Land-Rover Ltd, forges forward with new products, staying always in the front line of the 4 x 4 market, there is – in truth – no reason to make excuses for our home market agents. If 9 out of 10 blokes that you meet at Lode Lane can express so much interest in, enthusiasm for, and knowledge of the product, surely there is something sadly lacking in the method of distributing dealerships in the United Kingdom. In our experience, those franchise-holders entitled solely to sell Land-Rovers and Range Rovers are a completely different breed from the run-of-the-mill dealers/distributors: their involvement with the product equals that seen at Solihull, and is, without question, reflected in their order books. It is a constant disappointment to us that a company with such high standards in almost all areas, should apparently care so little how it is represented on the home market. If sales at home were booming perhaps one could overlook the generally poor salesmanship, but unfortunately an increase of vigour is desperately needed.

264

One way in which we suspect that Land-Rover could help itself in this area is by taking a leaf out of the book of certain German motor manufacturers, and offer a highly personalised customer collection service, whereby customers can order direct from the works, and once the machine is (custom-) built and ready, the customer collects, at the same time having a chance to see where and how it is manufactured, what else is being manufactured there, to inspect thoroughly his new vehicle, to have every feature explained and demonstrated, and to be the first-ever driver of that vehicle. In Germany such service includes free overnight accommodation for those travelling long distances but that might be slightly over-the-top for Land-Rover! (There may, however, be an argument for Range Rover customers receiving a touch of this VIP treatment: Birmingham Airport and a range of modern hotels are only a matter of minutes away from Lode Lane, and some package-deal could surely be arranged whereby Land-Rover foots the bill but without feeling it too badly. If the customer is as highly regarded as the product, the image of a product like the Range Rover, which already appeals to the top bracket of society, can only be nicely enhanced).

Apart from the slight saving of avoiding delivery charges by having new owners visit the works and pick up their new vehicles, the benefits of forging such an individual and personal relationship with the customer would clearly be seen in developing a loyalty to the product which could be life-long. And why not get some mileage out of the very positive, and dynamic atmosphere created by Land-Rover's employees? It is, after all, rare enough these days. It would seem singularly appropriate to apply such a policy to a company which forms part of a nationalised industry; if it belongs to the nation, let the nation get a look in there and identify with some part of it for once.

Also, Land-Rover already has a unique demonstration team that travels throughout the world giving driving instruction, showing how to get the best performance out of Land-Rovers off-the-road as well as how to protect them from driver-abuse. Land-Rover's team is led by the enthusiastic Roger Craythorne who does a great deal for the vehicles' public image with his little crew of experts (who also have to be masters of patience, tact and diplomacy!). This must be one of the best teams of its kind when compared to other 4 x 4 driving demonstrators, who tend to be much more wary of handling their machines in the way they have been built to be handled. In our capacity as expedition advisors to Land-Rover, we frequently need to arrange for expedition drivers to be shown all the niceties of off-road driving by Roger's team, who have their own 'Jungle Track' with the diverse conditions required, and the experience invariably proves to be very valuable for the expeditions concerned.

Of all the 4-wheel-drive vehicles that have evolved in competition to the Land-Rover, Toyota poses the biggest threat. Once the Japanese began producing 4 x 4s, it was only a matter of time before they started exporting to the developing countries where the importance of built-up cars was

Range Rover chassis assembly.

Body frame assembly of the 4-door Range Rover in the new North Works.

The new Land-Rover engine building and assembly line.

Land-Rover engine storage is now controlled by computer.

prohibited, but not of utility vehicles. Their network grew so fast that they are now the world's most prolific 4 x 4 manufacturers, with Toyota well in the lead. The trend towards increasing sales was helped immeasurably by the fact that the yen/sterling balance permitted Toyota to sell the Land Cruiser at between 10 and 60% per cent less than Land-Rover could afford to sell their own vehicle for – but even this did not daunt Mike Hodgkinson. He commented at the time that as Land Cruisers are built with steel bodies that rust, and Land-Rovers are built with aluminium bodies that don't rust, the Land-Rover's life is at least one-third, if not two-thirds longer, and a lot of Land Cruiser buyers are now returning to Land-Rovers.

Opposite: Body assembly in the more spacious new assembly plant.

Pallets are moved by robot stackers and conveyors.

Every Land-Rover engine is tested on a TV visual display unit.

Range Rover bulk stores.

Final assembly and inspection of the Range Rover.

The Jeep, the forefather of them all, and other American 4 x 4s, such as General Motors' Chevrolet 'Blazer', and Ford's 'Bronco', have all been suffering from a heavy drop in demand in the United States, particularly in the 'leisure sector', caused by major fuel price rises which have inhibited the use of thirsty 4-wheel-drive vehicles just for fun. Sales of all-wheel-drive vehicles in the United States fell dramatically in the early 1980s, including the traditional

Jeep. The prospects for the Jeep are encouraging, however, since it is virtually managed by the French firm of Renault, now joint-owners of the company with American Motors Corporation, and the new management's plans could spell closer-to-home competition for Land-Rover. However, having deserted the American market some years ago because of supply problems, there seems to be an increasing likelihood of Land-Rover getting back in, now that these problems are being solved, so perhaps the influx of Jeeps on the European market will be to some extent counter-balanced by the appearance of Range Rovers in the United States especially in view of Jaguar's success across there! Nissan's 'Patrol' vehicle, and the Daimler-Benz 'Galaendewagen' (produced with Steyr-Daimler-Puch in Austria) are two of the more serious attempts to compete with Land-Rover, but our opinion of the latter is that, considering all the engineering expertise that went into the mechanical functioning of the vehicle, it ought to have been dressed accordingly: the body-style leaves much to be desired, and the end product is in the Range Rover price bracket, while offering less than Land-Rover comfort.

Whatever the competition comes up with, there are those sectors of the Land-Rover's market that are fairly safe – six out of every ten Land-Rovers are sold to military customers, for example – and as a workhorse it has the advantage of a long-established reputation. During the 1970s it became obvious that regular customers were not enough, and at the end of that decade the then MD, Mike Hodgkinson, stated that 'although our vehicles are

A 110 on the new rolling road test cell at the factory.

arguably the best in their particular market sector, we are planning further developments on all fronts and I can promise a constant and steady development plan taking us right through the 1980s. Believing in progress by evolution, we are working hard on the next generation of vehicles, which will provide more comfort by advanced suspension, with increased wheel travel and better seating, together with improvements to visibility, braking and quietness – so the Land-Rover will still be the best of the 4 x 4 worldwide workhorse range.' So far, so good. Even though he is no longer with the company, his promise is holding good. Since he made that statement there have been a series of new developments emerging from the (very streamlined) Solihull premises, as detailed in the latter pages of Chapter 1, and in Chapter 4 regarding the progress on the Range Rover. In fact, a study of the entire Land-Rover organisation as it is today would undoubtedly reveal that it is ready for anything: ready to tackle whatever competition might arise with their own advanced products, ready to manufacture at whatever rate the market demands with the technologically modernised and compact, efficiency-orientated factory, and ready to maintain their exceptionally high standards under the watchful eye of the quality-conscious Mr. Gilroy, and ready even to be de-nationalized should that eventuality occur.

History has revealed that Land-Rover's fortunes went through an exacting few years during the 1970s. The Third World recession hit here as hard as elsewhere, and radical measures were essential for there to be any way out of the doldrums, and any prospects for competitiveness in the 4-wheel drive world. When Tony Gilroy, a soft-spoken Irishman from Cork, became Managing Director following Mike Hodgkinson, his first target was to get the production operation streamlined by 1985, which included the closure of satellite factories and complete centralisation at Solihull, encompassing the ex-Rover Car works there, and modernising every aspect of the organisation. The success with which the company was steered out of its prolonged 'hibernation' can perhaps best be shown here as it was shown to us, at the long-awaited launch of the new "Ninety" in May 1984.

Eastnor Castle is an imposing nineteenth century baronial mansion imitating the fortified tradition, in sombre grey stone. It sits at the end of a close-cropped green valley, 'master of all it surveys'; the uplands are densely wooded ancient forest, and it is this delightful pocket of the West Country that Land-Rover has the honour to use, by long-standing arrangement with the resident owners. We were ushered to a car park at the side then, somewhat circuitously, up stone steps inside a turret, along a parapet, and into the castle's Reception Room... through a window! At the presentation, in a darkened room guarded by gleaming suits of armour, it was announced that the purpose of the occasion was three-fold, but not until we were eventually herded down to the hall and out through the main entrance to the courtyard did the reason for our rather furtive initial welcome become really clear. The wide gravelled square, with the castle's keep beyond, was bedecked with spanking new shiny Land-Rovers and Range Rovers, in the new colour range – dozens of them. Predominant was the 90-inch in all its forms, from basic soft-top pick-up to the pert and streamlined 'County' station wagon, and this was the first time any of us present had seen the machine close up. 110s were represented to show off all their new features, also for the first time, and Range Rovers to demonstrate that "luxury need not stop where adventure begins". We were invited to pick a vehicle and drive off, following the route as detailed in our brief, which was 35 miles or so of road and motorway; we found ourselves in a 90-inch 'County' station wagon, with power steering, fitted carpets, unfamiliar windows, new dashboard, upholstered seats – and so on. Our destination was a hillside venue where we all changed vehicles. We hopped into a 90-inch hard-top diesel pick-up and were told to follow the route indicated by white dots, which led into the forest along an unmade lane which degenerated – by degrees – into crude track strewn with obstacles. There were four separate routes marked out to follow, weaving and writhing through the tangled undergrowth, each taking half an hour to an hour; white dots were the 'nursery slopes', through red and blue to black dots, which could only be tackled by those who knew just what they were doing as the course ploughed across flooded gulleys, up and down impressive inclines, through swirling mud like thick grey custard up to the door sills, and pivoting round hairpin bends at fearful angles.

Land-Rover had marshalls discreetly posted at judicious points in case of dire distress, and at the end of each course we selected a different vehicle, getting a chance to test all the new models as well as the new features of existing models. At about midday all vehicles converged on a woodland clearing, fragrant with bluebells, baked potatoes and barbecued meat, for a restorative lunch, before chugging back into the wilderness to search (in vain) for terrain terrible enough to flummox these work-horses. Whatever we were driving, however, was unstoppable in the face of every hazard. We were particularly impressed by the ride and handling of the 2.5 diesel 90-inch, but also by the dramatic improvement in comfort, on all models, with the superb suspension. In such severe off-road conditions you expect to incur a few bumps and bruises to the body, but we couldn't have had a safer, smoother and better-supported ride, which was inconceivable in a 4-wheel drive vehicle only a few years ago. Throughout the day Land-Rover's management team were on hand to chat over all aspects of their new products, and again we were struck by the guileless enthusiasm they all radiate. One of the ingredients contributing to the vehicles' success from its inception has been the camaraderie and product involvement of the work force at all levels, and this is as evident now, under the management projected by Tony Gilroy, as ever it was. He is a firm but quiet and agreeable man whose attitudes and high standards make him exactly the right person, leading Land-Rover from the front, to steer it on to further strengths and an even brighter future towards the year 2000.

Appendices

Association of Rover Clubs Ltd — G.R. Day Esq, 10 Highfield Rd, Bagslate, Rochdale, OL11 5RZ. Tel: (0706) 30200.

Anglian Rover Owners Club — Malcolm Tilling, 2 Queen Alexandra Road, Goldington, Bedfordshire. Tel: (0234) 210078.

Breckland Land Rover Club — Michael Plummer, 39 Northfields, Norwich, NR4 7ES. Tel: (0603) 57841.

Cornwall & Devon Land Rover Club — Mrs. Sue Retallick, Mill Combe, Islington, Newton Abbott, Devon. Tel: (036-46) 430.

Cumbrian Land Rover Club — Nick Wild, 32, Salcombe Avenue, Little Bispham, Blackpool, Lancs.

Essex Land Rover Club — Dave Bygrave, The Knoll, Bygrave Road, Ashwell, Nr. Baldock, Herts. SG7 5RH. Tel: (046-274) 2418.

Hants & Berks Rover Owners — Andrew Smith, 29, Silverdale Road, Tadley, Nr. Basingstoke, Hants. RG26 6JL. Tel: (073-56) 3395.

Lancashire & Cheshire Rover Owners Club — Chris Caton, 228, Prenton Dell Road, Prenton, Merseyside. Tel: 051-608 2848.

Land Rover Register (1947-1951) — Tony Hutchings, Bridge Cottage, 11 Tilmore Road, Petersfield, Hants. GU32 2HJ. Tel: (0730) 64977.

Land Rover Series One Club — David Bowyer, East Foldhay, Zeal Monachorum, Crediton, Devon, EX17 6DH. Tel: (03633) 666.

Leicestershire Land Rover Club	John Taylor, 78 Kilby Road, Fleckney, Leics. Tel: (0533) 403732.
Lincolnshire Land Rover Club	Reg Mason, Greensleeves, Walesby, Market Rasen, Lincolnshire. LN8 3UW.
Midland Rover Owners Club	Bob Rowley, The Old Thatched Cottage, Brown Heath Common, Nr. Droitwich, Worcestershire.
New Biggin & District Land Rover Club	Jack Gardner, 43, North View, Biggin-by-the-Sea, Northumberland. NE64 6AX. Tel: (0670) 852533.
North Eastern Rover Owners Club	George Atkinson, 9, South Drive, Cleadon, Nr. Sunderland. Tel: (0783) 362083.
Peak & Dukeries Land Rover Club	Bill Keen, 38, Woodhouse Lane, Chesterfield, Derbyshire. S44 6BL. Tel: (0246) 826532.
Pennine Land Rover Club	Brian Holland, 12 Granny Lane, Mirfield, W. Yorks. WF14 8LA. Tel: (0924) 493046.
Red Rose Land Rover Club	Peter Hartley, 5, Stockdale Crescent, Bamber Bridge, Nr. Preston, Lancs. PR5 6NA. Tel: (0772) 30282.
Rover Sports Register Club (Rover Cars Only)	Tony Holder, Blue Fir, Bellington, Chesham, Bucks. Tel: (0494) 783437.
Scottish Land Rover Owners Club	Miss Janet Campbell, 33, North Grange Road, Bearsden, Glasgow. G61 3AG. Tel: (041-942) 2088.
Somerset & Wiltshire Rover Owners Club	Ken Knight, Birdlymes Cottage, Porton, Salisbury, Wiltshire. SP4 0ND. Tel: (0980) 610776.
Southern Rover Owners Club	Mrs. Sandra Bourne, 124, Crescent Drive, Pettswood, Nr. Orpington, Kent, BR5 1BE. Tel: (0689) 39458.
Staffordshire & Shropshire Land Rover Club	Bill Hewitson, Grinfel, Pooles Lane, Bloxwich, Walsall, W. Midlands. WV12 5HJ. Tel: (0922) 76152.
Yorkshire Rover Owners Club	Mrs. Sue Whiteley, 10, Thorncliffe, Kirkburton, Huddersfield. HD8 0UG. Tel: (0484) 603564.
Association of Rover Clubs Overseas Liason Officer (U.K. Contact for Overseas Rover Clubs).	Bill King, 223, Chartridge Lane, Chesham, Bucks, HP5 2SF. Tel: (0494) 783809.

SPECIALIST EQUIPMENT and SPECIAL CONVERSIONS
Available from Land-Rover Suppliers

General

Engine Speed Governor (petrol only)
Tooley Electro Mechanical Co Ltd, Church St, Earl Shilton, Leics., England.
Telephone: 0455-42091.

Hydraulically Damped Bucket Seat (Land-Rover)
Bostrom Division Universal Oil Prod, Weedon Road Industrial Estate, Northampton, England. Telephone: 0460-55521 Telex: 31346.

Independent Heater (Land-Rover)
Eberspacher (UK) Ltd, Fibbards Rd, Brockenhurst, Hants, England.
Telephone: 05902-2678 Telex: 47674.

Roof Rack, Heavy Duty (all models)
Walter Broadley Machines Ltd, Kingsfield Way, Gladstone Road, Northampton, England.
Telephone: 0604 583191.

Roof Rack and Ladder, Jerry Can and Fixings (all models)
Unipart

Towing Equipment, Rubber Helper Springs, Free-wheeling Hubs, Undershield (Land-Rover, not V8)
Unipart

Overdrive (all models except V8 Land-Rover)
Unipart

Air-conditioning in-dash (all models – new vehicles only)
Land-Rover Ltd.

Air-conditioning (all models)
Hubbard Engineering Co, Hill View, Otley, Ipswich, Suffolk, England.
Telephone: 047 339 522.

Automatic Transmission (Range Rover)
Schuler Presses Ltd, High Street, Sunninghill, Ascot, Berkshire, England.
Telephone: 0990 20211   Telex: 848332.

Sunshine Roof (Range Rover)
Slideaway Roof Ltd, Tyburn Trading Estate, Ashold Farm Road, Erdington, Birmingham, England.
Telephone: 021 382 8811.

LPG (Range Rover)
Landi Hartog UK Ltd, Shay Syke, Halifax, West Yorkshire, England.
Telephone: 0422 58188.

Power Braking Systems

Compressed Air (all models)
Feeney & Johnson Ltd, Alperton Lane, Wembley, Middlesex, England.
Telephone: 01-998-4458.

Vacuum (except diesel)
Feeney & Johnson Ltd, Alperton Lane, Wembley, Middlesex, England.
Telephone: 01-998-4458.

Trailers

Power Axle (long wheelbase only)
Scottorn Trailers Ltd, Chartridge, Chesham, Bucks, England.
Telephone: 0494-782631 Telex: 837697.

Articulated (Land-Rover)
Scottorn Trailers.

Towing Equipment (all models)
B. Dixon - Bate Ltd, Bridge Works, Tarvin, Chester, England.
Telephone: 0244-24034 Telex: 61317.

Motor Caravan (all models)
Carawagon Coachbuilders Ltd, Thames St, Sunbury-on-Thames, Middlesex England. Telephone: 09327-85205 Telex: 917170.

Mobile Cinemas
Cintec Ltd, Wandle Way, Mitcham, Surrey, England.
Telephone: 01-640-2241 Telex: 946117.

British Films Ltd, Carlyle House, 235 Vauxhall Bridge Rd, London SW1, England. Telephone: 01-828-7965 Telex: 947165.

Mobile Radar (long wheelbase only)
Abbey Electronics Ltd, Charter Way, Hurdsfield Industrial Estate, Macclesfield, Cheshire, England. Telephone: 0625-29521 Telex: 667598.

Recovery Equipment (Land-Rover)
Harvey Frost and Co. Ltd, PO Box 16, Bishops Stortford, Herts, England. Telephone: 0279-53208.

B. Dixon-Bate Ltd, Bridge Works, Tarvin, Chester, England. Telephone: 0244-24034 Telex: 61317.

Security Vehicles (long wheelbase only)
Glover Webb & Liversidge Ltd, Hamble Lane, Hamble, Hampshire, England. Telephone: 042122-2811 Telex: 477527.

Snow Clearance (Land-Rover)
Atkinsons of Clitheroe Ltd, Kendal St, Clitheroe, Lancashire, England. Telephone: 0200-22211 Telex: 63211.

James A. Cuthbertson Ltd, Biggar, ML12 6DQ, Scotland. Telephone: 0899-20020 Telex: 778185.

Spraying Equipment (Land-Rover, not V8)
Evers and Wall Ltd, Lambourn Woodlands, Nr Newbury, Berkshire, England. Telephone: 0488-71444 Telex: 848658.

Stake-sided Body, Wooden (long wheelbase only)
P.D. Stevens & Sons Ltd, Adderley Rd, Market Drayton, Salop, England. Telephone: 0630-2396.

Welders (Land-Rover)
Tooley Electro Mechanical Co. Ltd, Church St, Earl Shilton, Leicester, England. Telephone: 0455-42091.

Workshops (long wheelbase only)
Tooley Electro Mechanical Co Ltd, Church St, Earl Shilton, Leicester, England. Telephone: 0455-42091.

Winches

Auto Capstan (Land-Rover, not V8)
Plumett Ltd, Worthing Rd, West Grinstead, Horsham, Sussex, England. Telephone: 0403-86310 Telex: 8771780.

Capstan (Land-Rover, not V8)
Fairey Winches Ltd, South Station Yard, Whitchurch Rd, Tavistock, Devon, England. Telephone: 0822-4101 Telex: 45324.

Unipart

Drum (Land-Rover, not V8)
Fairey Winches Ltd, South Station Yard, Whitchurch Rd, Tavistock, Devon, England. Telephone: 0822-4101 Telex: 45324.

Electric (all models)
Ryders Auto Service (GB) Ltd, Knowsley Rd, Bootle, Lancs, England. Telephone: 051-922-7585.

Hydraulic Auto Capstan (Land-Rover, not V8)
Plumett Ltd, Worthing Rd, West Grinstead, Horsham, Sussex, England. Telephone: 08926-3000 Telex: 88891.

Hydraulic Drum (Land-Rover, not V8)
Unipart

Manual Jockey Winch (all models)
Tirfor Ltd, Halfway, Sheffield, England. Telephone: 0704 482266.

Winch Fitting and Accessory Service (all models)
Spencer Abbot (Engineers) Ltd, 51 Tyburn Rd, Birmingham, England. Telephone: 021-327-2711 Telex: 337217.

Winch Accessories (all models) *and Ground Anchors* (Land-Rover)
Unipart

Hydraulic Power Systems (all models)
Spencer Abbott Engineers Ltd, 51 Tyburn Road, Birmingham B24 8NN, England. Telephone: 021 327 2711   Telex: 337217.

Aeroparts Eng Co Ltd, Commercial Road, Hereford, England. Telephone: 0432 67636.

Centre pto, Bottom pto, Rear pto and Pulley (Land-Rover, not V8)
Unipart

Air Compressors (large compressors are only suitable for long-wheelbase diesel)
Airdrive Ltd, London Rd, High Wycombe, Bucks, England.
Telephone: 0494-30021 Telex: 837959.

Ambulances (all models)
Herbert Lomas Ltd, Handforth, Wilmslow, Cheshire, England.
Telephone: 0625-25258 Telex: 668913.

Pilcher-Greene Ltd, Victoria Gardens, Burgess Hill, West Sussex, England.
Telephone: 04446-5707 Telex: 877102.

Armoured Patrol Vehicle and *Armoured Personnel Carrier*
Short Bros and Harland Ltd, PO Box 241, Airport Rd, Belfast, Northern
Ireland. Telephone: 0232-59271 Telex: 74688.

Dropside Body, Tipping Rear Body (long wheelbase only)
P.D. Stevens & Sons Ltd, Adderley Rd, Market Drayton, Salop, England.
Telephone: 0630-2396

4-door Conversion (Range Rover)
FLM (Panelcraft) Ltd, 32 The Arches, Broughton Street, London SW8, England.
Telephone: 01 622 2080. Telex: 911780.

Pilcher Greene Ltd, Victoria Gardens, Burgess Hill, West Sussex, England.
Telephone: 04446 5707 Telex: 877102.

110-inch and 120-inch 4-door Conversion (Range Rover)
Glenfrome Eng Co Ltd, 115 Glenfrome Road, Bristol, England.
0272 557727 Telex: 449639.

6 x 6 Conversion, 125-inch and 139-inch (Land-Rover 109 inch)
SMC Eng Ltd, Simmonds Building, Hambrook, Bristol, England.
Telephone: 0272 564533 Telex: 44274.

Expedition Consultants
K.& J.Slavin (Quest 80s) Ltd, Collow Abbey, East Torrington, Lincoln,
England. Telephone: 0673 858274. Telex 32497

Filming Unit, Cine (long wheelbase station wagon only)
Cintec Ltd, Wandle Way, Mitcham, Surrey, England.
Telephone: 01-640-2241 Telex: 946117.

Filming Unit, Video (long wheelbase station wagon only)
Cintec Ltd, Wandle Way, Mitcham, Surrey, England.
Telephone: 01-640-2241 Telex: 946117.

Fire Fighting/Crash Rescue (Land-Rover)
Carmichael Fire and Bulk Ltd, Gregory's Mill St, Worcester, England.
Telephone: 0905-21381 Telex: 338039.

HCB Angus Ltd, Southampton Industrial Park, Testwood, Southampton,
England. Telephone: 0703-865766 Telex: 477052.

Chubb Fire Security Ltd, Victoria Road, Feltham, Middlesex, England
Telephone: 01-890 6401 Telex: 261402.

Pilcher Greene Ltd, Victoria Gardens, Burgess Hill, West Sussex, England.
Telephone: 04446 5707 Telex: 877102.

Firefighting/Crash Rescue (Range Rover)
Gloster Saro Ltd, Hucclecote, Gloucester, England.
Telephone: 0452 69321 Telex: 43134.

Generators (details from manufacturer)
Tooley Electro Mechanical Co Ltd, Church St, Earl Shilton, Leicester, England.
Telephone: 0455-42091.

(long wheelbase only)
Allam Generators, Callywhite Lane, Dronfield, Sheffield, England.
Telephone: 0246-419165 Telex: 547776.

Hydraulic Platforms (long wheelbase only)
Simon Engineering Dudley Ltd, Dudley, West Midlands, England.
Telephone: 0354-70180 Telex: 338568.

Spencer and Sons (MH) Ltd, Great Bowden Rd, Market Harborough, Leicester,
England. Telephone: 0858-63253 Telex: 341966.

Lubricating Workshop (long wheelbase Truck Cab only)
Tecalemit (Engineering) Ltd, Plymouth, Devon, England.
Telephone: 0752-701212 Telex: 45124.

Mass Radiography Unit (long wheelbase only)
Anglo Coachbuilders Ltd, Station Rd, Batley, West Yorkshire, England.
Telephone: 0924-476421 Telex: 55220.

TOTAL SALES PER YEAR

Year:	Land-Rover	Range Rover
1947-48	48	
1948-49	8,000	
1949-50	16,085	
1950-51	17,360	
1951-52	19,591	
1952-53	18,570	
1953-54	20,135	
1954-55	28,882	
1955-56	28,365	
1956-57	25,775	
1957-58	28,656	
1958-59	28,371	
1959-60	34,168	
1960-61	35,148	
1961-62	37,139	
1962-63	34,304	
1963-64	42,569	
1964-65	45,790	
1965-66	47,941	
1966-67	44,191	
1967-68	44,928	
1968-69	50,561	
1969-70	47,538	86
1970-71	56,663	2,537
1971-72	52,445	5,510
1972-73	49,724	6,519
1973-74	45,169	8,604
1974-75	54,298	10,516
1975-76	58,523	12,207
1976-77	44,562	9,039
1977-78	48,342	11,498
1978-79	43,200	11,610
1979-80	51,337	10,153
1980-81	40,669	10,037
1981-82	39,845	13,104
1982-83	28,182	12,053

TOP 20 EXPORT MARKETS – LAND-ROVER LTD

	Market	Volume
	1980	
1	Iran	4,406
2	Italy	3,090
3	Nigeria	3,029
4	Arab Gulf	2,267
5	Algeria	2,149
6	Netherlands	2,030
7	Malaysia	1,845
8	Kenya	1,815
9	Saudi Arabia	1,757
10	Australia	1,734
11	Angola	1,682
12	Morocco	1,662
13	France	1,611
14	South Africa	1,373
15	Tanzania	1,258
16	West Germany	1,017
17	Portugal	1,008
18	Oman	957
19	French West Africa	884
20	Switzerland	855
	1983	
1	Iran	4,489
2	Algeria	1,260
3	Jordan	1,113
4	Oman	968
5	France	861
6	Italy	689
7	Iraq	647
8	Tanzania	522
9	United Arab Emirates	516
10	Zimbabwe	461
11	Switzerland	433
12	Zaire	412
13	Belgium/Luxembourg	402
14	Sudan	352
15	Zambia	350
16	French West Africa	325
17	Nigeria	323
18	Somalia	316
19	South Africa	304
20	New Zealand	289

The position of Managing Director of the Rover Company has been held by the following men since 1933:

1933 - 1956 Spencer B Wilks.

1956 - 1957 Spencer B Wilks and Maurice Wilks.

    (Spencer Wilks was Chairman from 1957 until 1962, when he retired from the Chairmanship to become the company's President, which title he retained until his death in 1971.)

1957 - 1960 Maurice Wilks and George Farmer.

1960 - 1962 Maurice Wilks.

1962 - 1969 William Martin-Hurst.

1969 - 1973 AB Smith.

1973 - 1975 Bernard Jackman.

    1975: Partial nationalisation of British Leyland, abolition of Rover as separate entity.

1978-1982 Mike Hodgkinson

1982 to-date Tony Gilroy

Index

Terry Davey